NEW APPROACHES IN SOCIOLOGY
Studies in Social Inequality, Social Change, and Social Justice

Edited by
Nancy A. Naples
University of Connecticut

A ROUTLEDGE SERIES

NEW APPROACHES IN SOCIOLOGY
STUDIES IN SOCIAL INEQUALITY, SOCIAL CHANGE, AND SOCIAL JUSTICE
NANCY A. NAPLES, *General Editor*

THE EVERYDAY LIVES OF
SEX WORKERS IN THE NETHERLANDS

Katherine Gregory

Routledge
New York & London

Published in 2005 by
Routledge
Taylor & Francis Group
270 Madison Avenue
New York, NY 10016

Published in Great Britain by
Routledge
Taylor & Francis Group
2 Park Square
Milton Park, Abingdon
Oxon OX14 4RN

© 2005 by Taylor & Francis Group, LLC
Routledge is an imprint of Taylor & Francis Group

Printed in the United States of America on acid-free paper
10 9 8 7 6 5 4 3 2 1

International Standard Book Number-10: 0-415-97234-5 (Hardcover)
International Standard Book Number-13: 978-0-415-97234-5 (Hardcover)
Library of Congress Card Number 2005016650

Library of Congress Cataloging-in-Publication Data

Gregory, Katherine.
    The everyday lives of sex workers in the Netherlands / Katherine Gregory.-- 1st ed.
        p. cm. -- (New approaches in sociology)
    Includes bibliographical references and index.
    ISBN 0-415-97234-5
    1. Prostitution--Netherlands. 2. Prostitutes--Netherlands--Interviews. 3. Transsexuals--Netherlands--Interviews. I. Title. II. Series.

HQ211.G74 2005
306.74'09492--dc22
                                                2005016650

Taylor & Francis Group
is the Academic Division of T&F Informa plc.

Visit the Taylor & Francis Web site at
http://www.taylorandfrancis.com

and the Routledge Web site at
http://www.routledge-ny.com

Contents

Acknowledgments

I want to extend my gratitude to the following individuals whose care and generosity propelled my graduate work and this manuscript forward: Professor Fay Akindes, Sietske Altink, Professor Sari K. Biklen, Professor Robert Bogdan, Dr. Sharon Brierley, Prof. Richard Breyer, Prof. Marjorie De Vault, Dr. Angelo Cacciuto, Prof. Larry Elin, my maternal grandparents, the late Aferdita Mina and Peter Efthim, my paternal grandparents, the late Andrew Krisulla Kallini Gregory, my mother and father, Kristo and Mary Gregory, my sister Jennifer Gjulameti, Emile and Freddie Gregory, Dr. Deborah Hall, Henriette Heimgaertner, Dr. Henia Johnson, Prof. Jonathan Laskowitz, Prof. Sy Leventman, Prof. Julia Loughlin, "Magdalena," Prof. Diane Murphy, Prof. Nancy A. Naples, Dr. Marie Pace, Prof. Stephen Pfohl, the late Janet Rizzo, Sister Maria Alfonsia, Cheryl Spear, Prof. Thanh-Dam Troung, Prof. Susan Wadley, "Victoria van der Way," Jan Visser, and the Director of the Living Room in "Den Apelhaven." Their encouragement and assistance saw this project to its fruition.

I dedicate this manuscript to the sex workers who invited me into their lives.

Chapter One

Introduction

Magdalena's window curtain was drawn when I arrived. She was with a client, and there was nowhere for me to stand without brushing up against male pedestrians searching the windows along this narrow alleyway. I stood near a medieval doorway where a mature bleached-blonde Dutch prostitute was soliciting for clients. I asked her how she was doing and she replied, "okay, but could you stand over there," pointing to Magdalena's place on the other side of the walkway. My presence as a female pedestrian in the street was affecting business. Finally, Magdalena reopened the window curtain, recognized me and then invited me into her room.

The ceiling was low but the basement room contained many luxuries not found in any window I had entered. The workspace was equipped with a double bed and ceiling mirrors hidden behind a curtain of muslin. There was a microwave, television, and kitchenette with a refrigerator. There was also a small shelf containing Hummel figurines. Dildos garnished the window, and dangling from the wall were poultices of garlic.

Today there is little business. Magdalena–an Afro-Brazilian transgendered prostitute operating in the Red Light district of Amsterdam- makes clicking noises with her mouth calling out to would-be clients straining their heads to figure out who is inside the basement's window. Her efforts are mostly in vain in part because of the sound proof quality of the room and the reflective tint over the window. *"Makado,"* she calls them when they fail to respond, then she turns to me and we explode in laughter. The joke is on them.

Magdalena grows frustrated with her lack of street visibility and after a dozen or so men have passed by, but failed to make eye contact, she acknowledges that there is a problem. Finally, she gets up from her ornate throne and begrudgingly decides to sit on a stool near the door after an older Dutch cab driver passed by commenting that he could not see her.

Making an effort to be visible from the street compromises Magdalena's pride. With an attitude of contempt for clients she quips, "if they want it, [sex], they can enter the room." Any effort to lure customers with clicking noises and hand gestures waving her price—a standard practice she and other window prostitutes use to communicate with customers- seemed largely for my behalf. After awhile, we realized would-be customers were focusing on the wrong person: me, as I could be seen from the street through the half opened door.

This afternoon Magdalena barely generated enough earnings to pay for her 200 guilders ($85 or 85 Euro) per day window rental. The previous night, however, was more productive when she worked in another window at ground level. There, clients could walk by four or five times, make gradual eye contact, and then begin the negotiation for services. Despite this favorable location, she had little choice in the room she rented since her landlord, a middle-aged Antillean prostitute, whom she identified as a transsexual, controlled most of the rooms used by transgendered sex workers.

The previous passage describing the interior of Magdalena's window illustrates some of prostitutes' daily practices, and hints of how the space influences relations and meanings shared among agents engaged at that site. Magdalena's window provides a unique perspective to understand Dutch window prostitution. I witness, firsthand, the art of commercial negotiation through a mixture of gestures and nonverbal communication. This dance between consumer and provider reveals patterns of codes and rules producing a window prostitution culture different from other types of sex work. Magdalena understands and rationalizes her own commercial value and operates to maximize her earnings. As an agent in prostitution, she has developed different skills to attract would-be clients. Her articulated window performance and her ability to communicate and negotiate clearly manifest her material interest in the sexual exchange for money.

This book concerns the everyday lives of sex workers and addresses the significance of looking at sex work in the Netherlands by arguing three main points. First, sex workers like Magdalena represent the cultural and social diversity of prostitutes working in various types of legal commercial venues in the Netherlands. Sex workers' experiences are complex, and therefore they do not represent a uniform group. For this reason the study focuses primarily on transgendered sex workers, however the narratives of female sex workers, both Dutch and non-Dutch are also presented. Second, prostitution is legalized and standardization is implemented as a way of controlling and profiting from the industry at local and national levels. It is key to know what legalization can do for marginalized groups. Many of the narratives gathered for this study come from social groups, such as migrants and transgendered people, who are largely absent from qualitative research on this topic. Third, legalization has made the Netherlands a desirable place for many Third World and transgendered prostitutes to migrate to and to survive in, however this system does not solve all of the problems related to prostitution. Recently, a massive influx of immigrants and undocumented migrants has produced tensions with the dominant society, and as a result, immigration policy reforms now threaten many migrants with deportation. This scenario produces a two-tiered system with different experiences of sex work in the Netherlands. While legalization grants rights and benefits to some sex workers, others, mostly migrants, face working conditions that produce inequalities under this system.

The Dutch system is at the vanguard concerning prostitution policy. This "rational" approach to the subject warrants exploring from the perspective of different types of sex workers to understand their quality of life and how they benefit or not from rights and privileges granted them. Although the Netherlands is the location of many studies on prostitution (Van Haastrecht et al, 1993; Altink, 1995; Pheterson, 1996; Chapkis, 1997; Wijers and Lap-Chew, 1997), I was drawn to this site because of ongoing changes in the representation of sex workers. Dutch prostitution requires continuous reevaluation of social, economic, and spatial relations because diverse social factors—such as a sex worker's citizenship, gender identity, language acquisition, erotic parameters, that is, what sexual services the sex worker is willing to perform or not perform, and ability to negotiate with clients—when intersected with this context can dramatically affect conditions for prostitutes.

A BRIEF HISTORY OF PROSTITUTION IN THE NETHERLANDS

Documentation of prostitution in the Netherlands dates back to the 1500s. Even at that time local city and State officials tolerated concentrations of this type of commercial activity in most mercantile centers. Although the practice remained stigmatized in the centuries that followed, the commercial exchange of sex for money became public in window-brothels within consigned places such as the Red Light District.[1] State regulation of prostitution as an institution, rather than a de facto practice, began to occur during the 1700s when the French occupied the Netherlands. During this period, control over spread of venereal disease was achieved through testing and quarantine of women working in the sex trade (Mr. A. de Graaf Stichting, 2002)[2].

Social movements[3] that considered prostitution a form of sexual slavery attempted its eradication. The industry, however, thrived despite these measures. Brothels existed inside "legitimate" businesses and prostitutes discretely worked out of their homes. Prostitution was tolerated as a part of social and economic life in the Netherlands because it posed little disruption to "public order," and was easy for officials to "ignore" it.

We can see signs of this early "tolerant" approach to the sex industry in current Dutch public policy. From a legal standpoint, full decriminalization of Dutch prostitution occurred as far back as 1810. In 1911, a "moral law" was passed, penalizing third parties (brothel owners and managers) for their participation in prostitution (Mr. A. de Graaf Stichting, 2002). Since 1993, stricter legal definitions and standardization of different forms of erotic labor have determined criminal codes prohibiting illegal trafficking or coercion of persons for the purpose of prostitution.

Although legal terms distinguish between prostitutes who work in the sector and third parties who organize and profit from the industry, this pragmatic approach to erotic labor does not eliminate unequal relations between sex workers and brothel managers ("Between the Lines," 1997).[4] Until twenty years ago, said one informant,[5] it was impossible to work in prostitution without a "middle-manager."[6] Today, Dutch and EU prostitutes in the windows and streetwalking areas mostly work for themselves.[7] This is, however, not the case with many Eastern European women working there.

How this greater autonomy came about has largely to do with advocacy groups. In the last thirty years, concern for sex workers' social rights has given rise to a union organized by prostitutes themselves (Altink, 1995; Pheterson, 1996; Chapkis, 1997; Wijers and Lap-Chew, 1997). The politicizing of issues concerning sex workers has shaped dialogues taking place between activists, sex workers, local public health officials, the International Labor Organization, and the Department of Justice in the Netherlands. As of 2000, the Dutch government has recognized sex work as a form of labor, granting full legal status to the occupation. As a result, sexual labor in the context of the Netherlands requires understanding the sector from the standpoint of a regulatory system (Mr. A. de Graaf Stichting, 2002).

An estimated six thousand sex workers provide erotic services in commercial venues throughout the Netherlands (Mr. A. de Graaf Stichting, 2002).[8] They perform their work in a variety of locations that I refer to throughout this book as "sexualized spaces." These sexualized spaces include windows, sex-club-brothels, and streetwalking zones. Among prostitutes each site assumes different social meaning deriving status from the type of clientele the site attracts, the location of the sexual exchange, the presence of hard-drug addicts, and how client negotiation takes place.

Dutch "windows," used for commercial sexual purposes, consist of a small single room in a basement, ground or second floor location, overlooking the street. In Amsterdam, they are clustered in the Red Light District and in "satellite" commercial areas near the Jordan and De Pijp neighborhoods. Individual sex workers sit, stand, or dance in the window to draw customers. As with the room I described early in this chapter, the room is equipped with a bed, sink, and window curtain drawn when providing services. Most rooms connect to a common kitchen and bathroom shared with other prostitutes working in the same building. At night, a red or florescent violet light illuminates the person who is in the window and indicates that the site is a commercial sexual location. Sex workers rent windows on a weekly basis for an eight-hour daily shift at a cost of 150 to 200 Fl ($75 or 75 Euro to $150 or 150 Euro) per day at the time I conducted my research between 1998 and 2001.

There are between six hundred and seven hundred sex club-brothels in the Netherlands. These venues are not confined or restricted to the Red Light District or where commercial sex is concentrated. Sex-club owners are encouraged to register with local municipalities, however this is on a voluntary basis. An estimated 3,500–4,000 prostitutes (out of a total of 6,000) work in these venues (Mr. A. de Graaf Stichting, 2002). Conditions in the sex clubs vary from places that have live music and require sex workers to give thirty to fifty percent of their total earning to the "bar" to places were women parade on stage wearing numbers pinned to their panties or bra for clients to identify them and where club prostitutes must perform any and all sexual requests made by the client for a duration of thirty minutes.[9]

Lastly, streetwalking zones are designated areas where street prostitution is permitted. Streetwalking in public areas, however, has mostly been prohibited. The exception has been the Red Light District where it was temporarily tolerated. In the 1970s, increased use of heroin, and later crack-cocaine consumption in the 1980s, led to the degradation of residential areas as drug-addicted prostitutes sold sex to keep their habit. To maintain "public order" and prevent recidivism of drug-addicted prostitutes in the criminal justice system, streetwalking zones were designated in ten major cities across the Netherlands to monitor and concentrate this population (Mr. A. de Graaf Stichting, 2002).

At the beginning of the 1980s, a large number of undocumented women began entering the country to work in prostitution. Undocumented prostitutes[10] not permitted to work in the windows without proper residency papers, flooded the streetwalking areas, the only sites where they could work without the threat of deportation.[11] This phenomenon disrupted the preexisting order set up to regulate sexual labor. Debates around sexual exploitation and coercion were reopened due to the presence of Dominican, Columbian, Thai prostitutes, and other ethnic groups that followed. This new social arrangement, in fact, exposed deficiencies in the existing regulations (Altink, 1995; TAMPEP, 1996; Mr. A. de Graaf Stichting, 2002). In truth, despite the legal status of prostitution and the demand these "foreign" women filled, they were denied residency in the Netherlands (Para. 3 Dutch Alien Labour Law, "*Uitvoeringsbesluit van de Wet arbeid vreemdelingen*" quoted by Mr. A. de Graaf Stichting, 2002). As a result many undocumented migrants have been forced to seek underground economic employment and to risk becoming victims of coercion, totally spoiling the intent of the regulatory system. This precarious situation continues to cause a rise in illegal migration, overloading the capacity of the Dutch social system to absorb it.[12]

Uncovering how complex social groups share common and disparate identities and make collective and individual meaning out of their everyday activities requires employing ethnographic methods (Machin, 2003). The "everyday" in this case is the manner in which sex workers are socialized for the purpose of "managing in the system" of regulated and quasi-regulated Dutch prostitution (Essed, 1991: 3). But embedded in this qualitative approach to understanding "mundane" practices of sex workers is the question of whether is it possible for a researcher to "linger" anywhere long enough to grasp patterns and processes of any given culture and not overstep the limitations of their findings. This, of course, is under the assumption that prostitution cultures share common interests, memories, desires, and drives as well as a similar relationship to place. Enabling a researcher to gain a sense of the ordinary helps to provide this knowledge, but whether or not it is possible to listen to and engage with subjects for the sake of understanding how people go about their "everyday world" will always be met with an unanswered question of how the researcher selected the moments she chose to represent as meaningful to her subjects and whether those experiences are reproducible or anomalous to that social world. By avoiding all universal claims, at best, the results of which could produce a partial knowledge on different prostitution communities working in a variety of commercial sexualized sites.

To my knowledge, a detailed ethnographic study of Dutch prostitution describing how sex workers cope with their everyday lives is missing from the Dutch literature on the subject. Most of the literature focuses on statistical policy analysis or the effectiveness of public health campaigns. My work presents a descriptive, first-hand account of how sex workers are adjusting to many social and economic changes to their work place. The logical method of gaining greater understanding of their experiences drawing on an

ethnographic approach, or "hanging out" with them, as a way of comprehending the meaning sex workers gave to the social changes occurring in
commercialized sex. This sample is skewed, representing largely the perspectives of transgendered sex workers. Of the twenty-two sex workers
whom I interviewed, seventeen are transgendered[13] and five are born-
females. Fifteen of them are immigrants or migrants. In their recounts,
issues of sexual identity, migration, and erotic labor intersect exposing their
material reality. Sex workers shared their experiences with me through
story telling, one-on-one interviews, and casual conversation, conveying the
complexity of their social arrangements in their professional sphere and in
their personal lives.

Before the data gathering stage of this project, I consciously decided to
approach this topic from a standpoint that would validate the narratives of
sex workers because their experiences and knowledge cannot be disentan-
gled from the production of sex work. By recovering Foucault's "subjugated
knowledges," the point of departure becomes that of the experiences of
transgendered and female sex workers through their story telling and "wise
resistances" to hegemonic ways (Clough, 1994: 91). This method affords
my informants a sense of dignity and respect for their own knowledge production. Nonetheless, there are multiple theoretical lenses imposing an interpretation on all forms of erotic labor, including Dutch sex work. Some social
theories contradict the overriding messages found in this book. For this
project, I am suspending the use a radical feminist lens in which the "sexual
ideology of patriarchy" explains the normalization of all forms of commercial sexual practices under the matrix of "eroticized domination and submission" (Dines, et al, 1998: 2). I do not deny prostitution's historical origins in
the "sexual ideology of patriarchy." What I contest to in this framework is
the blanket assumption that all commercial exchanges are a form of eroticized subjugation; that sex workers are not agents in their own lives; and
why erotic labor is deemed as demoralizing to the person who performs it.
This radical feminist framework should be used to illuminate the normalization of power relations, as they are relevant to victimology studies on
human trafficking and other forms of "involuntary" erotic labor. It is not
possible, though, as Dworkin (1981, 1987) and MacKinnon (1988) would
like us to assume, to impose the same treatment of pornography to all
aspects of erotic labor and on all gendered bodies that perform commercial
sex. If a "system of sexual subordination and oppression of women" plays a
role in sex work how does this framework apply to transgendered prostitutes or sexual practices that do not conform to heterosexual paradigm?
(Dines et al, 1998: 1) And even if parallels are made in the relations between
sex worker and client, is it that easy to index everyday practices as "systems

of oppression" (Dines et al; 6)? In the case of a radical feminist framework, all forms of gendered violence are lumped together across gendered bodies and the border between pornography and sex work narrows when framed as a "privatized sexual entertainment" (12). But this model is too neat and rigid for all types of erotic labor or circumstances under which individual sex workers enter the industry, or even for that matter, the motives that drive clients to seek out sexual services to fit into.

Throughout this text my "take" on sex work in the Netherlands recognizes prostitution as a form of labor or series of services requiring a performance from the sex worker. This is not to suggest that sex workers do not struggle against discrimination and social stigmatization. "Sex Radicalism" supports such an interpretation (explained in more detail in Chapter Two) of prostitution. This approach acknowledges that a sexual order is embedded in commercial relations, however also suggests that sex work can undermine existing sexual hierarchies or elicit forms of resistance to sanctified heterosexual relations. Does sex work undermine "hegemonic familial structures" and "reproductive heterosexist roles" or is prostitution another form of "institutionalized heterosexuality" (Purvis, 2004; Ingraham, 1996)? Certainly the marginalized social status and symbolic power of sex workers are inextricably tied to the "organizing principles of institutionalized heterosexuality" (Ingraham, 1996). I would surmise, however, the presence of transgendered sex workers servicing "heterosexual" male clients might suggest ways that some sex workers undermine the "heterosexual imaginary"[14] so closely tied to commercialized sex (Ingraham, 1996). What the theoretical leanings of Sex Racialism do is give me analytic room to recognize how the label "prostitute" has served as a totalizing inscription to stigmatize both the activity and the individual providing the act. Questions arise whether it is possible to "re-territorialize" language for those groups who have been labeled by the dominant society. It leads me to ask: who gains from these labels and stigmatizations? Under the thesis of "resignification," the terms "sex work" and "sex worker" transform the meaning attached to erotic labor as a "legitimate activity" but have the old remnants of stigmatizing thought really been dissolved?

Theories of Pierre Bourdieu also inform my research as to how space mediates social relationships between prostitutes and other actors. His "method" of interpreting complex social systems links micro practices of everyday life to larger social forces. Bourdieu's approach suggests society is made up of "fields" (sometimes also referred to as "markets") in which agents struggle to accumulate status (Bourdieu, 1998: 34). How social groups emerge in the field and struggle for power emphasizes ways structures and practices are part of everyday activity in the habitus (Thompson,

1999: 25). Internalization of a social order keeps those from different classes or groups from crossing into more desired fields, resulting in repro-duction of structures—the relations of unequal power. Tension occurs when individuals in each field occupy positions determined by the types and amounts of capital they possess, producing a struggle for position, domina-tion, and agency.

Applying Bourdieu's theory to Dutch prostitution reveals how it oper-ates as a complex field in which many spheres—city, state, labor, public health advocacy groups, EU wide institutions and individual agents- with varied interests strategize to regulate diverse modes of erotic production and accumulate forms of capital—symbolic or material—from it. This applies to sex workers as well. Inside the culture of Dutch prostitution, there is a hierarchy of prostitutes who hold and vie for different social posi-tions and amounts of symbolic capital, that is, cultural and social forms that legitimate subjects. This is determined by factors that include whom sex workers service; the conditions under which they provide a sexual exchange; how the commercial exchange takes place; how prostitutes artic-ulate their habitus through gestures, attire, and bodily movements; and, their legal status.

To understand how domination occurs in this setting, it is helpful to consider Foucault's depiction of the "disciplinary body" that reveals how all bodily movements are "socially qualified" (Margolis, 1999: 70). "Knowledge" is assigned to the body in its spontaneity and fluency, making it a site of "incorporated history" (Thompson, 1999: 14) through which "performative" forces are received. The "main mechanism of domination" says Bourdieu, "operates through the unconscious manipulation of the body" (1998: 15). Bodily techniques, as well as language restraints, are imposed by dominant classes, and manifest how individuals and groups relate to the social world (Bourdieu, 1993: 83). At the same time, "bodies and pleasures," Foucault insists are sites of "resistance to power," however use of this analysis becomes difficult to hold when "sexual diversity" is pro-duced as a result of "disciplinary deployment of sexuality" reverting back to the "frame from within the very discourses it seeks to subvert (Jackson, 1996: 19). The most obvious examples are found in the communication techniques used by window prostitutes to solicit clients. Society reads this behavior as appropriate conduct for a prostitute, and as a result, sex work-ers replicate it as a standard way to act. In another example, public health measures are set up to regulate sex workers' behavior throughout the Netherlands. This illustrates how sex workers internalize the precepts of STD and HIV prevention through self-management of their sexual behav-ior. In a third example, relations between Dutch citizens and "migrants" are played out in the disparate rights granted to each group. Dutch street-walkers displayed their privileged social position by controlling entry of new migrant groups through demarcation of sidewalk space. Not all relations, however, are about one-way domination and internalized codes of prescribed conduct. Some sex workers, particularly transgendered people, resist marginalization through their "disruptive" gendered performance. They manage to renegotiate their roles as providers, especially with clients who were vested in protecting their heterosexual status.

In Foucault's writings on "discourses of power" he stresses the interrelationship between "political mechanisms" and public ways of thinking (Nesvig, 2001; Foucault, 1990). To grasp the diverse social groups who are living and working in the Netherlands and their presence in this study requires acknowledging how institutionalized pluralism conceptually functions to maintain Dutch hegemony. The "ideology of pluralism" has its historical origins dating back to early religious tolerance in the Netherlands and manifests today in the form of cultural, racial, religious, and national diversity, otherwise labeled as ethnic pluralism (Essed, 1991: 15). In this case, ideological pluralization is deployed as a type of "ethnicism" producing "colonial paternalism, structural marginalization, and cultural assimilation" and suppressing how power relations operate similarly to racism (Essed, 1991: 2, 15). Given that the focus of this study is on the "everyday" routine of sex workers lives, mundane aspects of life that are normalized as a means for inhabitants to "manage" within any social system are a way to make connections to greater "structural forces" at play (2). Managing in the system, therefore, translates into navigating around a Dutch hegemonic hold that organizes in to a Dutch way of life (2). Here, the "dominant group assum[es] that Dutch norms and values are superior and not subject to change" (6) and whereby "cultural control" is concealed in the "emptiness of the promise of cultural pluralism" that never materializes for many immigrants, especially those ethnic groups who arrived in the Netherlands solely for the purpose of filling menial and informal labor markets (6). I became acutely aware of this "contradiction" firsthand while living with undocumented migrants during the data gathering stages of this study, and again, when I became a resident of the Netherlands during the year in which I wrote the first draft of this manuscript as my dissertation.

Many of the racist mechanisms in place are vestiges of postcolonial relations with former Dutch colonial subjects (Essed, 1991). The Dutch government provided social services and programs and citizenship to these groups. But there are other ethnic and social groups living and working the Netherlands, and in some cases, many of them hold undocumented status. Some of the undocumented and recent immigrants in this study identified themselves as originating from Brazil, Ecuador, Nigeria, Rumania, Ivory Coast and Somalia, which might "mark" their appearance as physically different from the dominant Dutch society. Rumanians whom I interviewed claimed to be Romany, situating them as part of underclass across Europe, however a few sex workers who are mentioned peripherally as part of the prostitution scene are from other parts of Eastern Europe. They are working illegally in the Netherlands and hold an ethnic status that marks them as "Other" or as "outsiders" in this society. Hence for the purpose of this book, when migrant status is assigned to a sex worker, it can be assumed that this person has been marked as "other" in the context of the dominant Dutch society but that a "racialized" difference may or may not be signified based on the Dutch social construction of ethnicity.

Recognizing how "ethno-racism," a term I have coined to acknowledge the interlocking structures that work in concert in the Netherlands, operates as an intersecting system of oppression and identity rather than "as separate and discrete systems of hierarchy" with gender and sexuality (Gamson et al 2004, Collins, 2000, Glenn, 1992) in the realm of Dutch sex work suggests greater complexity to the treatment of the issues raised in this text. While institutional ethno-racism, sexism, and heteronormativity are reinforced every day in not so subtle ways, and extend to the origins of sex work as a manifestation of Dutch colonial and patriarchy relations, to understand how master social categories materialize in the micro-practices of life renders them, for most part, as invisible forces. One way to shed light on social inequities produced in the commercialized sex industry begins by identifying a two-tier prostitution industry that benefits some sex workers, namely Dutch citizens and other European Union residents, with rights and excludes others, namely undocumented migrants. Listening to Dutch informants talk about their experiences on the streets and the mobility of their social roles gives some indication of how white status is conferred to some sex workers but not others in Dutch society. This privilege leads to heightened expectations of personal success and the ability to navigate through different social institutions, forcefully advocating for themselves as indications of how invisible privilege operates through knowledge systems and access. But to grasp the nuanced dimensions in which ethno-racism, sexism, and heteronormativity and how these systems are replicated through social interaction with different institutions and social groups would have meant that I was to conduct a different kind of study.

To determine what is normalized in Dutch life might reveal ways in which ethno-racism, sexism, and heteronormativity are reproduced, sanctioned, and regulated. I will never fully grasp the internalized emotive response many undocumented workers have when in contact with the police, social workers, public health workers, clients, and Dutch citizens. For such a sex worker to explain to me how these systems of oppression are played out in their everyday working experiences did not occur in such an obvious way. This is, however, where symbolic metaphors play a role in treating how power relations are deployed within Dutch prostitution. For instance, the historical symbolism of Latin American female sex workers providing waged sexual services to European male clients reveals a pattern of historically situated colonial sexual relations of domination and servitude. On a micro-level I might ask why did a Latin American female streetwalker end up the victim of being paid in counterfeit currency when Dutch streetwalkers were not? This becomes apparent in my imagination when I take a step back from the figurative prostitution window or streetwalking zone, and ask myself how am I supposed to frame contemporary commercial sexual relations when the parties involved in the exchange are "immigrants" or in some cases when both client and sex worker are immigrants? The symbolic reality that I witnessed over a two-and-half-year period was not so obvious as a reproduction of post colonial relations, or even patriarchy as it is defined. How does this configuration shift when the sex provider is a transgendered person and the client is Turkish? The lens that locates remnants of colonial relations is more difficult to hold steady in this context where the parties keep changing representation. Hence, the fluidity of identity and social relations within the commercial exchange lends to a challenging undertaking for any study that intersects the topics of migration, race, sexual identity, and erotic labor.

"TRANSGENDERED" AS AN UMBRELLA TERM

The longstanding feminist project (Lorber, 1994; Sedgewick, 1994; Butler, 1989; Rubin, 1975) challenging the naturalization of all sexual dualisms in western society has with some success done so by theoretically dismantling the "hegemonic hold" sexual binaries have on conceptualizations and assumptions made about gender and sexuality. The fixed rationale under question has been up until now concealed within the matrix of reproductive heterosexuality (Lorber, 1994: 25). Reframing gender and sexuality systems as historical social products makes it possible to reconceptualize genders and sexualities as fluid and flexible forms emerging under changing societal conditions over time. Judith Butler, in particular, asserts a social constructivist stance treating gender and sexuality as a fluid state and influencing the direction of this study. In particular, Butler calls for subversion, or "gender trouble," to expose how gender performances are enacted and reproduced in everyday life. Resistance, therefore, is achieved through parody to destabilize notions of a "naturalized" gendered self. Subversion, Butler argues, occurs explicitly through drag, linguistics, and an "incoherent" gendered body.

Many queer theorists, activists, and transgenderists alike have contested this notion of who and what constitutes as transgendered (Gamson, 1995; Broad, 2002). For some groups the definition of "transgendered" only includes "those who change their gender but not their sex" (Broad, 2002: 248). For others, it is a matter of "not fitting" into either a traditional idea of what is masculine or feminine. Because of the broadness of this concept, the process of transgendered "identity building strategies" might suggest that no universal identity claim applies to this group or that a transgendered performance functions more as a "identity-blurring" tactic (Gamson, 1995: 590; Broad, 2002: 244) than the formation of a "collectively identity." The master category of gender is, therefore, challenged by transgendered identity politics taking on "gay/lesbian ethnic identity" by using "queer deconstructive politics" (Broad, 2002: 243).

It is necessary to address the number of identity claims attached to the word "transgendered." Usually, the term transgendered identifies the following: "transsexual,"[15] "pre-operative transsexuals," "*travesti*"[16] and/or "transvestite/cross-dresser." Throughout the book the word "transgendered" is used as an inclusive, umbrella term. My use of this term represents my viewpoint unless indicated otherwise.

In the streetwalking zone, the gender identities of streetwalkers are labeled according to how local human service agencies demarcate the sidewalk. Enforcement of gender labels determined where streetwalkers stood on the curb. Transgendered and transvestite prostitutes stood on one side of the street while women and transsexuals worked on the more visible side of the strip (this situation is explained in greater detail later in this chapter). Most streetwalkers I spoke to identified themselves according to how they were classified in the organization of the zone. Distinctions between the different groups represented as "transgendered" are made in a number of ways. In the streetwalking zone where I gathered data, for instance, informants identified "transsexuals" as women who have had a sex reassignment (male-to-female) and stand on the same side of the street as other female prostitutes. Of three transsexuals I interviewed, most defined themselves as "operated-women."[17]

"*Travesti*" is a common term used in Latin America (Kulíck, 1996). In addition to wearing female coded clothing, *travesti*s have had some "body modification" to enhance their feminine appearance. Many *travestí*s, particularly those from Latin America, ingest female hormones purchased in the underground economy, and have industrial silicone injected into their hips, buttocks, and possibly their breasts (Kulíck, 1996). They do, however, retain their male genitalia and during sexual exchanges with clients sometimes perform with their penis depending upon the request of the client. During the course of my data gathering, Dutch "*travestís*" refer to themselves as "transgendered." As a result, I use the terms interchangeably when referring to them. The other group present on the street were transvestites and/or cross-dressers who dress in women's clothing when streetwalking at night but "live" and identify themselves as men. Both *travestís* and transvestites are spatially segregated from female and transsexual prostitutes and share the "transgendered" section of streetwalking areas. In my research, I focus exclusively on transgendered prostitutes who rent windows in Amsterdam and female and transgendered streetwalkers who work in an unregulated streetwalking zone in the city of Den Apelhaven.[18] Based on my skewed sample, the dominant perspective, however, is transgendered rather than female.

Many Dutch and EU sex workers complain regularly that the presence of migrants has changed the demands of the business. They argue that prior to the migrants' arrival, sex workers were only expected to perform either oral sex or genital sex, never both for the price of an exchange. In addition, they also criticize migrants for undercutting prices set and accepted by most Dutch sex workers. As a result of these new conditions, the "rules" or expectations have changed, or intensified, requiring all sex workers to provide oral stimulation to the clients' genitals as well as genital or anal sex.

Most of the data I gathered refers to transgendered prostitutes and their sexual practices. These distinctions between types of people performing erotic labor in some cases reflect the different services they provide to clients. Whether in the windows or street, the sexual performance has become somewhat standardized. With the exception of fulfilling specific client fantasies, most window prostitutes and streetwalkers usually perform what they call a "suck and fuck" for 50 Fl ($25 or 25 Euro). This involves beginning the transaction with oral stimulation to the male client's genitals and then after he becomes aroused, performing genital-to-genital sex if the sex worker is anatomically female. Transgendered sex workers perform oral genital stimulation and then engage in anal sex in the role of "insertee" or "inserter." As part of the unofficial contract, the client is given ten minutes to have an orgasm. If the client seeks any other physical contact with the sex worker the exchange goes back into negotiation.

THE LAYOUT OF THE BOOK

The next two chapters respectively deal with literature relevant to my research and methodological issues, procedures, and processes specific to my fieldwork. Chapter Four—Space and Place: in the Windows, grounds the text in the sites where I gathered data. It details an auto-ethnographic account of my experiences entering sexualized spaces, my role in the sites near or where sex work occurred and also how sex workers understand those sites. The physical locations described include the Red Light District in Amsterdam, and interior of windows used for commercial sex. The Chapter Five- Space and Place: in the zone details my observations inside of a community center, in and around the vicinity of a streetwalking zone, and inside the residence of an informant. To understand how these spaces are organized and how relations are mediated in them, I draw on the writings of Pierre Bourdieu.

Chapter Six -Victoria van der Way, is entirely devoted to the life story of a Dutch transsexual. She embodies multiple social roles as a middle-class Dutch citizen, transsexual, geriatrics nurse, streetwalker, advocate, and property owner. Her life story becomes emblematic of how a subject adapts to diverse conditions and environments. Perhaps most importantly, her life challenges mainstream approaches to identity and sexuality, or "pathologized/victimized" prostitution narratives so often found in academic texts (Heyl, 1979).

This chapter is written in a structure and style intended to bring out Victoria's personality and cadence. The structure of the chapter chronicles the development of my relationship with her during multiple interviews together. Most aspects of her life story are reconstructed in the order in which they were revealed, however some themes have been condensed into cohesive tales because of a pattern in our dialogues that often returned us to previously discussed topics. Victoria's speech is animated and spontaneous. Without the use of an electronic recording device, I had to take notes furiously as she spoke to capture exact language used when reconstructing events in her life. This strategy of using a conversational tone of writing is intended to make her present in this chapter.

The last data chapter, Chapter Seven—Coping strategies for economic, physical and emotional survival on the streets and in the windows, focuses on the coping strategies used by sex workers to optimize economic, social, and/or emotional benefit. It reconstructs data gathered during observations and conversational interviews with prostitutes. Those interviews varied in length and complexity, concentrating primarily on the meaning transgendered and female sex workers gave to their experiences on the streets and intimate relations. Different subjects share how they are "making out" in the world, especially with lovers, police, clients, and other actors on the scene. The chapter begins with the story of an "unsuccessful" female Dutch prostitute, Anke, whose life experiences prove to be a tale of defiance and individualized cultural practices. Central to her story, and those of some others like Ramona, an Ecuadorian *travestí*, are the ways sex workers cope with alienation and intimacy in their professional and personal lives. Finally, in the conclusion, I discuss the relevance of my work to understand window and streetwalking prostitution in the context of the Netherlands.

Chapter Two
Changing Perspectives on Prostitution

Research studies reviewed in this chapter served a number of purposes in my education on the subject. First, they were useful to illustrate how varied theoretical positions framed prostitution under diverse sets of cultural and historical conditions. Second, they provided examples of different methodological approaches used to establish relations between researcher and subject, and diverse ways of crafting data into analytic findings. Third, they gave me the foresight to navigate through tense political circumstances when I entered the Netherlands.[1] And finally, they radicalized me as I embraced or rejected them, eventually leading me to my theoretical home in the selective readings of sex radicalism and first-hand narratives of sex workers.

To my knowledge, most of the literature on Dutch prostitution written in English (the only language I can read) is limited to historical recounts on the trafficking of women, commonly referred to as "white slavery," (Altink, 1995; Pheterson, 1996; Wijers and Lap-Chew, 1997), focuses on public health initiatives gauging success rates of safe sex initiatives among migrant and EU sex workers (Van Haastricht et al, 1993; EUROPAP, 1997; Tampep, 1997, 1996), or evaluates policy agendas (Bindman with Doezema, 1997; Mr. A. de Graaf Stitching, 1997; Haveman, 1998; Doezema, 1999; Wijers and van Doorninck, 2002) determining whether voluntary entry into prostitution really exists or whether legalization simply conceals elements of coercion, how best to define human trafficking and to develop strategies that benefit migrant women. This is mainly due to the fact that the dominant framers[2] of Dutch prostitution take a legal standpoint to determine how to proceed around the topic. Apart from few exceptions (Chapkis, 1997) to date no detailed ethnographic studies of sex workers have been undertaken. Moreover, a coherent set of narratives describing current patterns in Dutch prostitution is missing or if available is not accessible to me due to language.

It must be acknowledged that as a non-Dutch person, I entered the field with a myopic focus on prostitution. What I lacked was a sensibility around how the Dutch construct their social reality or how they think and respond to prostitution based on the series of ideas produced within their society. The purpose of my work, however, far from being an attempt to challenge the logic of Dutch prostitution policy, is to present first hand accounts of sex workers' experiences in a regulated environment to a wider audience.

A large body of literature presenting North American narratives on prostitution is accessible and continues to shape the way researchers think about prostitution. Although the American studies cited in this chapter refer to a context where, unlike the Netherlands, prostitution is criminalized and may not directly apply to my research issues, they serve as a background to understand various modes of thought around prostitution.

The early sociological studies on prostitution (K. Davis, 1937; Maurer, 1939; Whyte, 1943; N. Davis, 1971; Skipper and McCaghy 1971) provide insight into what dominant cultural values and problems concerned researchers sixty-five years ago, exposing both short-lived preoccupations and longstanding unanswered questions. I then discuss how recent studies have readdressed prostitution filtering it through different and, at times, antagonistic theoretical frameworks. Here I discuss multiple feminist perspectives from abolitionists, who declare all prostitution as a form of male domination and sexual slavery (Shrage, 1989; Barry, 1995; Dines, 1998), and "Third World" feminist activists (Kempadoo and Doezema, 1998), Regulationists (O'Neill, 2000), to Sex Radicals (Chapkis, 1997; Nagle; 1997) who recognize the resiliency of prostitution and therefore advocate greater rights to sex workers. My "take" on sex work in the Netherlands is to recognize prostitution as a form of labor or series of services requiring a performance from the sex worker. Therefore, I have adopted the "Sex Radical" interpretation acknowledging that sex work can undermine existing sexual hierarchies or elicit forms of resistance to sanctified heterosexual relations.

Later in the chapter I devote a section to the analysis of writings on economic globalization and development (Troung, 1990; Eloe, 1992; Pruitt and LaFont, 1995; Kempadoo, 2000) that examine complex forces linking historical colonialism, consumerism, and tourism to prostitution. I do so because some of the issues are relevant to my informants, as many of them are undocumented workers who illegally migrated to the Netherlands to work in the sex industry. While some of this analysis might get lost in my descriptive depiction of practices on the streets and in the windows, however it is a reminder that these social relations did not occur in an economic or political vacuum.

Included in my review are also first-hand accounts of sex workers' experiences of erotic labor (Alexander, 1995; Nagle, 1997; Eaves, 2002; Delacoste, 1998) and research conducted on the social meaning gay sex workers attribute to their performance (Browne and Minichiello, 1995) as I plan to construct an understanding based on sex workers' knowledge of prostitution. Both bodies of work helped me reflect on modes of erotic interplay from the perspective of the sex worker and influenced the shape and form of my inquiry in the field.

The last section of the chapter reviews writings on transgenderism (Kulíck, 1996; Pettiway, 1996; Prieur, 1998) and is perhaps the most relevant to my research as many of my informants are transgendered. These writings played a key part in my understanding of gender role-playing during a commercial sexual exchange. Most of them approach prostitution and transgenderism using an ethnographic method in which the researcher lives among this community. They are richly descriptive and researchers give ample room for the voices of their "co-collaborators" to be heard. Furthermore, this qualitative approach brings into focus the identity politics that every researcher brings to the field, suggesting that sometimes a shared identity claim seals relationships with informants and other times not.

CURRENT DUTCH STUDIES

Studies on Dutch prostitution focus on theoretical debates over "voluntary" and "involuntary" participation in sex work (Altink, 1995; Doezema, 1995, 1999; Pheterson, 1995), ways of approaching trafficking of women (Doezema, 1995, 1999; Wijers and Lap-Chew, 1997; Haveman, 1998; Wijers and van Doorninck, 2000), and public health issues concerning undocumented workers (TEMPEP, 1995, 1996, 1997, 1998; Municipal Health Services, 1997; EUROPAP, 1997). Legalization of prostitution in the Netherlands is grounded in the right of self-determination established by the International Committee for Prostitutes' Rights (Doezema references Pheterson, 1995). Accordingly, only "voluntary" prostitutes have the legal right to work. Therefore, the definition of "voluntary" prostitute is central to argumentation for legalization. Doezema calls attention to racist and classist assumptions embedded in notions of voluntary entry into Dutch prostitution. A "voluntary" prostitute is one who participates in sex work by economic "choice" and without coercion. This assumption almost exclusively includes white, Dutch women or citizens of the European Union. Third World and migrant women who enter prostitution because of limited economic opportunities are framed in a completely different way. They are seen as victims and are a priori denied any agency in the debate around voluntary versus involuntary entry. Doezema points out that there are multiple realities of sex work and that the real abuse stems from how prostitutes are treated and stigmatized by society rather then the institution itself.

Current anti-trafficking campaigns concentrate on exploitation of Third World women forced into the sex industry in Europe. Some researchers question the "criteria for criminalization" when addressing traffic of persons in the Netherlands and rhetorically ask what "function" criminalization serves and whom it holds accountable (English summary, Haveman, 1998). Other studies (Wijers and Lap-Chew, 1997; Wijers and van Doorninck, 2000) stress strategies for approaching trafficking of women so that policy might not worsen conditions or erode much needed rights for migrants and other women already working in prostitution. They challenge how each framework, from "immigration, organized crime, human rights, to the feminization of poverty," constructs related issues to undocumented sex work and whether a policy agenda benefits the real needs and concerns of migrant women (Wijer and van Doorninck, p. 1). Anti-trafficking law enforcement data helped me better understand punitive risks undocumented sex workers face each time they work in the streetwalking zone. This policy approach shows even less interest in the rights and possible abuses of migrant and "Third World" women who "voluntarily" enter prostitution in the Netherlands. The problem of undocumented workers, therefore, rests in the framing of their presence there and throughout the European Union.

There are a variety of ways in which undocumented prostitution is framed. When the topic is understood as a "migration problem," the focus is on preventing entry into Western Europe and devising measures against illegal workers from working or living there. When the problem is framed as an issue of "organized crime," the migrant is constructed as a victim and a form of physical "evidence" of a criminal act. Either way, these studies suggest that both interpretations can have repressive results for migrant women, and propose to provide greater rights for all sex workers regardless of their legal status.

A plethora of Dutch public health research (Municipal Health Services, 1997; EUROPAP, 1997) focuses on STD and HIV prevention activities. Migrant and transgendered communities working in streetwalking zones are targeted to determine their knowledge of STD/HIV transmission. Other projects (TEMPEP, 1995, 1996, 1997, 1998) aim for community outreach to Latin American, African, and Eastern European populations to develop a greater understanding of their working conditions, recruitment into Dutch prostitution, and how best to serve their health needs. Identifying these studies locates who are the dominant framers of Dutch prostitution and what is the locus of attention for most Dutch research.

SHIFTING PERSPECTIVES OF PROSTITUTION

This section provides insight into the historical development of positions on and language used to define prostitution. I divide this section into two parts. The first part is devoted to a brief discussion of early studies on prostitution and the second part lays out current feminist debates around the topic as both a local and global issue. Although not directly related to my research setting, the first part serves as background material to the reader and identifies preconceptions still held regarding prostitution. The second part, meanwhile, presents a spectrum of contemporary feminist positions that I critique and inevitably position myself within to set up a perspective through which to frame my work.

EARLY STUDIES

Early studies (K. Davis, 1937; Maurer, 1939; Whyte, 1943; N. Davis, 1971) frame the phenomenon of prostitution - and the actors involved - through various theoretical models often constructing prostitution in opposition to "legitimate" heterosexual institutions. Whether prostitutes were described as impoverished female victims of industrialization or "lower class degenerates" partaking in organized crime (N. Davis, 1971), sociologists have historically used a rigid causal framework through which to problematized prostitutes in society. Kingsley Davis identifies social mechanisms controlling how sexuality is conceptualized, analyzing how society "encouraged" and "forced" participation in institutionalized heterosexuality. He does this by illustrating how societal forces "discouraged" subjects from having (hetero)sex outside legitimate institutions such as marriage, and how society enforces strict incest taboos. He concludes that marriage is a "chief cultural arrangement" and without positive and negative norms attached to it and other sexual practices there would be no institutionalized way of controlling sexuality. This framework identifies dominant cultural values of the time and how morals are reinforced in everyday socialization as well as in the assumptions researchers make about commercial sex.

Other studies (Maurer, 1939; J. Bryan, 1962; Skipper and McGaghy, 1971) reflect similar historical assumptions and use an authoritative tone or moral judgment on both the topic and the human subjects under study. Clinical distance in the design and interpretation of the earlier works reflects every attempt of researchers to take an "objective" stance. Some social scientists (Skipper and McCaghy 1971), moreover, refer to female subjects in language replete with evaluative determinism ("alienated" and "deviant") and dismiss the subject's interpretations of her sex performance or meaning she gives to commercial interactions (N. Davis, 1971; N. Jackson, 1963). The subjects who claim a positive status attached to commercial sexual activity are described as morally suspicious or defined as "promiscuous" (N. Davis referencing Thomas, 1939). In yet another study (Maurer, 1939), prostitutes are portrayed as a "culture-less" group of women lacking the intelligence to develop their own argot or strategy for finding higher status criminal activity within the informal sector.

These early works function as a way of holding me in check as I contemplate ways in which I have been socialized inside the dominant culture to assume what is "normal" sexual behavior and what happens to those who subvert the ideals of compulsive heterosexuality. As a result I have tried to validate the social meaning sex workers give to their work without moral judgment and to write about myself as an actor inside the field site rather than as a detached authority.

In the 1960s and 70s, a theoretical movement challenged many of the tenets previously found in the sociology of deviance (Lemert, 1951; Becker, 1963; Liazos, 1972). What emerged from these writings is known today as labeling theory. A central tenet of labeling theory identifies how individuals or groups from marginalized positions in society are often subjugated to exclusionary practices and/or made the object of studies that reproduce existing assumptions about them. The internalization of a deviant label "marks" the individual who then "organizes" his/her deviant identity around a set of prescribed behaviors or actions socially interpreted as "deviant" (Pontell, 1996: p. 61). Moreover, the implications made by labeling theory addresses how certain actions or individuals become marked as abnormal, while other types of behavior get overlooked. As a result, the "interactionists," as they were called, focused part of their inquiry on how social values become naturalized in society and how that standard enforces the categorizing of others. Becker, in particular, identifies how "rule creators" and "rule enforcers" determine and perpetuate their own interest in the labeling process.

During this period, a significant study came out on the role of the American "madam" in the professional indoctrination of "house prostitutes"

(Heyl, 1979). Heyl explores "career processes" through her use of life-history methodologies and accomplishes this feat without the moral judgment found in previous prostitution studies (Heyl, 1979; 155). This research focuses on the perspective of informants, departing radically from the deviant identity model when interpreting findings. Here, the author uses language of her informants to identify individuals and the acts they perform. This study supports my choice of language and the powerful meaning attached to language such as "sex work" and "sex worker," and the meaning ascribed to activities from the perspective of the informant.

FROM "DEVIANT" TO "VICTIM" AND "SEXUAL RENEGADE"

Feminist theories that have emerged in the last thirty-five years have organized around various positions on prostitution. One of the dominant voices comes from a European-American feminist project that focuses on gendered subjugation by male domination and patriarchy. In the writings of Andrea Dworkin, Kate Millet, and Kathleen Barry all forms of heterosexual relations have been classified as male violence against women (Clough, 1994: 14). This includes consensual heterosexual relations, pornography, prostitution, rape, child pornography, and unpaid domestic labor clustered together under a heterosexual matrix. In the interim, the prostitute was transformed from "deviant" to "victim" of exploitative male sexual violence and prostitution interpreted as a human rights issue addressed before the United Nations (Clough, 1994; Chapkis, 1997; O'Neill, 2001).

Dialogues between Radical Feminists and organized sex workers have taken place over the years but often have amounted to miscommunication. This schism identifies how differently the two camps understand and interpret sex work. Sex workers have criticized radical feminists for misrepresenting their concerns and dismissing their understanding of their experience as uneducated or lacking an enlightened heterosexual consciousness. They have also charged radical feminists with stripping all women who enter prostitution of any agency (Toronto Women's Conference, 1985).

In the dialogues that ensued between Canadian and American sex workers, they began expressing their own needs which include decriminalization,[3] exemption from punitive consequences, rights to fair wages, physical safety, and control of their enterprises (Bell, 1985). With this said, Radical Feminists still question whether decriminalization improves conditions or worsens them even if these basic needs were granted in North America as they are (partially) in the Netherlands. Radical Feminists fear that "legalized" conditions only "normalize" the institutionalization of sex work, particularly in places where limited labor market alternatives exist for women (Barry, 1995). This "academic" stance fails to exhibit solidarity with the struggle of sex workers, and for this reason, my politics lean toward presenting the views of sex workers as a primary filter to understand this topic.

In *Live Sex Acts: Women Performing Erotic Labour*, Wendy Chapkis broadens debates over the meaning of prostitution and the rights of sex workers in the United States and The Netherlands. Again, the laying out of the different points of view exposed the politically charged environment in which I entered. While Abolitionists[4] and the Anti-Sex[5] and Pro-Sex-Positive[6] movements contend that all "commodified sex" represents a form of sexual violence, Chapkis, stating a position in the Sex Radical movement,[7] interprets sex work as a way of undermining an existing sexual order and define "recreational sex" as a "libratory terrain" (Chapkis, 1997: 1).

As Chapkis and others point out (Kempadoo, 1999; O'Neill, 2001,), depictions of women as passive agents under a heterosexual matrix (Chapkis, 1997: 15), drain the commercial sex exchange of any resistance or subversion, "flattening" whatever "dialectics of struggle" may exist into a "seamless system of male domination" (Chapkis, 1997: 20). Moreover, when a "First World" feminist framework is used to understand prostitution and the lives of women in the "Third-World," it generates a dehumanizing representation in line with a language of victimization, hence "join[ing] forces with power it seeks to challenge" (Chapkis, 1997: 14; Kempadoo, 2000).

I am indebted to Chapkis for putting herself and her point of view out into the general dialogue on erotic labor practices and performativity.[8] Chapkis' presence gives me the confidence to contemplate new ways of framing sex work, and to discover subversive ways of understanding erotic labor without betraying (the false perception of) a uniform feminist project. After all, Chapkis' intention was to "heal the schism with feminism" around commercial sex (Chapkis, 1997: 1), and to expose dichotomies translating into a language and terrain with loaded meaning and intentions.

Chapkis' comparative study of erotic labor in San Francisco and Amsterdam samples across the occupation of "erotic labor." In this instance, Chapkis cleverly blurs the definition of prostitution under a "wide range of occupation locations" of sex work or erotic labor to present a unifying front while at the same time adamantly acknowledges that the experience of sex work is contextual (Chapkis, 1997: 7). The results are largely shaped by her interviews with "women performing erotic labor" and with politicized activists and friends in the sex industry who share her "sex radical" perspective (Chapkis, 1997: 7).

Chapkis does not disclose in her book, but did so during an interview she gave me in 1998, her limited direct access to potential informants in the Netherlands. Local Dutch prostitution advocacy organizations denied Chapkis direct access, and as a result, she had to submit her survey questionnaire to be handed out by employees at an anti-trafficking organization, never meeting some of the subjects who answered her questions.

What Chapkis does with her data is equally significant and political in nature. Chapkis makes an effort to "acknowledge the power of the writer" when editing interview transcripts. Interview narratives are fully intact without her interpretation from the author. In attempt to "confront her own agenda" rather than using sex workers' stories to simply authenticate her own position, (p.7), she draws on the perspectives of "dissenting voices" of erotic laborers, who do not share her view.

Some of my fieldwork experience parallels the obstacles Chapkis faced while conducting her study. My data gathering, and more specifically, the persistence with which I had to endure to complete my fieldwork follow in the footsteps of Chapkis. My own attempts at contacting Dutch prostitution advocacy organizations under the assumption that I would gain access through them failed. This forces me to circumvent these institutions and to operate as a sole-researcher making contact one-on-one with window and street prostitutes. Taking this approach was crucial for the completion of this study and only felt personally justifiable after I learned first-hand from Chapkis of what was missing from her comparative study. As for her "intact" interviews in which informants submit or record a response to the researcher's questions, I felt it would be of value to write about the environments in which prostitutes work and live, and to include myself in the reconstruction of the events and the conditions under which life stories were told to me. In some ways, this approach to writing ethnographic material gives greater validity to the tales and narratives as they were communicated to me without an electronic recording device.

Other significant writing from the Sex-Radical group comes from the personal narratives of sex workers themselves. In Jill Nagle's *Whores and Other Feminists* (1997) sex workers and activists share their labor experiences. The compilation of first-person accounts of working in the sex industry stresses the need for constructing knowledge from the standpoint of erotic laborers. Nagle deconstructs linguistic binaries that reproduce stigmas attached to prostitutes. Based on the resignification of sex work and solidarity among all erotic laborers she reclaims the word "whore," and introduces "whore feminisms." This standpoint approaches sex work from a positive location, declaring how working in the industry can be fulfilling for erotic laborers.

One personal narrative in *Whores and Other Feminists* stresses the meaning of understanding erotic labor from a first-person depiction. This narrative and others like it inform me of how erotic laborers experience being on display in the windows. As a filmmaker and erotic dancer, Vicki Funari's "Naked, Naughty, Nasty," holds as a memorable auto-ethnographic narration identifying bodily performance as a form of repetition drained of eroticism. For Funari, sensual acts are imbued with lifeless commercial exchanges leaving her to ask why male clients seek out and purchase simulacra and other "fiction of female desire" in the first place (Funari, 1997: 26). Funari makes contrasting analogies to filmmaking and erotic dancing. The control she has in constructing images behind the camera contrasts with disempowerment she experiences while dancing or maybe it is only another "fiction" as she loses personal control while fulfilling the fantasies of clients (Funari, 1997: 26). In the end, Funari wonders if the organization of strip clubs and their actors, as a symbol of perversity, serves to "normalize" the "outside" world, or whether the commercial exchange simply mirrors societal norms (Funari, 1997: 26).

In *Prostitution and Feminism: Towards a Politics of Feeling*, Maggie O'Neill proposes a multi-method approach to conduct research on prostitution. O'Neill reviews feminist debates on prostitution and then presents ethnographic data collected while working for a local magistrate in the UK. Although her initial use of the data was intended for a clinical audience for institutional purposes, to analyze her data for this book, she draws on a "critical feminist standpoint" and then deploys a Participatory Action Research (PAR) methods approach, along with ethno-mimesis (from Adorno's writings on art). Her application of "hybrid" methods or "interpretive ethnography" suggests the value of multi-methods approach. Given the constraints of her research design, however, I question how she uses these methods in her study of drug-addicted British teenagers. Despite these shortcomings, O'Neill's proposition relates to my own project in a tangible way. In the chapter on coping strategies, I focus on "coping" practices that directly make links between "multiple micro realities" that expose day-to-day negotiation taking place between sex workers and their clients and sweeping socio-cultural relations that allude to broader economic forces.

O'Neill also claims there is room within the social sciences for using "visual/artistic re-presentation" to convey the experiences of sex work (O'Neill, 2001: 2). She is motivated to evoke an emotional response in her reader/viewer giving examples of the emotive force of performative art on stage. Her identification of "psychic processes" – "feeling, meanings, identities" – connects to macro processes, and identifies the goal of research to transform experiences through "art, life-story narratives, and film" (O'Neill, 2001: 5, 7).

Here, I described a number of studies presenting feminist positions on prostitution. I recognize, like the Radical Feminists, that prostitution, in some instances, is a human rights issue. This is especially the case when involving children and human trafficking. Nevertheless, this depiction of prostitution inextricably connected to coercion and exploitation is not universal and may not apply to all conditions under which people enter and work in the industry. There are elements, of course, of an underground economy even in the Netherlands, [9] however the Dutch are trying to enforce a regulatory system to organize and control this part of the industry. Overall, this site is a place where sex workers have greater rights and benefits, and therefore, in line with the Sex Radicals, I recognize a person's right to work and earn money with her body. Cases of informants who profited from the needs and desires of clients can be found in my interviews. Their experiences, far from being without any agency, represent examples of multiple ways dominant sexual hierarchy may be subverted.

POST COLONIAL RELATIONS AND SEX TOURISM

As mentioned in the preceding section, the last two decades have seen an influx of migrant sex workers from "Third World" countries to the Netherlands. As a result, the make-up of people working in this sector presents new and complex issues challenging the regulatory system. Each person arrived in the Netherlands under different social and economic circumstances. Literature on post colonial relations and sex tourism serves as background material for understanding what events might have precipitated their arrival.

Critical writings (Truong, 1990; Enloe, 1992) on the subject expand to colonialism and sex tourism in other "Third World" regions where economic and social relations are tied to the "First World." In particular, *Global Sex Workers: Rights, Resistance, and Redefinition*, (Kempadoo and Doezema edited, 1999) examines globalization of sex work (Kempadoo and Doezema, 1998: 2). Their thesis is based on issues of national economics and debt repayment that give impetus for the creation of and increasing dependency on tourism. "First-World/Third World" dualisms are also challenged. "Neo-colonial" and "un-nuanced" feminist writings identified as "First World-Anglo" feminism are charged with racism for reconstructing a dialogue on sexual exploitation in which the "victim" must be rescued (Barry, 1984) or depicted as passive, exoticized Other (Kempadoo and Doezema, 1998: 11).

Reproduction of post-colonial relations through sex tourism is not exclusive to European and North American males seeking out "Third-World" prostitutes. Pruitt and LaFont (Pruitt and LaFont, 1995: 423) describe a "suspended reality" of commercial sexual exchange between economically mobile European and North American women and marginalized Jamaican "Rastamen" or "Rent-a-dreads" who provide sexual "services" to the women while they are on vacation. Following notions of Western "courtship" in the form of "gift-giving," the two parties reproduce inequalities they interpret as inconsequential or simply ignore. These sexual relations in this context intersect gendered structures of power with race and class, producing new "asymmetries."

Similar to most commodified forms of leisure time, material realities are layered under a fantasy, temporarily eroding social conventions regarding racialized and classed romantic restrictions. Thus European or North American female tourists achieve a new social reality as they appropriate resignified symbols of indigenous Jamaican culture – represented by Rasta culture and Caribbean lifestyle - and experience a form of cultural transformation (Pruitt and LaFont, 1995: 431). Commodification of the culture presented may be a misrepresentation or reconstruction of Jamaican life, however in this instance the "Rasta's" performance is a form of survival.

In this last example, Rastamen exchange "romantic" sexual relations for westernized economic status. Part of this exchange involves a reproduction of the "naturalized" world where Rastamen claim to originate and where European or American women desire to gain entry through sexual relations (Pruitt and Lafont, 1995: 428). Lying at the center of the transaction, however, is an analogy to economic relations between "First and Third World" spheres (Pruitt and LaFont, 1995: 428). While I do not take a political economy approach in my research, I signal how racial, class, and cultural relations play out in Dutch prostitution. In effect, these writings identify both historical colonial relations that facilitate modern prostitution, and how economic development strategies affect the daily lives of "Third World" citizens, presenting incentives for entering prostitution either in their countries of origin or abroad.

THE MALE SEX TRADE

Analysis of the male sex trade broadens the way I think of prostitution and who performs the sexual exchange. I do not suggest that the experiences of transgendered and gay sex workers are synonymous, however identity issues unveiled in this literature apply to most of my informants as well. To date, few studies have focused on the gay sex trade. Most data concentrate on public health and HIV transmission, juvenile incarceration, and substance abuse (Browne and Minicheillo, 1995: 30-32). In a rare instance, Browne and Minichiello (1995) have produced a significant series of articles on the social meaning gay sex workers give to their sexual performance and how they distinguish "personal" from "commercial" sex and other "modes of interaction" between client and provider (Browne & Minichiello, 1995: 598).[10]

Gay and bisexual prostitutes challenge notions of agency and any overarching theory of prostitution as a gendered division of labor (Browne and Minicheillo, 1995: 599-601). Identity politics, however, still play a key role in their professional concerns. For instance, if subjects claim a gay identity inside a heterosexual space, then the label carries a stigmatizing meaning for them. This social position may also result in devising strategies around how to avoid permanent negative effects of working in the sex industry (Browne and Minicheillo, 1995: 599-601). Many gay male sex workers gain a sense of agency from their relationships with clients because they have greater flexibility regarding whom they choose to sexually service. Greater economic agility exists for this group because many of them provide sexual services on a part-time basis or hold formal employment during the day (Browne and Minicheillo, 1995: 598).

This research addresses how gay sex workers grasp prostitution through their bodily parameters (Browne and Minichiello, 1995: 611). As a boundary between personal and professional sex, the condom symbolizes "work equipment" and integrates into the "act" of pleasure for many sex workers. By constructing a "false sex" with a barrier, the service is understood as a performance, allowing sex workers to maintain emotional boundary management[11] (Browne and Minicheillo, 1995: 603). Other performative acts prior to the sexual exchange, including nonverbal communication and intuiting as a way of interpreting client needs, were identified by gay sex workers and substantiated in my data gathering.

Like the gay sex workers who maintained mental and emotional "space" through personal boundaries and "self programming," (Browne and Minichiello, 1995: 611) my informants talked about their use of a "sixth sense" largely in the context of safety issues or when "sussing" out how much money a client had to spend on sex. To my knowledge, all the transgendered and female sex workers whom I interviewed used condoms in a professional context, and, perhaps because of extensive sex education in the Netherlands, often used safe sex tactics in their private relations as well. Despite their use of condoms, I inquired into how female and transgendered prostitutes demarcate their "private" and "commercial" realms and ascribe meaning to the types of sex in which they engage.

ETHNOGRAPHY & TRANGENDERED PERSONS

Studies on transgendered prostitution have great relevance to my study because nineteen of my twenty-two informants identify as transgendered. The three primary studies of interest are a life-history of five drug-addicted, transgendered African-Americans (Pettiway, 1996), Prieur's ethnographic study of a brothel in Mexico City (1994), and an ethnography conducted among transgendered Brazilians (Kulíck, 1996).

Pettiway explores the construction of gender identity, race, and drug-use through the experiences of five African-American, "gay" (as the author defines them), drug addicted, sex workers (1996). Each subject is characterized as a "deviant" who "commits" sex work (Pettiway, 1996: xxiv). This vocabulary used to describe the activities his subjects partake in suggests that Pettiway understands prostitution and drug consumption through a criminal justice model.[12] The researcher also lays out a set of assumptions about what is a normative cultural value and what it means for an individual to "fail" at entering mainstream society. Although he "refrains from speaking with authority," his preconceptions interfere with Pettiway's ability to approach his subjects in a "non-judgmental" manner (Pettiway, 1996: xxi). Specifically, his criminology framework affects his ability to evaluate his definitions of what is "dysfunctional" behavior and how he categorizes his subjects as examples of "disorder" (Pettiway, 1996: xxii).

It is also relevant to consider the approach used for gathering data. Pettiway interviewed his subjects in a "room" for one hour with a desk and tape recorder between him and his subjects. During all interviews Pettiway was addressed as "Doc," distancing himself from his subjects. At no time did Pettiway attempt entering their everyday living arrangements or working conditions. This approach appears limiting in terms of research design and the kind of rapport he shared with his subjects. How does Pettiway achieve understanding of their daily lives given his moralistic and physical distance from his subjects? Even with Pettiway's "coaxing" during his interviews, and his reflections as a gay black man, he dissociates himself from his informants through his education, academic position, and disciplinary framework. Pettiway is confined to writing about "criminal justice discourse" (Pettiway, 1996: xxiv), however when he deviates and reflects on his own life experience he shies away from the rigidity of his academic position to reveal his humanity for those whom he has chosen to study (Pettiway, 1996: xxvii). What this might suggest, therefore, is that "identity politics" of a researcher may or may not be an adequate window to ethnographic results.

This piece, as an exercise in ethnographic methodology, required that I reflect on what responsibility researchers have when entering the field. This includes what kind of design they use and what groups they "choose" to feature. If they decide to "study" a marginalized group, I question how this study will benefit the informants or whether knowledge produced simply supports preexisting stigmas and prejudice. There is also the question of entering the field with a theoretical commitment and how that filter shapes the way a researcher views her subjects. On this matter, I find illuminating Kulíck's book, *Travestí: Sex, Gender, and Culture among Brazilian Transgendered Prostitutes*. His ethnography, like Annick Prieur's, *Mema's House: Mexico City on Transvestites, Queens, and Machos, Travestís*, focuses on transgenderism and prostitution in the context of Latin America.

When sexual identities, practices, and meanings are framed as "social products" from different cultural and historical perspectives rather than universalized tendencies, the normalization of multiple gender configurations begins to provide new dimensions to the politics of desire and the body. A substantial amount of current research has been written on sexualities in Latin America that support this claim (Cantú, 2002; Sigal, 2002; Nesvig, 2001; Balderston et all, 1997; Kulíck, 1996; Carrier, 1995; Prieur, 1994; Almaguer, 1993; Mendès-Leite, 1993). The scholarship reaffirms distinctions found in the sexual typologies constructed across Latin American cultures and how they differ widely from Western discourse on sexual identities. This contribution is of relevance to this study because of the large number of Latin American informants included in my sample and the impact Latin American *travestís* have had on client demands for their sexual services in the Netherlands.

Prieur (1994) amply identifies various subgroups that frequented a Mexico City brothel where she conducted her ethnographic study. Here, too, issues of power and functionality are central to the discussion of sexuality. But unlike the Western definition of "homosexuality," which is based on the biological sex of the partners involved, the Latin American social construction of "homosexuality" is defined by the roles that each partner performs. A gendered dichotomy is then reproduced through "active" and "passive" sexual roles played out by each participant. In effect, the labels identified in *Mema's House* both reinforce a heterosexual model on queer and transgendered relations and simultaneously expose marked distinctions in Latin American sexual identities. Each label reflects the multi-dimensional aspect of sexual practices and its impact on heterosexual status retention, masculinity, and *machismo*. Prieur's six month study illuminates how such social labels in Mexican culture distinguish between *jotas* who are biologically born men that "dress and act like women," and *vestidas* who are defined as "transsexuals and transvestites," both of which do not define themselves as "homosexuals". The most notable are *mayates*, who are men who perform penetration in the dominant role but are not socially defined as "homosexuals" because of their "active" role and the fact that many of them are "socially heterosexual" and married to women. Further distinctions reveal how "passive" partners carry a stigma wherein they are socially perceived as having relinquished their masculinity and therefore carry the negative labels of *jotos, puto, juco*, and *maricon*. In some instances anal sex between *mayates* and *jotos* is considered a "stand in" for the absence of women. Prieur concludes that "socially heterosexual" males who commonly perform bisexual practices with other men rarely acknowledge their participation in same-sex relation outside of queer designated spaces because of possible stigmatization in dominant heterosexual society (Nesvig, 2001). In this portrayal of bisexuality and "homosexuality" many contradictory messages are produced about Mexican social life, as Nesvig attests, exposing the acceptance and intolerance of such practices.

Kulíck's contribution to the study of transgendered prostitution should not be underestimated. This anthropological ethnography involved twelve months of well-funded fieldwork in Salvador, Brazil, where Kulíck spent eight months living among thirteen *travestís* in a boarding house (Kulíck, 1996: 11). Rather than focusing on representations and practices, Kulíck explores central elements in the construction of sexuality and gender. His subjects reconfigure a gendered social order by resisting and negotiating their identities in and outside the *travestí* community. The study takes the position that "transgenderism constitutes a privileged vantage point from which it is possible to oversee how sex and gender are conceived and enacted in everyday life" (Kulíck, 1996: 10) and, through such production, gender is both exposed as a performance and debunked as an "illusion that we are products of some natural process" (Kulíck quoting Judith Shapiro, 1996: 10).

Self-admittedly, Kulíck made a "naive discovery" upon arriving in Salvador. He recognized that "*travestís* did not conform to standard northern Euro-American sexual typologies."[13] They considered themselves neither transsexuals nor transvestites (Kulíck, 1996: 12). I have chosen to use Kulíck's definition to identify intersexed subjects and distinguish them from transsexuals and transvestites in my own research. But Kulíck is not the only researcher to document gender fluidity in Brazilian culture. "Shifting [gender] borders" are recognized in the writings of Mendès-Leite (1993) who refers to this phenomenon as "ambigusexuality" because it stresses how gender roles are based on performative aspects of "appearance" rather than sexual practices that remain "ambiguous" (Nesvig, 2001). Hence the gendered performance of the *travesti*, as a feminine identity, is affirmed by the presence of a hyper-masculinized, "heterosexual" male companion or client, however this public performance does not reflect what sexual roles each person is assigned in the sex act (Nesvig, 2001), as those roles are blurred or altogether changeable based on Mendès-Leite's account (Nesvig, 2001).

This ethnography tackled numerous methodological concerns that I face in the field. Kulíck faced an instant language barrier, not unlike my own circumstances, and for the first few months of fieldwork could speak only a few words in Portuguese. Mastering the language of his informants he realized that his "linguistic incompetence" actually generated tremendous stress for him as a researcher (Kulíck, 1996: 13). I cannot underscore enough the strain of my linguistic barriers communicating with informants in their native language. For Kulíck, however, a "barrier" made him dependent on other forms of shared communication similar to what I experienced with Spanish-speaking informants in the Netherlands.

The poverty levels in Brazil proved a shocking discovery for the researcher's Northern European standards of living, redefining the ethnographer's concept of a scarcity of resources. Other cultural differences between the researcher and his informants proved to be an advantage for him in the long-term. His Scandinavian origins made it impossible for him to "pass" as an inside member of the local community, however his appearance gave him an added exoticism that drew favorable attention from many informants (13). These discrepancies, along with his initial linguistic limitations, worked in his favor among some *travestís*, evoking sympathy, mystique, and eventually a rapport as his language skills developed.

Many of Kulíck's informants believed the researcher represented a Scandinavian ideology of "tolerance" and a more "cultivated" perception of sexual identity. His personal biography as an openly gay man created, from his perspective, a sense of trust between his informants and himself. Questions regarding his sexual identity and social position inside the transgendered community arose early in his dialogues with would-be informants. When informants asked whether he was a *viado* (meaning "gay" and closely related to the word for "stag" in Portuguese) and he answered "yes," his subjects then positioned him as "one of the girls," thus disqualifying him as a potential sexual partner (15).[14] In this instance, the identity politics of the researcher, as a "shared" identity claim, provides favorable conditions on which to build rapport with his subject. As I explain in my

Methods Chapter, I struggled with my representing multiple social positions in the field, and conclude that at any given moment, each claim can
translate differently depending upon cultural and geographic context and
who is responding to my presence in the field.

Kulíck claims his findings look different from the only other two
ethnographies on a similar subject written by two female researchers,
Annick Prieur and Neuza de Oliveira. Prieur conducted her doctoral fieldwork in Mexico City where she interviewed transgendered prostitutes living in a boarding house and later published her work as a book (1994). De
Oliveira wrote her master's thesis on *travestís* in Salvador, Brazil and was
largely responsible for sparking Kulíck's interests in the subject and the site
as a field setting. Unlike Prieur's and de Oliveira's identities as researchers
and their findings, Kulíck believes that his status of a *"viado"* facilitated his
ability to delve into *travestís'* intimate relationships to produce original
data (Kulíck, 1996: 15).

Transgendered sex workers were open to discussing their regime of
hormones and surgical modification in the context of a gender migration.
Regarding my own research, discerning what informants might have omit-
ted from our conversation about body modification or intimate relations is
impossible for me to gauge. Given what informants did disclose, I cannot
determine whether their openness was a result of my gendered identity or
"outsider" status.

The core of Kulíck's study consists of "spontaneously occurring conversations" between *travestís* and the researcher. To document his conversations, Kulíck tape-recorded extensively; he collected fifty hours of recordings
with sixteen informants (15). This method is described as "no more inher-
ently intrusive than attempting to reconstruct conversation from memory"
(17). This option was not a luxury I could reproduce; as a result my fieldnotes are based on reconstructions or note taking that occurred in real-time.

The bodily practices described in Kulíck's data are of great value to
understanding of the social reconstruction of gender inside and outside the
travestí community. In particular, he enhances a knowledge of body modification and links those practices to an economy that has grown around
injecting industrial silicone directly into the tissues of the body, hormone
consumption, and hair extension. These consumeristic bodily practices are
described as deployed across gender identities, and in effect help to identify
the image of *travestís* as a symbol of Brazilian femininity.

His research contributes to Queer Theory in a number of ways. *Travestís'* relations with their boyfriends, challenge Western constructs around

identity labels relegating certain sexual practices to the realm of "homosexuality." *Travestís* neither consider their male lovers "gay" nor their relationships as "homosexual," instead gender and sex roles are interpreted through the filter of "passive" and "active" positions.[15]

Kulíck warns against imposing his own outside model on the reality that he describes as "co-constructed" by all subjects involved in this ethnography. He achieves this approach when he denies wanting to "speak for them," and then pastes large chunks of conversational transcript for his subjects to "speak for themselves" as a way to present a focus on "bodily and social practices" as understood by them (18). This approach is reminiscent of Bogdan's "autobiography" of Jane Fry and her first-person narrative. In my own work, I've tried reconstructing social interaction with the intention of giving a sense of who is present and what is happening around us at the time of an observation or interview.

Overall, *Travesti* is a politicized work depicting acts of resistance under tremendous police violence, a high incidence of AIDS transmission, and social stigmatization. This ethnography goes to great lengths to identify how race and class inequalities impact the daily lives of Kulíck's subjects and how they must "continually reassert their rights to occupy urban space" (30) in the most defiant of ways.

CONCLUSION

The texts surveyed expose the complexity and ever-changing contexts in which prostitution takes place. Each study suggests how both sex workers and researchers understand social and economic forces that influence prostitution. Each study also exposes how we, as researchers, must take responsibility for knowing our subjects not in the abstraction of discursive analysis, but through shared understanding communicated explicitly by those working on the streets and in the windows. Without exposure to this first-hand experience, researchers cannot fully realize sex work as a material form and the end results will be more colonizing of marginalized human subjects with theoretical impositions.

Based on what experiences are absent, excluded, or undiscovered there exists space in which to produce new research and greater understanding of daily practices of sex workers. From this review of works, new methodologies, fieldwork excursion, and general understanding of new social and economic complexities provide ample room for new research to come to fruition.

Chapter Three
Finding My Way into the Field

INTRODUCTION

Over a six-to-eight month period between the summer of 1998 to the winter of 2001, I gathered data on prostitution in the Netherlands. By all accounts, the process of entering the field, making contacts with informants, and then gathering ethnographic material before reconstructing my study might appear seamless to any onlooker, however what is not apparent in the write-up is how the fieldworker, especially as a lone-researcher, must constantly negotiate her role to hold legitimacy in the field. The methodological procedures and challenges that I encountered during my fieldwork liken my experience to that of ethnographers who entered the field during tense neo-colonial transitions (see for example Rabinow, 1977: 151). In my case, intellectual gatekeepers and activists who contested and reshaped policy around prostitution and immigration initially foiled my entry into the field. Without losing sight of my research plan, I adapted to my share of methodological challenges, making my participation in the field a standpoint from which to reconstruct my data gathered on the daily experiences of migrant and transgendered window prostitutes and street-walkers in the Netherlands.

Reconciling with the privilege of conducting research in an international setting is central to my fieldwork. Recognition of my privilege as a US trained researcher requires that I confront ways in which the "investigated" is situates as "other," and lends to the stance that all research is a form of global intellectual capital and packed with historically situated relations. The unwritten process of gathering data would reveal the historical and material arrangements between the researcher and the object of her focus. What is often not articulated in the reconstruction is how the researcher's presence can inflict a type of "violence," albeit symbolic in nature, on any community under study (Rabinow, 1977: 151). My research is no exception. In particular, my interviews with informants, and even my presence in some sexualized spaces, represent a linguistic or cultural hegemony as a US citizen conducting research abroad and communicating mostly in English. My informants, in effect, had to conform to my language rather than speak in their mother tongue. Thus, my reliance on the cultural interpretations made by informants is an attempt on my part to counter any "symbolic violence" on this community.

This chapter also illustrates how informants' assumptions about the identity politics of the researcher can, on first appearance, obstruct or facilitate contacts in an international setting. In particular, I consider how my role as a social actor in the field required negotiating aspects of my citizenship, ethnicity, sexuality, age, and gender and shaped my methodological actions in the field. As a result, identity issues are discussed in regard to how they unfold between researcher and her informants, as well as interview procedures that transpired.

Similar to Rabinow's methodology, my research produces a reliance on informants as interpreters of local knowledges, Dutch prostitution norms, and transgendered cultural practices. In effect, the reflexive tones found in my reconstruction of events, understanding of prostitution culture, and transgendered practices signal a hermeneutical quandary revealing how analytic interpretation reflects a "comprehension of the self by detour of [a] comprehension of the other" (Rabinow, 1977: 6), situating myself as a central figure in my own ethnography.

WHY THE NETHERLANDS

Early in my graduate coursework, I developed an interest in transnational migration and its impact on informal labor sectors in Western Europe. My research interests narrowed on prostitution in Europe after attending a conference on sex tourism in Kingston, Jamaica.[1] In 1998, I embarked on preliminary research in Amsterdam, the Netherlands. Legalization of Dutch prostitution and the appearance of "transparency" around this topic provided what appeared to be a stable environment where data gathering on the experiences of sex workers could occur. Choosing a site where the sex industry is heavily regulated would materialize as a location where I could educate myself on the impact of legalization, and gain awareness of how and what subjects operate inside and outside this framework.

ACCESS AND THE GATEKEEPERS IN THE NETHERLANDS:

Over the course of two and a half years, I have made eight trips to the Netherlands. Personal savings and student loans largely funded my doctoral research, imposing strict time constraints (research was conducted during summer and winter breaks). Part of the time was spent securing stable places to live and attempting to make contacts in the field. I interviewed various advocates at agencies including the Institute for Prostitution Issues, Red Thread, GGGD (the public health department), a law expert at Leiden University; STV, an anti-trafficking organization in Utrecht; NISSA, a research center in Utrecht, and Gilbert Herdt who introduced me to other researchers in the area. These agencies, and the advocates who represented them, were informative about the existing conditions and problems facing people working in this sector, but no contacts inside the windows, clubs, or streetwalking zone were made accessible to me though each agency offered an "affiliation." Administrators and advocates, alike, foresaw my presence having little influence on Dutch policy, and therefore believed that research in the Netherlands would not amount to much since "it had all been done."

Advocates warned me that intellectual gatekeepers, operating through public health organizations, controlled intellectual turf throughout most of Western Europe. Suggestions were made that I should travel south of Turin, Italy, where my research findings could have a greater impact on "policy."

At this early stage in my research, I could be easily deterred, and upon the advice of the Dutch advocates, I made two trips to Rome assuming I would pick up my research there. During a two-month stay, I resided in the Nigerian quarter, less than a block from Stazione Termini and Piazza Vittorio Emanuele and made significant contacts with private social agencies eager to provide outreach services to Nigerian and Albanian prostitutes. Most organizations, however, had limited funding and had little success making contact in those closed communities. The harsh conditions would have required a long term commitment to making contacts, and a substantial amount of money and time that I did not have available to me.

ACCESS

Access to my early informants could be described as coincidental in nature, yet the experiences gave me the impetus to continue with my fieldwork. Early in my research, enroute to the Netherlands, I visited Reykjavik, Iceland. While there I informally observed the interior of an erotic dance club where I met an Estonian stripper named Jennifer. After I complimented Jennifer for her acrobatic choreography on stage, I approached her at the bar and asked her if we could talk. Jennifer was eager to speak to me in English, but the house rules of the bar required that I purchase a twenty-dollar drink charge expected of male customers wanting to meet with the dancers. Jennifer talked at length about her dancing in different Scandinavian countries for short-term assignments and how she supported her son back in Tallinn. From that experience I realized how mutually fulfilling a conversational interview could be for informant and researcher. Shortly after I crossed that threshold of insecurity and uncertainty, I was in Amsterdam where I met an Afro-Brazilian *travestí* who invited me into her window and later took me to her home for dinner. Again, a mutual affinity between my informant and me launched a two-day interview into a relationship that developed into a significant contact over the course of two years. Through my relationship with Magdalena, I met other transgendered sex workers. It was this emotional generosity of those early contacts whom I met during the second summer of research that gave me the personal confidence to follow through with my fieldwork.

The type of relationships that I needed to develop for my ethnographic research took time to establish. But a time constraint imposed on these relationships intensified the intimacy between us as well as produced a degree of superficiality in the arrangement between subject and researcher. This issue is explored in greater detail in a latter part in this chapter, where raised questions around developing common meanings shared through language, cultural symbols, and gestures between informant and researcher (Rabinow, 1977: 153). In retrospect, I feel these early attempts to contact informants were awkward for me as I did not want to invade their privacy and professional space, and to negotiate how to reciprocate the emotional exchange that was required of me.

I continued making contacts in the windows until my fifth trip to the Netherlands, when I gained access to a Dutch streetwalking "zone." After I met with social welfare and public health agency workers eager to discuss streetwalking conditions, confidentiality issues prohibited me from accompanying them on their weekly rounds. Some public health workers suggested that sending my resume and a letter explaining my intentions would elicit a response in a few months. I contacted the director of a "living room" or "*huiskamer*"[2] in an urban setting to inquire whether she might permit access after a public health nurse suggested that I call directly. The director invited me to the center under the condition that I maintained the anonymity of the people whom I interviewed and not reveal the location of the site.[3]

At the *huiskamer,* I filled the role of volunteer, preparing sandwiches, serving coffee, and distributing condoms. During my observations at the Living Room, I experienced ease in the presence of many transgendered streetwalkers who used the space for changing clothes or for respite before setting out to work on the street. I finally spent 48 hours observing the *huiskamer* in Den Apelhaven where I informally spent from thirty minutes to several hours interviewing individually each of the seventeen streetwalkers I refer to in my study.

During a return visit to the *huiskamer* the following winter of 2000/2001, I spent three weeks observing commercial venues in two Dutch cities. During this period, I followed up with an interview with Magdalena; spent upwards of one-hundred additional hours observing at the *huiskamer;* spent between fifteen to twenty hours talking to Victoria, with whom I remain in contact via email; I also followed-up on the experiences of twelve sex workers whom I had met the previous summer. In January 2001, I visited Victoria at her home for an eight-hour visit; in spring 2002, Victoria visited my home in Amsterdam.

To date, I have spent over one hundred and fifty hours at the Living Room where I interviewed seventeen transgendered and drug-free women, of which eight to ten were of "immigrant" status, discussing aspects about their lived experiences performing sex work and daily social practices. As stated, some interviews lasted hours at a time, while others were fragmented, often disrupted by the sex worker's need to return outdoors to work on the street. My shortest interviews were no less than thirty minutes each, but usually occurred more than once with the same informant. Overall, during a single shift at the Living room, I spent between eight and twelve hours during each observation and communicated with each informant up to six times during that same period.

Due to social barriers with female sex workers, the majority of my contacts were with transgendered prostitutes. This occurred because of a number of factors. First, through my contact with Magdalena, I was introduced to other transgendered window prostitutes working in Amsterdam. During my observations at the Living Room, I observed primarily in the transgendered dressing room used by transgendered and females who were not drug-addicted. As a result of my proximity to a transgendered space and my early contacts in the field, my interviews largely represent the views of the transgendered community working in the sex industry.

From June 2002 to June 2003, I became a resident of the Netherlands and wrote drafts of this manuscript as my dissertation.

LINGUISTIC HEGEMONY

The English language is commonly used in negotiation between client and sex provider as well as during communication between sex workers if one party is a non-native Dutch speaker. Most of my informants possessed intermediate to advanced English language skills. Communication was never a barrier with Dutch informants as most spoke English with great fluency. Many non-Dutch sex workers, who had lived in the Netherlands for over a year, were accustomed to communicating with clientele in English. Despite the pervasiveness of English spoken on the streets and in the windows in the Netherlands, I cannot presume shared understandings between researcher and informant as all of my interviews were conducted in English, a second or third language for all of my informants. As a result, "finding themes and meaning in everyday practices that are often taken for granted" required clarification of informants' statements to avoid misinterpreting what appeared "obvious" for expressive nuances used for descriptive purposes and vice versa. Ultimately, an interpretive risk had to be taken as I faced the arduous task of reevaluating what I thought were shared cultural signifiers and artifacts (De Vault, 1990: 100). If such cultural disjunctures existed, then other social determinants were also affecting speech and nonverbal communication taking place. This would lead to further "linguistic incongruencies" while transcribing and interpreting my fieldnotes (De Vault, 1990: 100).

In addition to possible misinterpretation of intended meaning, other forms of linguistic or symbolic violence may have taken place. This linguistic violence compares to Rabinow's use of the colonizer's language (French) before his acquisition of Arabic when communicating with his informants during his first few months in the field. Nonetheless, my use of English was a form of linguistic hegemony that I consider as my shortcoming.[4]

Another tension arises because of the language used to describe sexual practices. This is limited by our present ideas/vocabulary around sexual acts, desires, and feelings. "Linguistic coding" and "social policing" reveal how most of our "sexual vocabulary" reconstitutes dichotomies (heterosexual/homosexual, fetishist/Sadomasochism, monogamous/polygamous) excluding many sexual acts and feelings that exist outside our cultural construction of sexuality (Delany, 1995). In fact, most of what is experienced in the sexual realm still remains without linguistic conventions. Therefore, as participants, actors, and researchers, we are constrained in retelling informants' "selection," "narrative form," "their referents, their texture, and their structures" of any sexual tale (Delany, 1995: 21).

IDENTITY POLITICS

Much can be assumed about the researcher and her relationship to her subjects under the rubrics of identity politics. Cultural or physiological markers of the researcher may or may not legitimate her presence in the field. Often informants understand the researcher's identity outside the context of her social locations. Whether or not shared physical or cultural attributes communicate a shared knowledge and experience between researcher and informant can be challenged. Some researchers make an effort not to attach themselves to essentializing claims around their identity but still assume "legitimacy" because of national origins or sexual identity practices. This stance could, however, disguise other disparate economic or social incongruencies or a lack of mutual relatedness not necessarily articulated (Olesen, 2000). The interpretive status of a researcher in the field leaves me wondering how much control any one of us has negotiating our identity in the field.

Rosalie and Murray Wax's fieldwork on Pine Ridge Reservation (Wax, 1979) identifies the influence of the researcher's codification and social position when data gathering. Rosalie realized that numerous personal factors shaped the design and quality of a few studies she and her husband carried out on various reservations. Two personal factors, age and gender, became evident as advantageous identity markers for Rosalie as she entered certain types of field settings. For example, her identity as a "mature woman" translated into access to sex segregated groups that otherwise she and her husband could not enter together. Her role as a "mother" facilitated communication with women with children, informants who might have otherwise denied her access because her membership in the dominant Anglo society (Wax, 1979: 513).

More recent post-modern and post-colonial critiques have systematically interrogated and revised any such claims based on fixed social locators. The writings of Trinh T. Minh-ha and Gayatri Chakravorty Spivak have drawn on discourses of "hybridization" and mutability of identity rather than essentializing or imperializing effects to establish, for example, a master category of woman for political gains or access (Clough, 1994).

Despite this theoretical attempt to destabilize social binaries exposing reproduction of master categories, a researcher still must negotiate how subjects whom she encounters in her field setting will interpret her embodiments and markings. For example, I experienced confusing circumstances around my own position in the field. My identifiable presence has been scripted to communicate a particular gender, class, ethnic, and sexualized subject positioning that created opportunities and constraints when gathering data. This intersection of social markers that I embody also meant that I had no control over how my identity was interpreted in the field.

Different groups reacted to me in dissimilar ways. My most challenging response came from would-be female informants who took greater time to establish a connection with me. This could be explained through their reading of my gendered coding, or their awareness of my resistance to partaking in certain modes of femininity practiced by many female sex workers. The fact remains that there were many social variables at work, making identification of a single factor difficult to determine. As a result of these barriers with female sex workers, I focused my efforts on the transgendered community that was more accessible to me.

For the most part, my "gendering" in the field was mediated through commercial spatial relations, positioning me as an actor inside my fieldsite rather than just as an observer. For example, as I stood waiting for an informant to finish performing services from inside her window, a female prostitute asked me to move across the street because I was a "distraction" in her commercial space. And yet in the early stages of my fieldwork, when walking through the Red Light District, my eyes met those of window prostitutes, and not knowing the protocol between prostitutes and female/non-client, I smiled in acknowledgment. Sometimes the women seated in the interior rooms returned the greeting, other times they treated me as an invisible presence. Whether my presence was "invisible" because of my non-consumer potential or rather because I represented a "commercial distraction" is contestable.

There were also fieldwork incidences during which my gender coding posed an actual physical threat to me. While enroute on foot to a streetwalking zone, I encountered would-be clients slowing down their automobiles to evaluate my commercial desirability. On a few occasions these same would-be clients tried running me down with their vehicle because—as one transgendered streetwalker[5] explained—the drivers understood my presence as "just another [disposable] drug-addicted female streetwalker" making her way to the zone. In each example, the spatial context rendered me as a "commercial entity." This suggests that the sexual order I entered reinforced my position as a gendered subject. Therefore, controlling my social position was an organizing sex/gender system that "recognized" me as a prostitute by definition of my embodiment at that location.

The previous examples lead me to suggest that the way I interpret my gender performance as a researcher can have little bearing on how informants or other actors interpret my identity in the field. The performative aspects of my gender position largely explain my tenuous relations with female prostitutes, but can this identity claim explain my two most developed relations with contacts (that have lasted over two years) who were transgendered? Perhaps my gender performance had no impact on these relationships? When each informant welcomed me into their home they did so because I treated them and their work with "respect," "dignity" and "without judgment," that facilitated a degree of trust.

Another example of a researcher/informant relationship that transcends presumed social difference between the two parties could be found in the writing of the autobiography of Jane Fry (Bogdan, 1974). Throughout the duration of the writing project, Bogdan maintains his professional distance, denying a "friendship" developed between the collaborators, however a mutual trust "transcends" whatever attributes are assigned to Bogdan's gender identity or social position as an academic. Their mutual respect suggested that whatever "dissimilarity" exists between researcher and informant, Bogdan genuine intentions for greater understanding and desire to confer dignity upon his subject without added attention to any gendered differences that exists between informant and researcher took precedence over of a shared identity.

To describe the standpoint of trust between researcher and informant does not take into account the process that the relationship must endure to reach that shared state. This required that I endure a brief stage during which informants "sussed" me out. During this initial contact, my informants discovered additional social locators embedded in my gendered identity such as my status as an "unmarried" and "childless" woman in her late thirties. Age as a social location leads me to suggest what I consider to be the significance of age, as identified by Wax, when fieldworkers enter a site. Exploring issues around prostitution, in particular, requires some degree of maturity and sophistication around sexual politics. Certainly mature sex workers were apprehensive when a young, inexperienced researcher or social worker entered the field.

In the end, personal "factors" that have shaped my life translated into "life currency" solidifying affinities and encounters. Additional disclosures of personal information, such as my first-generation Albanian-American ethnicity, my eight years without health insurance, my "sexual literacy," or my living in illegal accommodations with undocumented migrants, produced, albeit temporary, legitimacy in the field. Thus, each personal articulation was a weighed choice on my part and a means of qualifying my position after experiencing a cool reception from some informants of my initial disclosure of holding the position of researcher.

In hindsight, I am convinced that my ability to respond with attentiveness and respect toward potential informants opened many doors for me while in the field. When Victoria disclosed early on in our relationship that she could envision my "starting a center like this *huiskamer*, because you have the heart, the right intentions," she invited me into an emotional engagement transcending whatever might have been assigned to the politic of difference or sameness. Such a judgment on my part became subjective guesswork and was determined largely by what information informants choose to disclose or omit to me. On occasion, the judgment can involve second-hand information from another informant that either substantiates or refutes the original claim. For example, one Dutch female streetwalker, Anke, described at lengths her struggle to survive on the poverty line without ever disclosing to me that her economic position was partly due to her gambling. Only through another informant did I learn of Anke's monetary losses through this activity. During our multiple interviews together, Anke, herself, never disclosed this information about her life to me. On another occasion, an informant talked at lengths about having a sex reassignment, but only later did I learn, again, from another streetwalker that the informant had been talking about her gender migration for years but had not taken appropriate steps to have the procedure done.

Time spent with informants and observation of relationships between prostitutes made it possible to determine what informants were "trusted" by their peers and staff workers at the Living Room. My observations, however, did not preclude informants from embellishing and/or lying to me. During some interviews, I took a leap of faith and accepted their stories and experiences at face value or at least with the realization that I was hearing a partial truth with other points of view or interpretations missing from the reconstruction.

CITIZENSHIP

During the course of my research, I transported my North American status to a Northern European country with a diverse ethnic and immigrant population. My privilege as a North American sometimes required offsetting a global-wide perception that all North Americans from the United States have a myopic imperialistic world-view. Assumptions were often countered by the way that I quietly carry myself in the field and the political perspective that I espoused.

My informants' response to my presence may have been due to my "alternative" take on US domestic and foreign policy. Among informants there was an almost disbelief in criminalization and conditions under which prostitution operates in the United States. Sharing my sentiments conveyed solidarity with sex workers and their rights and by publicly airing my views on prostitution and a number of other issues, they were able to "suss" me out.

PRIVILEGED ACADEMIC

The greatest negative reaction I received around my North American status came from Dutch activists and staff workers at the Living Room. Anti-American political and economic sentiments were not the only motives for such resentments. Instead, subtle hostility was directed toward my privileged access to the facility as an "outsider," and my opportunity to travel abroad.

Similar to most facilities that provide off-hours services, the staff worked on rotational shifts that produced a certain amount of internal tensions based on scheduling. Their director was transitioning out of her position, and was rarely present, therefore leaving certain senior members in charge of operating the facility. My presence, however, though initially welcomed, was interpreted as an extension of the director's decision-making power. Whether I aligned myself with this person politically was not the point: I was this person's "guest" and that translated into some social meaning.

Also, my status as a "researcher" meant in some capacity I was "commodifying" the very surroundings staff took for granted as an everyday occurrence. Whatever educational discrepancies there were between the staff and myself only magnified my privilege in the field. Most staff had the equivalent of a LPN license (Licensed Practical Nurse), RN (Registered Nurse) status or was on the brink of gaining a Master of Social Work.

FIRST GENERATION ALBANIAN-AMERICAN

Whether my social class was understood through my means to commute between North America and Europe, or my graduate education represented a class marker distancing me from sex workers and staff at the Living Room, my social location was communicated through cross-cultural markers understood by my informants and the staff at the Living Room. Some of this "reading" depended upon the cultural location of the person interpreting my gestures and utterances. I am still left to wonder why I was welcomed kindly by Dutch staff of Caribbean or Surinamese descent? It is possible that many Dutch and non-Dutch ethnics understood my physical marking as a "Westernized" performance of a Middle-Eastern identity. In the context of Northern Europe, with existing tensions around "immigrants," my "ethnic" representation re-qualifies my social category in a real way.

Clearly, my identity as a first-generation Albanian-American translated into a social repositioning, offsetting crystallization of my US citizenship. In the context of Europe, making an identity claim as "Albanian" holds an entirely different set of social locations, and largely that of a negative construction.[6] Although Albania is technically part of Eastern Europe, and formerly a part of the Eastern Bloc, this mostly Muslim ethnic group has been racialized. Although my coding doesn't immediately identify me as North American or Northern European, this piece of identity became a beneficial "repositioning" when in the field.

IS THERE A DOMINANT IDENTIFYING SOCIAL CATEGORY?

Identifying my multiple social positioning in the field leads me to question whether any single identity factor needs to be shared between researcher and informants. Under the premise of a shared national or ethnic identity between researcher and informant, can other social determinants, such as sexual identity politics, take priority over cultural membership in the context of prostitution, or can an unobtrusive characteristic of the informant or researcher invert assumptions about dominant social categories? What occurs if a researcher addresses the topic of "sexual identity" when the subject under consideration cannot be separated from its national or cultural manifestation? For example, Antonia Young (Young, 2000) conducted research on Albanian female virgins who live as men, challenging the intersection of cultural and national forms, and transgendered identities. Assuming this researcher is "Anglo-American," and her heterosexual identity doesn't offer her any legitimating claims or membership in that group, what is then her legitimating position in the field?[7]

When showing Young's text to a few Albanian-Americans, they questioned the intentions of the researcher. Some members were fascinated with the topic, while others expressed horror at this textual representation on their ethnic community. They also assumed that a member of this ethnic community would never have sensationalized or published potentially stigmatizing elements about their culture. Albanian members also questioned why an Anglo researcher might have had an interest in what they "read" as a curiosity of Albanian culture rather than a cultural norm. They did not read this topic as a concern about transgenderism, but rather a phenomenon representing an aspect of their ethnic culture. What I am suggesting is that members of a cultural group can interpret the presence of an "outsider" researcher from a different perspective, regardless of how forthright a researcher may be with her subjects or whether a social factor is the guiding principal identifying she concern for her research topic.

In the writings of Wendy Chapkis, Leon Pettiway, and Don Kulíck, the authors make essentializing identity claims that distinguish their sexuality as a legitimating factor for their research on prostitution in a transnational context (Pettiway, 1996; Chapkis, 1997; Kulíck, 1997). Based on their self-declared status as a "sexual minority" or "sexual renegade," they presume a great deal about what constitutes a commonly held experience among female and transgendered sex workers, drawing on the "legitimacy" of one dominant cultural signifier. Their assumptions do not take into account cross-cultural contexts that can produce tensions or how social and economic forces might otherwise influence the status of an informant. In fact, the cultural and social context of each researcher's fieldsite could undermine whatever "universal experience" might be assumed about what it means to be "gay" or "lesbian," especially at a cultural location where sexual typologies hold a different set of social meanings. As a result, assumed shared experiences can be shaped by other factors, weakening what otherwise might be assumed as a shared identity claim between researcher and subject.

When writing about prostitution, contexualization of the topic is necessary, as it does not guarantee automatic entrance or shared meaning even between researchers who have experienced sex work first hand or for those who have been at the "border" of the sex industry. Jo Doezema's (Doezema, 1995; Chapkis, 1997; Kempadoo and Doezema, 1998) identity as a former prostitute and union activist, and now as a graduate student in the United Kingdom, gives her a certain kind of legitimacy among activists and scholars. Academics perceive Doezema's position as an "insider," not unlike some of the first-person texts written by sex workers themselves, but her position does not guarantee instant legitimacy within all prostitution communities. Sometimes the group under study rejects the "insider." During my observations at the Living Room, a nursing staff member, who formerly worked as a sex worker, experienced difficulty asserting professional authority with the streetwalkers. On occasion, when she attempted to impose house rules on her former colleagues, they dismissed her as a "hypocrite." In actuality, the streetwalkers in the Living Room might have seen her as a "traitor" who had opted for greater social and educational status by leaving prostitution, or they could have seen her as someone who was permanently marked as a "prostitute," regardless of having left the industry and moved on to another occupation. Conversely, the nurse represented to her new colleagues someone who had "insider" knowledge with a legitimate perspective on issues about prostitution. Nonetheless, her standpoint required straddling two social positions that proved at times challenging to negotiate, suggesting how the role of "outsider" or "insider" sometimes comes with both "advantages and disadvantages" when working with or gathering data on any given population (De Vault, 1995).

The previous scenario might offer an example of how little cultural or social stability exists in the field, even under the domain of familiar sex/gender/sexuality systems. "Hybridization" of identity and cultural practices is taking place all around us. Should any qualifying social factors lead to admission into any given research setting? Virginia Olesen (Oleson, 2000: 227) cites numerous examples in which a social attribute shared between researcher and subject did not carry enough social meaning to produce a common unifying identity. Olesen refers to Patricia Zavella's (1996) failed attempt to interview Mexican factory workers with whom she shared a common Mexican lineage; Ellen Lewin's (1993) study on lesbian mothers who identified "the surpassing of motherhood over sexual orientation" as a dominant social category; and Dorinne Kondo's (1990) experiences conducting fieldwork in Japan (Oleson, 2000: 227) as examples of presumptions made when determining a research setting.

Throughout the data-gathering phase of this study, it was impossible for me not to feel self-conscious of how my multiple identity claims might be "read" by informants. Sometimes I could "control" how others might categorize me, or so I thought, by carefully editing disclosures about myself or skillfully framing my ideas, however in the end I had little influence over how an informant would "read" my self presentation. My multiple social positions put me in a precarious position most of the time, identifying me as a potentially entrusting presence or causing an inhibiting effect on communication with contacts. Perhaps this speaks of the hard-edged "nature" of the industry or simply my awkward presence in it, but during the interviewing phase, on occasion there was a sense that both researcher and subject were still uncovering social characteristics about each other, and that mutual trust was a delicate process that couldn't be instantly sealed. Sometimes at an emotional level there were unconscious reactions or cross-cultural miscommunication operating between the parties involved. An example of this fragile process might explain why some female sex workers seemed reluctant to make contact with me. Whether this distrust was in reaction to the type of woman they assumed that I represented or the gendered script that I performed, the relations might suggest why some of those same contacts did not open up until my follow-up visit six months after initially making contact with the person. There were also benefits to this situation. The precariousness of these social bonds could also shift in my favor as when public health workers from local agencies or police officers suddenly would enter the Living Room. Their presence would abruptly reorient my position as confidante to one of the streetwalkers because without warning I was someone outside of the bureaucratic and institutional domains that controlled the space. In either instance, other actors' presence transformed the social meaning of who I was in the space. The spatial relations, in effect, were constantly in a state of flux in the zone, sometimes easing my relations with the members and other times facilitating obstacles when other intimacies were expressed in this dynamic flow of converging lives and institutions.

CONCLUSION

Methodological processes facilitate the production of all knowledge about a given topic and therefore should be given greater emphasis as an insepa-rable part of all findings. Often methodological considerations are taken for granted, or undervalued, once the data gathering has been accom-plished and the outcome has been highlighted. Hence is the significant role of reflexivity to a study. Consider, for instance, how data gathering is bound by our own cultural assumptions, and that might include the multi-ple social identities of researchers as well, and ask how under the most aus-picious conditions, are we capable of producing a "partial knowledge" that brings meaning and fairness to those whom we have studied? It has been suggested that if greater significance were given to the way in which con-tacts are made in the field and data are collected there might be less space for misinterpretation and authoritative claims (Punch, 1986: 85), resituat-ing the subjective nature of qualitative inquiry. This process, in particular, exposes how ethnography is "actively situated between powerful systems of meaning" that are forever requiring (Clifford, 1986: 2) decoding and interrogating, with the ethnographer at the center of her field experiences. Identity claims, therefore, are legitimated and deconstructed by a series of factors that sometime make sense to the researcher, but other times leave them wondering how they arrived at a particular place in their research. Given the amount of "acknowledged difference" (Olesen, 2000: 228) and "liminal culture" that functions as "dialectic space" through which "par-tial (cultural) reconstructions between the knowledge, linguistics and sym-bols of an informant and that of the researcher" takes place (Rabinow, 1997: 155), we are fortunate to have any amount of textual artifact of the lived experiences shared at all.

Chapter Four
Space and Place: In the Windows

INTRODUCTION

This chapter explores the role of physical space in shaping commercial sexual relations in the Red Light District in Amsterdam, inside and outside of prostitution windows. The physical characteristics of this setting and that of the zone, described more fully in the next chapter, underscore how social arrangements are reinforced and challenged, and how each site provides material opportunities for prostitutes working inside those spatial conditions.

The Red Light District is internationally known for its concentration of commercial sex venues. Sixteenth and seventeenth century buildings are home to window prostitution, sex shows, million-dollar residential property, restaurants and markets catering to a local Asian community and tourists alike. Over the course of two and a half years, I returned to the area to learn how informants interpret their working environment and to unmask for myself what they commonly take for granted about commercial sexual relations in the windows. The chapter begins by focusing on spectators and clients as they interact with window prostitutes. From the exterior of the Red Light District I shift the perspective to inside the window where I give an account of a relationship that I developed over the course of two years with a transgendered sex worker named Magdalena. Her narrative provides a perspective of what it is like for a prostitute to work inside a window and reveals how she constructs private space in her personal life.

ON THE OUTSIDE LOOKING IN: VOYEURS AND CONSUMERS

The sidewalks around the Red Light District are a public space. Gazing at sex workers displayed in the windows is a dominant practice of pedestrians.[1] Of the people walking through the district only a small percentage of them intend to pay for commercial services. Subtle distinctions in this ritual distinguish *voyeurs*, who are there to watch sex workers, from *customers*, who enter the District with the intention of paying for services. While women were not precluded as consumers and gazers of erotic labor, most of them were in mixed groups or with companions as tourists attracted by the street folklore.[2]

In the marketplace, commercial sex and cultural sensibilities intersected with constructions of heterosexual desirability, sometimes evoking new longings for male tourists traversing the District. Fair to say, like all of us, male tourists carried into the District an internalized, corporeal sensibility around the desirability of prostitutes. They also dominated the area through open conversation intended to engage a consensus among friends and strangers watching women and *travestis* in the windows. On more than one occasion I overheard men using a peer rating system devised to quantify the value of women in the windows.

The following example illustrates what kind of conversations I overheard during my observations. In this instance, a group of five Italian men in their late-twenties apply their cultural construction of heterosexual desirability to window prostitutes while walking down various streets in the Red Light District.[3] The group defined sex workers as either "robots" because "they all make the same moves," in reference to prostitutes dancing while standing in windows, or as "hot" enough to appear "in a calendar." In the former instance, the men found impersonal standardized hip and shoulder movements commonly performed by many sex workers undesirable. Paradoxically, bodily gestures that should have shattered a frozen impression framed by the window and the fluorescent glowing light produced a different interpretation of their movement. Women identified as appealing to spectators' corporeal sensibility, were exalted to a representation in another visual medium. This practice of gazing upon a window prostitute from a distance, coupled by the transference of her impression onto another visual representation, not only reifies sex workers but tells of the powerful impact visual media occupy in our fantasy realms. What I am suggesting is that embedded in the cycle of visual consumption is the replication of a representation of the prostitute as an image. The result elicits a fantasy that never amounts to any human interaction or physical consummation but rather to a loop of visual consumption from one layer of reification to another.

When voyeurs crossed over in their communication with other male groups, their talk was for the purpose of imposing a cultural interpretation of the bodily forms before them. One African-American man strolling through the streets with five other (North) American friends declared to an audience that the woman positioned behind a window "[had] no booty at all." At another street level window, this same man asked a stranger standing next to him if he could ask the prostitute to move "her string bikini over a little [to expose her genitals]." Spectators' public declarations confirmed their heterosexual status, permitting them to "share" with other male strangers a common heterosexual desire based on a culturally scripted value on to what a desirable body is supposed to resemble. These same comments allowed for clusters of heterosexual men to assemble together in the context of a sexual quest without threatening their masculine identities.

From the first time I entered the Red Light District for this project, I equated this spectacle that I have just described to a Disney world for adult males. This is a commercial place promising new desires, consumption habits, and gratification or disappointment depending upon the results. There is a value judgment in this statement, not towards the window prostitutes but towards some men who enter the space with a sense of entitlement and disrespect[4] for the window workers and other female pedestrians who are in the area.

INSIDE MAGDALENA'S WINDOW

The interior of prostitution windows provides a unique perspective to understand how this functions as a commercial operation. My research project physically and conceptually expanded at the point at which I gained entry to the interior of a window. This could not have happened without the consent of an informant. Over the course of two-years, I gained access to one particular window as a direct result of such an invitation that also evolved into a long-term relationship with a Brazilian transgendered window prostitute named Magdalena.

One afternoon in the early summer, walking through the center of Amsterdam, I took a wrong turn down "Kriegstraat."[5] There, I passed a window in a series occupied by *travestís*, making eye contact with an Afro-transgendered sex worker sitting in her window. Rather than continue walking, I turned back and knocked on her door. The person standing at the closed glass door looked confused by my presence, but opened it with polite reception. I asked how much it would cost to talk to her. "Fifty guilders for fifteen minutes," she said in a strong French accent, still perplexed by my request. I explained my status as a student researching prostitution and my desire to talk to her about her experiences working in the industry. She understood saying it wasn't necessary to pay but inquired why I was interested in the subject. After elaborating on my project I was invited into an airless small room filled with cigarette smoke and the thick scent of body oil.

The person went by the name Magdalena, and towered over me. She then invited me into her 10 ft by 7 ft room, including a single bed tucked in the corner and a shelf on which stood a shrine of penile prostheses of different shapes and sizes. Those same statues produced an erotic ambience in an otherwise, clinical room. They belonged to Magdalena who toted them to work each day.

Magdalena presented herself in a streamlined performance wearing a black rubber bustiere exposing her cleavage and matching rubber shorts riding high on her long thighs. High black boots added to her domineering presence. She also wore amber contact lenses and a long brown wig, producing a creolization of her appearance.

Magdalena said she came from Paris by way of French Guinea and Brazil. When asked how long she had been working in prostitution her face becoming unguarded turned to a look of despair as she raised nine perfectly manicured fingers. "Nine years," I said. And she nodded with a solemn "yes."

Magdalena shut the door behind me continuing our conversation as she walked to the back of the room to lower music blaring from behind a door. She told me that she hoped to do this kind of work for six more years. Her enormous hands went up and six fingers confirmed the number of years she would continue to work in the windows.

THE GAME

A potential Turkish client walked by as we stood in the window together. Without dropping our conversation, Magdalena flicked a tuft of hair behind her shoulders, flashing her eyes quick enough to make contact with the man. Right before me, the dance between potential client and sex worker had begun with a series of ritual gestures. This window/street interaction consisted of verbal and nonverbal communication lasting twenty minutes before culminating in a sexual exchange. When the would-be client passed the window for a second time, Magdalena knew well enough that the man was not a casual voyeur, flashing her extended hand up to indicate fifty guilders for services.

There we were standing together in a cramped area the width of the window, just inches from the curb. As our conversation progressed, I was still psychologically and spatially adjusting to the shift in perspective from being on one side of the pane of glass looking in the window to the other inside of the window looking out on the street. I tried to keep my composure and not to appear as if this was my first time in a window. As pedestrians passed and gazed at us, I read their eye contact as reproachful moral judgment, indifference, or sexual predilection that consumed Magdalena or my form. At ground level, I could not escape from feeling exposed to activity on the curb, which, I suppose in hindsight, made the location more convenient for clients and easier for sex workers to attract business. Only after minutes passed did my awkwardness of being on display subside and I could focus on what Magdalena was communicating to me.

Magdalena identified herself to me as a "female" but with male genitals. Her breasts were sore she said because she had just had them both re-augmented. Without notice, she gently pulled out her left breast and then her right one that was bandaged around the nipple where an infection had begun to cause her pain. Her breasts were for visual presentation to support her image, however were never accessible for consumption because clients, she declared, were "not allowed to touch them." Her clients, she said, were largely men who claimed they were not gay, but expressly wanted to "suck" her male genitals. She charged 50 guilders ($20) for 15 minutes, and only for a "suck," she said, because if clients wanted more they would have to pay for additional services.

Suddenly an intensification of negotiation occurred as the Turkish man made his way past the window for the third time. At this point, all communication was non-verbal through physical gestures, however bound to their symbolic interaction was a shared understanding between client and sex provider. Magdalena's hand and eye movement confirmed the price and in a welcoming posture waved the man to enter the room. She was playing a game with a prior knowledge that the potential client did not practice wearing a condom and would try negotiating an exchange without one.[6] Magdalena smirked, dismissing him for his high-risk sexual behavior, but continued the game. She knew of the man's penchant from previous failed negotiations together. His behavior prompted commentary on her Middle Eastern clients. Magdalena was not alone in her views. Many prostitutes who worked in the windows and on the streets openly refused to accommodate Moroccan and Turkish clients because of their disinclination to wear a condom, but also because of their cultural practice of price haggling.

Magdalena invited me to sit down on the edge of her single bed covered in white sheets, turning her back to the street as she continued to sit on her throne-like chair in the window. I asked about her frequency of condom usage. Looking me in the eyes she expressed in rehearsed fashion the necessity of wearing condoms with everyone, including her boyfriend.

As I looked around me, I wondered what meaning this room would hold were it not for the presence of a prostitute operating inside behind a glass partition? As an identifiable site for commercial eroticism, the prostitution window lingers in Western popular imagination as an emblem of legalized prostitution in the Netherlands. And in some respect the room conforms to what the public has come to expect of a commercial sex venue. Integral to the room's standardization, however, are sanitizing facilities meeting public health measures. In effect, this standard replication found in most rooms resembled what we have come to expect aesthetically from any low-cost hotel chain. The space remained functional and with little to define it as "erotic," especially in the interim between work shifts when the room appeared stark and meaningless until assigned to the next prostitute to enter during the course of three daily work shifts.

The window, in this respect, makes for more equitable conditions for sex workers who set a standard price for their commodified services. The overriding preoccupation entailed streamlining time management and protocol around paying for services before a sexual exchange takes place. Every aspect of the commercial process appeared controlled when Magdalena gave me the service for cost breakdown. Part of the commercial production of the room, therefore, required transforming this antiseptic and controlled space into a hyper-sexualized site. Magdalena accomplished this décor by maintaining an ambience she transported with her for every shift.

For many sex workers who engaged countless clients throughout the day, the space required compartmentalizing or disengaging the "personal" self from the professional work site. As part of an emotional management tactic, the demands of the transactional exchange left only small traces of the sex worker's personality outside the context of erotic labor. Not unlike the beauty contests recounted in Mark Johnson's ethnography on transgendering in the Southern Philippines (Johnson, 1997), Magdalena's physical performance appeared to be a highly staged and creative production achieved through costume and prostheses.[7] As a result, much of who she was in that space was bound by the role she portrayed.

Sex workers did not always conceal personal items, unrelated to work. As I found with many prostitutes whom I later interviewed, there were always small material objects that they either adorned themselves with or that came part of their accouterments that gave some inkling of who they were outside of the performance of sex work. An amethyst necklace around Magdalena's neck caught my attention. When I asked about her amethyst-gold necklace Magdalena eagerly displayed a matching ring. She said that these were gifts from her lover Maurice but countless customers were unaware of the significance of the ornaments. Perhaps this simple act of adorning the self with personal jewelry, I thought, reclaimed who she was even during a sexual transaction.

Just then, a group of North African men passed the window making eye contact with both of us. Like many sex workers who originate from countries outside the European Union, Magdalena spent numerous years working in other parts of Europe before settling in the Netherlands. In her nine years in the business, Magdalena said she spent five years working in Switzerland, where "money was good," and in Paris where she faced day-to-day violence on the streets. The opportunity of working in the windows, she said, ensured a safe haven compared to the street of other parts of Europe.

Contemplating the North African men who had passed, Magdalena turned to me and commented how they (North Africans) were "very bad" in France. When she worked on the streets of Paris, "the business was rough;" she and others experienced all sorts of violence on the streets. In fact, a close friend was stabbed to death working there. Contrasts between the streets of other European cities and Amsterdam were significant. The comforts of the window were important to her as she pointed with her long nails to a sink, a back kitchen, a bed, and a television at her disposal when she's not working.

This luxury was costly. The daily rental rate for an eight-hour shift cost 200 guilders ($90). In most cases, the rental required a six to seven day a week commitment or the room would go to another prostitute. Added to this condition, Magdalena also pointed out that as a transgendered sex worker she paid 100 guilders more than what female prostitutes paid for the daily rental of a room. This rental difference, I later concluded, was blatant exploitation by the landlord who rented exclusively to a small transgendered community working in six or seven windows and providing a niche market. Compounding this discrimination, she also noted that many transgendered sex workers charged less for services, however she never specified why this discrepancy took place.

The Turkish client returned within our visual scope sticking his head in the door. His action of entering the room was a spatial liberty since I never observed an overt invitation from Magdalena for him to enter. As soon as he opened his mouth he pouted and whined about her demanding the use of a condom. The would-be client disappeared again after Magdalena refused to give in to his request. The game, however, was not over.

When I first met Magdalena, she had been in the Netherlands for only three months. Unlike many sex workers who migrate to the Netherlands having contacts in the business or working in close proximity to friends and family, she had yet to make friends beside her boyfriend. We talked about her lack of relationships for a while. She attributed her isolation to distrust of everyone in the sex industry. Other prostitutes, she explained, were motivated by a need for clients. The local sex workers wanted to engage her in conversation but she wouldn't speak to them. The cell-like design of the window fostered a degree of personal isolation in addition to the competitive spirit of the block.

Working in the window, Magdalena declared, was not about pleasure but about generating as much income as she could during her eight-hour shift. When asked whether she liked her work, she adamantly told me, "NO, work, work, work" then made a grimacing face. This was Magdalena's systematic response each time I followed-up with a similar question each time we met over the course of two years. Her work cycle was intensive, requiring her to comply with the window rental agreement of occupying her window six to seven days per week. This also meant taking between one and two months off for vacation each year. Whenever she returned to French Guinea or Brazil, however, she "never worked," meaning that she did not work as a prostitute in her country of origin. In fact, her family had no idea of what she does for a living in Europe. Like many other South American sex workers, she planned to return home for the months of October, November and December to avoid the harsh winter.[8]

Suddenly the Turkish man returned agreeing to wear a condom and to the price demanded by Magdalena. Although Magdalena suggested that I wait in the back room, I opted to stand outside. With that the client moved deeper into the confined space, and Magdalena closed the window curtain communicating to passersby and would-be customers that a transaction was taking place. I struggled with how to frame the act of closing the curtain and obstructing our view of the interior. Was this a "private" or "public" spectacle, wondering whether this constituted a "private" act? The spectacle left much to the imagination for those of us standing outside the closed curtain in public space. As I exited, a group of well-dressed British men noticed me from across the street. Standing outside the closed window, I grew self-conscious suspecting pedestrians were taking me for a prostitute just because of my proximity to a commercial venue.

TAKING UP SPACE AS A FEMALE RESEARCHER IN THE WINDOW

Standing in a window in this district positions the person as "on display," and as just described, possibly judged. The position also means having to hold your own in that space without apology. As the North African men glared at me looking in from outside the window, I felt a double-edged judgment of what I represented as a woman spotted in a window. There I stood at the "border" wearing formless baggy clothes, a black leather jacket, red-framed glasses and no make-up. By virtue of being female I was marked as either sexually available or as a stigmatized woman. As a researcher in the field, I was struggling to hold my position. My surroundings and the pedestrians passing through the space had greater power to define who I was in that moment than I could muster with my own self-concept. Upholding my right to be in that space, therefore, meant wrestling with the internalization of outside interpretations of what I represented and why I was there. As a researcher, and outsider to erotic labor, I knew it was important to resist internalizing what I imagine to be a sexual exchange outside the realm of mutual desire or to project it onto my own body. It's not uncommon for some researchers to equate sex work with demoralizing language to describe the exchange because they have internalized and projected the commercial experience imagining their own unaccustomed bodies as the instrument of the exchange. I disengaged and consciously diminished the weight of the exchange as a way to manage my own emotional boundaries in the field.

In hindsight, from the distance of that street I could take stock for a moment to ask myself what were the symbolic representations taking place between client and sex provider during my first encounter in the windows. To this day, up close, on a micro-level it appeared like any game of negotiation for goods and services with each party bringing to the table their own set of needs, wants, and skills. Only if I squint my eyes to blur what I had witnessed, do I ask if this a replication of colonial relations? Were not the European male colonizers sexually exploitative of indigenous women in Latin America? Did they not set up brothels throughout the region and in the Caribbean to have their sexual needs fulfilled by mostly indigenous women? The configuration didn't quite add up, though. In this case, Magdalena is a transgendered sex worker legally employed in the Netherlands and about to service what I'll assume to be a Turkish man who immigrated to the country to do menial work that most Dutch have no desire to perform. In the end, how does one interpret the blurred power relations between two "immigrants" where one is transgendered and the other is trying to publicly protect his heterosexual status? It appeared like a complicated dance, where Magdalena hooked the client in promising sexual satisfaction and the client acquiesced agreeing upon her price and condom usage in exchange to have his customized desires fulfilled.

I stood outside no more than two minutes when the Turkish man left. He strode briskly past me without raising his face to meet my eyes. Magdalena reopened the window curtain and, looking for me, waved for me to return. As I entered the window, Magdalena offered me a cigarette that I accepted. The room was heavy with the thick scent of perspiration as Magdalena pushed the condom into the trash with a ready pool cue.[9]

Magdalena and I continued sitting in the window talking together when a middle-aged, Dutch man expressed interest in her services. The would-be client passed twice, each time making eye contact before finally entering the room. During this brief negotiation the two parties spoke in English. Magdalena explained her costs, and without any haggling the client accepted the terms handing Magdalena 50 guilders for services. This time Magdalena escorted me to a back door leading to a kitchenette and bathroom. I sat on the edge of a dusty Jacuzzi listening to music from a portable radio while overhearing them negotiate in the next room. As the man took Magdalena's instructions, I heard a condom package tear. Then I heard the client ask Magdalena "to come" and with his request her response of a demand for more money. Who would have guessed the client was also inquiring about "your girlfriend" (me) waiting in the back room. Magdalena replied, as she told me later, that I "didn't work."

Suddenly the door swung open and Magdalena reached over to turn up the music. She obviously didn't want me to hear the client's request for her to have an orgasm. This request had thrown the exchange back into the negotiation stage while the two parties were partially undressed and in close proximity to each other on or around the single bed. Five to ten minutes passed when I heard the client orgasm. In the end, the transaction earned Magdalena over 200 guilders.[10] She later told me that the client would have paid another 200 guilders had I joined them. My response was awkward, but I tried to be nonchalant about my commercial unavailability without appearing offensive or judgmental.

In this instance, Magdalena dictated and enforced body management. The client played his role, too, as he understood and respected the rules for the duration of the transaction. Service prices mediated clear boundaries for the sex worker even after the client decided he wanted additional services. The sexual transaction, therefore, is based on the agreed upon acts in exchange for money rather than a time-based contract. For most window and street prostitutes, unlike erotic labor found in the clubs where services are determined by an hourly charge during which any service can be demanded.[11] Contrastingly, once a client initiates a transaction, even the act of looking at or touching a sex worker is transformed into a service deemed acceptable or not by the service provider herself. The codes of behavior were for most part respected by the regular clients. Only uninformed tourists that did not know the protocol of the prostitution windows or were too inebriated to care broke the codes of conduct.

After Magdalena disposed of the condom, and the heavy scent of perspiration exited the room, we talked about her impressions of the Amsterdam Police. They, too, held a significant role in the maintenance of window prostitution. I was then reminded of how the American press featured articles on Amsterdam Police whose function, among other things, was to inform tourists of protocol in the Red Light District. Magdalena told me that Amsterdam was a "good place" where the police didn't abuse their power. In Paris, however, she said that the police demanded either money or sex.

Hours passed and the summer skyline slowly darkened outside. Magdalena continued to communicate with me in English, however sometimes she used French words that didn't require translations or I interjected German or Spanish words that she knew.[12] Then, as Magdalena's work shift drew to a close, a tall, thin gentle-faced man, in his late-twenties, entered the room without knocking. His motion to enter the space without gaining permission first startled me. After all, there is an unspoken rule that prohibits potential clients from entering at will. Magdalena turned to me and said, "It's okay. He is my boyfriend." I shook the man's hand as he searched my unfamiliar countenance.

MAGDALENA'S PARTNER

A sex worker's partner also has a relationship to the workspace and the industry, in general. Maurice was quick to articulate his overriding longing for a life away from prostitution. After he greeted Magdalena in French, and then learned that I was a native English speaker, he lapsed into English telling me about his experience with her work. "I hate it," he declared, "because it causes me pain." However, he admitted, "it's work" and that the physical working conditions of the window were more desirable than her working on the streets of Paris. In France, Maurice made a point of telling me, he was in the printing business, however now he only "helped" Magdalena get to and from work.

Not unlike other sex workers I later interviewed, Maurice and Magdalena had a plan with a timeline that included a future life after her retirement from prostitution. He expressed wanting Magdalena to work only for another "two more years." Magdalena overhearing his declaration protested. When I asked about their future goals Magdalena turned to Maurice and warned him not to utter their secret dream for fear that saying it out loud might inhibit their new life from coming true. I agreed that this secret belonged to them and should remain private. Only later, Maurice told me of their desire to leave Europe and move to Santo Domingo where they would finally "get out of prostitution." In the meantime, Maurice agreed that they both liked Amsterdam for the openness and tolerance, but qualified that "we don't smoke marijuana."

We were not only in the city of Amsterdam, sitting in a window in a satellite commercial district, but also undeniably in an area where transgendered prostitutes were concentrated. The cultural influence of transgenderism on the immediate environment made it impossible to ignore issues of gender and sexual identity in the personal life of Maurice and Magdalena. He needed to articulate his distance from customers, gay men, and how the outside world constructs the transgendered person and their lovers. As Maurice talked about his relationship with Magdalena, he resorted to numerous heterosexist conventions. First, Maurice referred to Magdalena as "his wife." He went into elaborate detail telling me about how he was previously married to a woman with whom he had a child. Throughout our initial conversation, Maurice was protecting his heterosexual status insisting that he was "not gay" by reminding me "gay men don't want transgendered sex workers." His sexuality, much like the boyfriends of *travestís* depicted in Kulíck's *Travesti,* had been scrutinized by the outside world due in part to the gender status of his partner.

The politics of claiming heterosexual status for Maurice was centered on his use of language to describe his relationship with Magdalena and his emphasis on the desirability of certain bodily acts he expressed in his erotic life with her. He reaffirmed his own hetero-masculinity by virtue of what gendered body parts he qualified as undesirable. He made a point then, and again over dinner, to tell me how he was "not interested in the penis." "Magdalena is my wife; I don't like men," he said. The language we used around their personal relationship bound Magdalena to traditional heteronormative conventions regardless of how they, as a couple, might have broken out of the paradigm. This was not uncommon for transgendered companions to remain within a heterosexual script assigning one partner to the role of "wife" and the other to the role of "husband." In Don Kulíck's *Travestis,* similar language conventions are used to give symbolic meaning to the relationships between *travestís* and their boyfriends. In such case the boyfriends considered themselves heterosexual because the role-playing they perform. *Travestí* relationships documented by Kulíck also revealed how couples stayed out of public view out of fear of being defined and stigmatized by an outside world. As long as Magdalena and Maurice kept the outside world at bay, they could continue to define themselves rather than be defined by their social surroundings.

MAGDALENA'S TRANSFORMATION INTO THE PERSONAL SELF

A Latin American acquaintance knocked on the door informing them of her impending shift at another window up the street. Based on the person's mixed gender coding that seemed to be "in progress," I assumed she was a transvestite, wearing facial make-up that was only partially applied and still dressed in men's street clothes. The conversation continued on in Spanish and slowly became incomprehensible to me. Simultaneously, Magdalena began her own process of changing out of her costume, pulling out from her gym bag conservative articles of clothing she purchased earlier on her shift.

This was the first of many opportunities to watch transgendered sex workers transform in to and out of professional and gendered roles. Even during the early stages of my fieldwork, it was apparent that a large component of the transgendered performance involved the production of "getting ready." However, at this moment both actors were reassembling gendered and commercial appearances and seemingly going in different directions in terms of their representations. Whether or not this aspect of gender construction sparks such a "reading," multiple gender transitions were taking place before me, making this an operative moment of "deconstructive value" (Broad, 2002; 245). Theorists such as Bordo (1993), however, might fail to see the deconstructive value of this gender transition because first, it did not take place in the public sphere where spectators could witness the transformation, and second, there was no way of telling if the "reader" present would interpret the transition with the awareness of how gender is culturally produced (Bordo, 1993; 292). Perhaps, though, the transitions both reified and undermined fixed notions of gender. But Butler, like other postmodernists, would certainly "celebrate" this moment as an act of resistance, interpreting it as creative agency through the destabilization of gendered role playing rather than representing something "restorative" in terms of a gender system (Bordo, 1993, 290).

The ambiance of the soft lighting from a small cosmetic mirror illuminated the room and diminished the cramped confines of the space. Somehow I didn't feel claustrophobic as Maurice and I forged a discussion on my research in Amsterdam. He talked about my study within the context of "reportage" and saw value in telling the stories and experiences of prostitutes. Then the conversation drifted back to why he hated Magdalena's work.

Calling out from the back room, Magdalena invited me to visit her at another window where she planned to work the following day. She gave me directions to another window, a block over on a side street, and said she would be there from 10AM to 8PM. Magdalena then qualified that she never worked overnight shifts because "protecting" her cycle of sleep with Maurice was the only way to maintain normalcy in her relationship with him.

The room, like Magdalena herself, was in transition as her shift drew to a close. Watching Magdalena and Maurice work in tandem as they systematically disassembled the room revealed the strenuousness of the closing phase of a shift. While Magdalena changed out of her work clothes, Maurice packed all of her belongings, including the dildos, into a blue gym bag while continuing to speak of his experiences in the "printing" business back in France. As he spoke, Magdalena stepped into the bathroom. Maurice then turned to me confessing his being unemployed and spending most of his time tending to Magdalena's work needs. He then excused himself, heading across the street to buy condoms for the next day. A physically transformed Magdalena emerged from the bathroom wearing no make-up, her long hair conservatively pulled back. She wore a loose gray weave blouse and matching pants. With her gray contact lenses removed, she now wore a pair of wide framed glasses, perhaps seen on middle-aged European actresses.

The boundaries around how a person could enter the window were also changing. Without knocking, a Dutch woman came through the door. I soon learned that this person was the next worker to rent the space when she asked in English whether Magdalena planned to vacate shortly. When Maurice returned, we were ready to depart. Turning to survey the space, the room appeared stark with no remnants of the last eight-hour shift. We then proceeded to walk over to another window where Magdalena would be working the following morning. At the moment she needed to drop off her daily rent.

As we turned down a narrow alley, shouting could be heard between two parties just out of view. A confrontation was ensuing inside the same window where Magdalena had to deposit the rent. From outside we heard her "landlord," Diva, shouting in English at a drunken European (white) male trying to enter her window without permission. I recognized Diva as someone I had seen before on the streets. Her large, powerful frame towered over most clients, and with her penchant for wearing animal skin outfits, large wigs, and pronounced augmented curves, her persona created a memorable image. In fact, her personification was right out of a larger-than-life fantasy. Instantly, I recalled walking across town late one night and observing Diva standing on the pavement outside her designated window, nearly naked, intimidating men as they passed. She had all but prohibited passage without payment first. She had resorted to aggressive tactics that night because, as I imagine, business was slow.

MAGDALENA'S DEFINITION OF GENDER IDENTITY

Magdalena informed me that Diva owns three rooms, and operates as a major contact for *travestís* wanting to work in the windows. In fact, if a transgendered sex worker wants to work in the area, she has no alternative but to seek out Diva. She also described Diva as a transsexual who was "still selling sex," despite her rental earnings.[13] The economic circumstances of Diva perplexed Magdalena and Maurice for two reasons.

First, through property ownership Diva had a source of capital generated for her "passive" participation in commercial sex. Under similar circumstances, Magdalena and Maurice assumed a prostitute would cease providing labor-intensive sexual services after ascending to a "management" position. No one asked whether Diva actually enjoyed working as a prostitute. Instead, Magdalena and Maurice assumed material "greed" motivated her to remain on the streets.

Second, since having her sex reassignment, Diva's presence as a prostitute made "no sense" to Magdalena. "Clients want transvestites,"[14] she insisted, "they don't want transsexuals [because] they want the [experience of the] penis." She went on, "They—clients—don't want a transsexual when they can have a woman." Based on Magdalena's logic, if a client wanted vaginal sex why then would he seek out a reconstructed sexual organ? Her assumption reveals something about Magdalena's relationship to her own body as well as the borders she upheld against an onslaught of probing clients. In fact, Magdalena intended on having a sex reassignment operation to become a woman, however she would do so only after she ceased working as a prostitute. "It's for me, not for them. My penis is for work. It (her penis) means nothing to me. This is how I am naturally." Magdalena identified her penis as a source of income, and gave that part of her body no other social value. Her penis, therefore, functioned as a gravitating force drawing clients to her even though she was hyper-feminine and "feels like a woman."

Reflecting on her own gender and sexual identity, Magdalena understood that her success as a *travestí* prostitute derived from the exoticization of her inter-sexed body. Namely *travestí* sex workers hold a unique distinction by imparting hyper-feminine coding with "male gear." Magdalena believed that her male genitalia were her greatest source of income in the plethora of services she could provide. Based on Magdalena's commercial use of her body, her comments support Mendès-Leite's blurred model "ambigusexuality" that is evolving out of the *travesti* culture in which a hyper-feminine performance will give no indication of the sexual roles a *travesti* might perform during a sexual act (Mendès-Leite, 1993). For Diva, however, to have had a sex reassignment and continued selling her services as a transsexual meant that Diva no longer competed in the same market as *travestí* sex workers. Diva, like the transsexuals whom I later met in the zone, now competed for clients with other female prostitutes. Magdalena's understanding of these commodified desires and the bodily form meant that a "biologically born" woman had greater "cachet" than a transsexual who had been through a sex reassignment. The naturalized genitals of a female sex worker in this instance represented an "authentic" sexual experience and were assumed preferred to a "reconstructed" body modified by medical intervention. Imbedded in this notion are assumptions about the sexual preferences of clients and what type of sex worker holds greatest desirability to them and alluding to an essentialistic view of gender.

When we finally arrived at Diva's window, she was in the process of throwing a German sounding man out of her basement level window. Purportedly the man had entered Diva's space without permission, warranting her reaction. As he was forcibly removed he managed to throw out insulting comments about Diva's "womanhood." In a drunken state, the man repeated that Diva was not a woman but "*a man.*" At this point he sought affirmation from the growing audience hovering around the window decrying who could claim herself a woman and who could not. Countering his insults, Diva grew louder, threatening to beat the man up and challenging his masculinity by saying that he was "no man for her." Her space, like her gender identity, was hers to define: she won the battle with the volume of her voice alone.

As this spectacle unfolded only feet from us, Maurice turned to me and said, "*This* is why I don't like the business. This is what I worry about when she works."

After Magdalena paid Diva for the window, the three of us walked into the darkness. There was a sense of vulnerability of the unknown as a group of drunken restless males passed us. Magdalena then extended an invitation to their home for dinner.

When I asked how we were getting there, they simultaneously replied, "By cab." As we walked two blocks over to heavier traffic, again passing hordes of rambunctious young men moving in packs, Magdalena described the difficulties of catching a cab from this location. Implicit in her statement was a sense of their avoidance of wandering out on the streets at night.

We caught a taxi and I motioned for Magdalena to climb in first. My gesture was two fold in meaning. First, Magdalena had labored all day and was visibly tired. Second, my gesture ran along chivalrous lines which may have appeared odd for a woman to extend to a transgendered person, however Magdalena was doing a more "femininized" gender characterization than I. Under the conditions of late night, Magdalena may have also felt more vulnerable as a transgendered person than I as a female. Meanwhile, Maurice took a seat up front, conversing with the cab driver. As we sped off, Magdalena gazed into my eyes confiding to me that she had "no friends besides Maurice." Her glance was weary and I felt her isolation.

Maurice paid the cab driver with Magdalena's money. Approaching a four-storied brick building typically found throughout Amsterdam, nothing seemed unusual about the residence, but for Maurice pushing the unlocked door open with his hand. We climbed two flights up. The time was already 11PM.

THE SANCTUARY

We entered a one-bedroom apartment with a long hallway leading to an open living room and kitchen. The bedroom Magdalena and Maurice shared had a simple elegance. The walls were painted sky blue and above their white metal-framed double bed hung a picture of the Virgin Mary. In the main living area a kitchen table was neatly set for two. Hanging from the dark wood panel was a photo of Magdalena and Maurice standing with one of Magdalena's family members. Both hosts offered to take my coat, however I declined intending not to stay long. We sat on oversized beige leather couches forming a semicircle that faced a television. Maurice offered me an orange soda, and we all had a glass. Before drinking Magdalena and I toasted with our glasses.

For a couple who had only been in Amsterdam for three months, their living quarters appeared settled and decorated with a host of familiar items. Before finding this apartment through "a friend," Magdalena and Maurice spent an entire month living out of a hotel. Each person differed on how long they expected to stay in this space.

Surrounded by reminders of her past, Magdalena mentioned her family back in South America. She had five or six siblings. All knew her as a transgendered person. Her mother, whom she said was "*tot*" then "*muerte*" (dead in German and Spanish respectively) had been an entertainer from French Guiana. Magdalena learned to speak Dutch while she and her mother moved to the Netherlands in her early childhood. Her father, a Brazilian fishmonger still lived there. To this day Magdalena felt a strong distaste for the sight and smell of seafood from growing up around her father's fish market.

Maurice prepared all of the meals in their household. Perhaps he was compensating for Magdalena's economic position as the breadwinner. Maurice's eagerness to cook, however, might have been due to the role he played in their relationship rather than his economic contribution, or there lack of.

I asked whether her family had met Maurice. "Oh, yes," she said, their relationship was not an issue. In fact, before her death, Magdalena's mother had met Maurice and liked him very much. Her family was not aware, however, that Magdalena worked as a prostitute. How Magdalena concealed this information was unknown to me. A year or so later when meeting up with Jojo, a prostitute who was working in Magdalena's usual window, I then learned how they once danced together in a troupe back in French Guiana. Thus having a profession in the entertainment industry might have made it easier to conceal the erotic overtones of her work.

Magdalena talked at lengths about her sense of religiosity. She "strongly believed" in Catholicism, praying regularly, however dismissed the practice of *Santeria,* or Voodoo. Using a phrase in Portuguese or Creole, she mentioned how Diva regularly practiced a form of Voodoo.

Catholicism functioned as a stabilizing institution as well as a source of dignity in Magdalena's life. Whatever cultural continuity Catholicism meant to Magdalena, she lived her private life with a sense of grace. The absence of friends in the business allowed her to distance herself farther from whatever social meaning she gave to prostitution culture.

Magdalena found many prostitutes were too competitive with each other. For this reason she never disclosed to her peers when she was having a "good day" in the windows. She gave the following example of how competition undermines congenial relations between prostitutes working in the windows. If prostitutes were present during a negotiation with one of her clients and the client refused to wear a condom, other sex workers would openly offer services without the use of a condom. To support her claims Magdalena concluded that the Turkish client must have received sexual services without the use of a condom or else he would never have attempted to negotiate services without one.

Magdalena explained to me how she experienced isolation working in the individual window. This situation was coupled by a lack of friends outside the industry. People whom she knew "outside," she said, expressed either condescension or an overall attitude that her work life was "her problem." Magdalena made a symbolic gesture of wiping her hands together to rid her of complicated and painful relationships and then she searched my face for a response. At the time of this disclosure she also explained why she allowed me to enter her window to speak to her. In that moment, when we first met, she "sussed out" my character sensing "no judgment" from my part. The respect I treated her with opened the lines of communication between us. I felt deeply touched by this statement and received a long moment of silence between us.

Over dinner, the conversation returned to the sex industry. In particular, they identified the layers of actors who played various roles at the local sex trade. They returned to the central role of Diva, whom they said had become wealthy renting rooms. They interpreted Diva's continuing to sell sex as a type of "greed" or "love of money." "Money, money, money, that's all Diva cares about," Magdalena said. In their depiction of Diva, there was no mention of "organized crime" or Diva's relationship to organized crime, however they spoke cautiously about turf in the surrounding neighborhood purportedly controlled by a Serbian mafia.[15]

Magdalena then mentioned how a Czech woman once asked her to work for "them" but she adamantly declined. This proposition exposed Magdalena's greatest fear of having someone from organized crime entering her window and stealing her papers and passport.

How bad was it for people without "papier" (papers)? I asked.

She said that without papers, prostitutes were susceptible to being exploited. Magdalena then presented herself as a "fighter," as someone who could hold her own. I wondered whether this was the advantageous position of being a transgendered prostitute, or the privilege of having a French passport. Her repositioning left me wondering whether Magdalena could masculinize her stance when needed.

Shifting the conversation, I asked Maurice about his family. He mentioned that when he told his "old fashioned" mother that "my wife happens to be a prostitute," she took it very well. Overall, he said his mother was very accepting of Maurice's partnership. It was then I learned that Maurice was 26 years old, ten years Magdalena's junior.

After dinner, we then sat back down in the living room area where Maurice turned on the television to watch "Jerry Springer." I was spared viewing the syndicated programming since I was tired and needed to return home. I suggested walking, but Magdalena and Maurice recommended taking a cab. At this moment, I noticed that they were rationing the last of their cigarettes. Maurice motioned for Magdalena to hold off on the second to last one. Instead, they shared the one he was smoking. Suddenly, one of Celine Dion's videos came on, and Magdalena recalled telling me earlier in the evening how much she loved the French-Canadian singer. But Maurice was in control of the remote and changed the channel, passing over Dutch porn to find the French news.

My attention drew back to Magdalena who heaved a sigh from pain in her breast. She caressed herself, expressing to me her discomfort, and how taking her medicine could heal the infection around her nipple from her breast augmentation. Maurice called a cab company that kept him on hold. I then volunteered to wait on the phone for the dispatcher rather than inconvenience him. When the cab arrived, I thanked them again for their generosity. Magdalena reminded me that she would be working at 10AM, and "to please come by." We kissed three times on the cheek before I entered the cab. The time was after 1:30AM.

MAGDALENA'S NEW WINDOW

The following morning, I purchased a pack of Dunhills and a breakfast pastry to bring to Magdalena's window. When I arrived at Magdalena's new window location, I found her Latin American transvestite friend standing in the doorway, wearing regular men's street clothes with facial make-up. She assumed Magdalena was working on the main street.

On my way to the other window, I bumped into Magdalena and Maurice. Magdalena seemed perturbed by something, as if she were not present. Maurice, on the other hand, was happy to see me, and kissed my cheek four times. They invited me to follow them. We approached the basement window entering the dark cramped space. The air was heavy from the residue of body oils. Maurice made a face to convey a noxious odor. The Latina, still present, seemed surprised that Magdalena was working in Diva's window this morning.

The room, though more spacious than yesterday's rental, felt congested with four people standing there. Magdalena was late, and clearly needed time to prepare for her performance. I suggested coming back later after she dressed. Before leaving I gave Magdalena the pastry, and then the cigarettes. She smiled at me in gratitude that I had thought to bring her cigarettes.

When I returned to Magdalena's window, her shades were closed. She was with a client, and there was nowhere for me to stand without brushing up against male pedestrians searching the windows along this narrow alleyway. I noticed a Latina woman in the next window. Through eye contact and lip reading, I ask if I may enter her place. She welcomed me in, and we began a conversation. She was from the Dominican Republic and spoke little English. A veteran of the first wave of Dominican prostitutes who came in the early 1980s, she had no children to support and had the luxury of traveling home for the winter. The sun streamed into her room, and the whiteness of her lingerie illuminated a contrast with the color and abundance of her fleshy skin. She was a woman in her mid to late forties, competing in a market of young aggressive prostitutes. She seemed to welcome my presence, but I excused myself for concern I might be distracting her from clients. I drifted across the alley standing near a mature bleached-blonde Dutch prostitute whose flesh burst out from the seams of her attire as she stood in a medieval doorway. I asked her how she was doing to which she replied, "okay, but could you stand over there," pointing to Magdalena's place on the other side of the narrow walkway. I realized my presence as a female pedestrian in the street was affecting business just inches from her room. Perhaps I was preventing her from contacting customers, and when I mentioned this possibility to her, she said that it could be true.

I walked around the area passing the same men who continued to perambulate in an anticipatory sexual state. I averted their attempts to make eye contact with me. My body stopped projecting outward and I shrunk, doing all that I could to maintain my right to move through the space without completely disappearing. When I returned to Magdalena's basement window, the tint and reflection of the glass was so glaring, it was impossible to see her sitting on her ornate throne. All that could be seen was her tassel of long hair. Magdalena waved and I entered down the steps. The air was fetid. Magdalena seemed frustrated with the space. When I told her that I couldn't see her from outside she grew concerned.

Magdalena wore her signature black rubber outfit. It required, she reported, about thirty minutes to prepare herself. Today there was no business. As would-be clients strained their heads to gaze at who was in the basement window, Magdalena made clicking noises with her mouth and called out for them to "come in." Her efforts were mostly in vain in part because of the sound proof quality of the room, and the reflective tint over the window. When uninterested men failed to respond, she called them "*makado*" then looked at me before we both laughed in amusement.

Dildos garnished the window, and, with the door jarred open, I was the one who passersby saw as I sat at the foot of a platform where Magdalena reigned from a regal chair. Dangling between the door and the window were poultices of garlic hanging from the wall. Magdalena laughed aloud and noted that this was evidence of Diva's Voodoo practices. I noticed another small yellow pouch, perhaps with human hair, hanging above it.

The ceiling was low, but this room was larger and contained many luxuries not found in Magdalena's previous work site, or any other room I have since entered. The "work space" was equipped with a double bed and ceiling mirrors, hidden behind a curtain of muslin. There was a microwave, a television, and kitchenette with a refrigerator. There was also a small shelf containing Hummel statuettes. These accommodations buffered the long hours of boredom that would occur on a slow night and became a stable place where I could locate Magdalena in the years to come.

In fact, one year later, when I returned to the room looking for Magdalena, I was surprised to find Jojo, her French Guiana friend, working her window that day instead. When I entered Jojo was sipping a large glass of Malibu rum with coke that she had put together from a well-supplied liqueur cabinet.[16]

Today, Magdalena's face and posture gave her the appearance of being bored, sitting in her high throne and tapping the armchair with her long plastic fingernails. Time was wasting away and she wasn't making any money.

NEGOTIATING MY ROLE AS RESEARCHER

As I sat with Magdalena, more men began making eye contact with me, or at least appeared more aware of my presence. This was an odd occurrence since I wore red-framed glasses and my clothes were not form fitting. I asked if Magdalena preferred that I leave, and she replied "no."

Magdalena grew frustrated with her lack of street visibility. After a dozen or so men passed, and after each one tried gazing into the window but failed to make eye contact, she acknowledged there was a problem. Based on the searching glances of passersby that did not meet hers, Magdalena knew the reflective layer coupled by the diminished height of the basement window failed to produce any communication with would-be clients. But she had little choice in the matter as Diva insisted that Magdalena work that room.

Evidently Diva had some control over use of the space, and where Magdalena was expected to rent. There were questions I wanted to ask about their relationship, but I did not want to press the issue with her.

Finally, Magdalena begrudgingly decided to sit on a stool near the door. Her acquiescent move occurred only after an older Dutch cab driver passed by commenting that he could not see her from the street.

For Magdalena to make an effort to be visible from the street compromised her pride. With an attitude of contempt for clients she quipped, "if they want it [sex], they can enter the room," but otherwise, she was not going to accommodate them any further. Any effort to lure customers with clicking noises and hand gestures seemed largely for my behalf as her audience. We giggled together as she made commentary on unsuspecting male passersby. After all they were paying attention to the wrong person: me.

A middle-aged, Dutch man wearing a groomed beard and a conservative suit passed numerous times. Each time, the man tried to make eye contact with me. When Magdalena moved away from the open space retrieving something from the back of the room, during that brief lapse away from the window, a Middle-Eastern man attempted to make contact with me. The man came as close as the door when I called out to Magdalena to negotiate with the potential client. Immediately, without much of a dialogue, Magdalena recognized the direction of his interest telling him in Dutch that it would cost him 400 guilders to have a commercial exchange with me because, after all, I was a virgin. The client recoiled but not before he looked me over in amazement at my inflated value and virgin status. Magdalena and I laughed at her management style, but at that moment she made a point of telling me that it is all right for me to "do a little business as well."

This suggestion required a subtle response. I showed no facial expression each time Magdalena made her suggestion giving my standard reply not to partake because "I promised my professor, I wouldn't 'get into it.'" Perhaps Magdalena was testing to check my underlying reaction to exchanging sex for money. My response held in balance my perception around bodily boundaries, the status of those who performed commercial sex, and possibly my informant as well.

When the bearded man passed for a fourth time, Magdalena knew she had a potential customer and attempted to catch his attention with heightened window theatrics reaching for one of her dildo sculptures.[17] As foot traffic thinned along the narrow street, just feet from us on the other side of the street, the older blonde prostitute took the hand of a young male client guiding him inside her room. As the door shut and shades were drawn, I mentioned to Magdalena my earlier encounter with the woman. Magdalena responded with a look of contempt for her and all other sex workers of her class. Implicit in her reaction was an expression of disgust for what she perceived as a form of greed and a lack of taste in the woman's personal appearance.

My understanding of her reaction included her disbelief in the desirability of a mature, working-class prostitute. Through the woman's gesturing and physical presentation she was marked by a class inscription perhaps unlike transgendered prostitutes who applied elaborate aesthetic rituals to their daily commercial performance, or could simply position themselves outside a fixed social class system. By most accounts the woman's appearance was that of a "common prostitute" and unlike many transgendered sex workers, she ranked low on the theatrics. Much to Magdalena's astonishment the young client entering the mature woman's room was one of her regulars, seemingly unfazed by the sex worker's maturity or lack of panache.

Hours passed generating little business. By late afternoon, my presence was causing a distraction. Finally, without being harsh, Magdalena suggested coming back a little later. We kissed the customary three times and I left.

FOLLOW-UP VISITS OVER THE COURSE OF TWO YEARS

I have made numerous return visits to Magdalena's window over the course of two and a half years since having first met her. After our first meeting an entire year passed before my returning to Amsterdam. My first stop was a visit to the basement window, but this time I was traveling with a Spanish-speaking friend and wasn't certain whether I should pass an informant's window with a stranger tagging along. Magdalena immediately recognized me, as I knocked before entering the basement door. She waved for me to enter into the familiar thick air. Magdalena held the same repose as last time, looking bored as she remained in her chair. I approached and we kissed three times. My friend stood in the doorway when she invited him to enter.

In English and Spanish, Magdalena shared how she had worked seven days straight. When I asked about Maurice and whether he was working, she made a look of disgust, telling me that he had not found work.

Business was slow. As men passed, she referred to them as *"pepito"* (little penis) and each time the three of us laughed at the susceptibility of her potential clients. The joke was on them.

Penile paraphernalia and herbal poultices still hung from the window. Magdalena mentioned that she and Maurice had moved into a larger apartment. Two potential clients passed by, two or three times and I felt the tension of not wanting to interfere with Magdalena's shift. In the six or seven times I have been to her window, each time I have felt a sense of guilt for having the flexibility to leave at will, while she sat there bound to her chair for an eight hour shift. This sense of immobility can easily translate to most jobs held in the customer service sector. Certainly anyone who has worked at a reception desk knows similar feelings of not being able to walk away from one's desk at will.

Magdalena appeared welcoming but reserved in her responses. I wasn't certain whether she was suffering from exhaustion or wondering why I kept returning to her window every six months or so. Then I contemplated whether I was simply a reminder of another year passing. With the three of us in the confined space, my friend and I were "free" to leave.

Magdalena expressed wanting to go home, suggesting that I work her shift. Again, I was awkward and humorless in responding, though we all laughed at the possibility of recouping my travel expenses.

When I mentioned looking for a room to rent, she mentioned Diva having space above this window. Diva was the motivation behind Magdalena's heavy work cycle, or so Magdalena claimed. She said that Diva wanted her to work every day. It was Diva whom I would have to contact if I were to rent an apartment in this block. Luckily, the apartment was over 1,000 guilders per month, and beyond my budget.

During Magdalena's complaints about her never ending work schedule, I asked about how many more years she intended to work. She threw out three long polished fingers. Another year had passed but another year had been added to her commitment to stay in this sector. Then she mentioned having her breasts redone and enlarged in July, and visiting her family in August. Her plans were not unlike the endless cycle of work facing most of us, rewarding her with a trip home. Not knowing where to take our conversation, I asked if they now knew about her work. She was emphatic about them not knowing.

The following Monday I returned to her window to cancel a dinner engagement we had arranged the previous week. I was alone with Magdalena when she expressed explicitly how much she despised working in the window. Speaking in the voice of the client, she mimicked their standard response, "'Are you happy fucking me?'" And in her hapless voice as herself she responded, "Yes, I am happy."

Weeks later, while bicycling down a residential neighborhood far from the grind of the Red Light District, I noted two females selling "S/M" as a pair in a satellite prostitution window[18]. There was an international soccer tournament happening all over the city, and hordes of drunken soccer fans were expecting to descend on the city within minutes. One of the females was Magdalena who was now working with a Latina and hoping to capture some of the bon vivant atmosphere of the games. She asked me to stop by her regular window the following day. We managed to see each other again before my research took me to other parts of the country.

Six months later, arriving in Amsterdam during a heavy snowfall, I passed by Magdalena's window. She recognized me immediately welcoming me into her window. Lowering the volume of the television with a remote control we exchanged "air kisses."

All was well she said. She looked thinner and her breasts were newly re-augmented. Maurice, she reported, now worked in a gourmet shop. I asked how much longer she intended to work, and she replied "three more years." Then she suggested that I should work in her window to make some money with her but I declined. I was left with disintegrating remnants of the luster of our initial contact that I held so dear. Magdalena wanted to work, so I motioned to leave. She suggested that I come back at 8PM, but I was too jetlagged to return.

This brief encounter was the last time I visited Magdalena in her window. Nevertheless, I consider my two-year relationship with her a positive and meaningful experience for me. Whether standing in her window, watching her interaction with clients, or observing her relationship with her partner, each scenario contributed to my understanding of window prostitution. The details of this experience also gave me a perspective on how space shapes social relations in this type of prostitution. How sexualized spaces are organized in other venues, such as in a streetwalking zone, are significant to understanding how different sites operate and what conditions benefit sex workers more than others.

CONCLUSION

Dutch window prostitution represents a highly visible symbol of normalization. This is not to suggest that social stigmatization does not occur for women working in the windows. The Red Light District itself is an accessible neighborhood in Amsterdam where tourists, consumers, residents, and researchers walk through. Perhaps because of the area's public attractions, when tourists, for instance, are in the District, they bring with them their cultural values about erotic labor and their expectations of what a window prostitute represents. I witnessed firsthand how many window prostitutes resisted negative treatment from passersby, but also how they conformed their movements, gestures, and solicitation script to what society has come to interpret as "prostitute-like." Here, the prostitute is more visible to the public, but her language usage and physical markings still signify her as a prostitute.

Observation time spent inside Magdalena's window was priceless in my understanding of Dutch window prostitution, helping to forge a perspective from which I could write about sex work. This perspective from inside her window allowed me to witness, firsthand, the art of commercial negotiation through a mixture of gestures and nonverbal communication, supporting a favorable position for sex workers when negotiating services. Exchanges between consumer and provider revealed a pattern of codes and rules producing distinct characteristics of window prostitution from other types of sex work. Moreover, my being inside the window gave me access to real sexual transactions exposing ways sex workers commodify their services and maintain parameters around the body. My presence in this space was not without its challenges, as prostitution sites required renegotiating my role as a researcher throughout my fieldwork.

My fortuitous contact with Magdalena shaped this entire study in other ways. Her transgendered identity motivated a broadening of my inquiry to consider how transgenderism influences spatial and commercial relations. Like other transgendered informants whom I later met, Magdalena positioned herself as an exotic performer and therefore an anomaly existing outside social qualifiers that label prostitutes and sex work as negative or low status. In the window, Magdalena gave a disciplined gendered performance complete with fantasy costume that elevated her work in the window to a craft. But her gender and sexual mapping also gives evidence of how "cultural hybridity" unfurls in a fluid, unselfconscious manner (Lopez-Vicuna citing Carrillo, 2004). In effect "cultural hybridity" has an impact on notions of sexuality and operates as a product of both culture and economics, as the latter clearly played an instrumental role in how Magdalena utilized her body in the commercial sphere.

Magdalena's reading of transsexualism did not afford transsexuals that same fluid state in their physical embodiment and through their commercial sexual services as she did *travestís*. She ascribed an inferior meaning to the transsexual body while assigning a "naturalized" superior position to the anatomically born female. How she internalized her own physical embodiment in relation to genetically born females required a hyper-feminine performance of her in the window and a commercial justification for keeping her male genitalia. Magdalena's appearance, and, more importantly, her isolation and disassociation from other sex workers, afforded her additional status maintenance at her work site. An example of this was exhibited when she expressed contempt for "common" female prostitutes, such as the older blonde woman who worked in a window across the street from her, because she perceived them as permanently marked by their (lower) social class, longevity in the sex industry, and lack of aesthetic maintenance. But confining her work to the windows meant some degree of community as well. Other Latin American window prostitutes visited her or used her as a contact for getting into the business. Jojo's professional use of the window was an example of how social networks provide support and common interests.

Of equal significance was the privilege of entering Magdalena's domestic domain. Here, I gained a firsthand sense of how she lives her personal life. This standpoint allowed me to involuntarily witness how her companion copes with her profession, and revealed what concerns and preoccupations extend to indirect actors in the business. Was Maurice a "pimp" or a boyfriend who was helping out his partner in between his own employment stints? I would guess the latter given that Maurice finally established himself during the course of the two years I remained in contact with them. In terms of social positioning, in their isolation, Magdalena and Maurice illustrated a desire to uphold "French" etiquette, in the form of table manners, eating habits, and roles as hosts, while simultaneously distancing themselves from the sex industry. Their isolation afforded them other benefits and represented an arrangement that is not uncommon for many transgendered couples. They maintained a degree of isolation in order to control their distance from the sex industry but also as a way for them to define themselves. Because they rarely ventured out together in public, this arrangement gave them greater social agency in adopting a heterosexual framework in which to organize their roles around.

Overall, my field observations in the Red Light District contribute to an existing body of research written about Dutch prostitution (Altink, 1995; Pheterson, 1996; Chapkis, 1997; Wijers and Lap-Chew, 1997). Nevertheless, ongoing changes in immigration, standardization, cultural representation, and public health initiatives, set the stage for further investigation at this location to gauge the effects of legalization and shifts in consumer practices. Furthermore, my focusing on leisure habits of clients and the customization of desires implicates possible links to a larger cycle of consumption mediated through erotic venues.

Chapter Five
Space and Place: In the Zone

INTRODUCTION

Inside the framework of legalization, unregulated prostitution zones exist as a way to address the needs of drug addicted female prostitutes looking to satisfy their addiction and an influx of migrants working in the informal sector in the Netherlands. This chapter explores the role of physical space of the zone designated for streetwalking in the city of Den Apelhaven[1] shaped spatial relations. At the latter setting, I surveyed peripheral areas around the zone and the Living Room, called *huiskamer,* a center that provides respite, food, medical care, and clothes changing facilities for streetwalkers. I suggest that the social meanings and arrangements of this space are neither constant nor fixed for each agent there. Many determinants affect meaning attributed to the zone, including the presence of undocumented streetwalkers, drug addicted women, law enforcement, transgendered people, clients, and what agents utilize the area.

In the zone, females and transsexuals are segregated from transgendered streetwalkers who stand across the street in their own section of the cul-de-sac. Boundaries around definitions of transgendered identities and sexual praxis in this space represent in many ways the symbolic reproduction of existing sexual binaries. But I would venture to consider how this enforcement of the space, imposed upon by social workers and administrators of the Living Room, influences client expectations of sexual practices performed on both sides of the street, how transgenderism is enacted in the zone, and its impact on transgendered streetwalkers economic survival. This division not only separates one set of sex workers from the other but also makes it easier for clients to distinguish the different types of services they provide. The direct impact on the economic lives of transgendered streetwalkers is immediate. As informants explained, many of the clients who frequent the transgendered side of the street were men who defined themselves as socially heterosexual. Clients who needed to protect their heterosexual status concealed their desires in a number of ways. The different interests of each actor involved in this exchange amounted to complex relations between transgendered sex workers and their clients and have wide reaching social and economic effects on all parties involved.

Applying Butler's performance theory of multiply gender identities and sexual practices emerging from the zone are put into praxis, and could suggest a stabilizing effect on the "transgendered identity," signaling a "normalization" of a third gender (Borenstein, 1998) or more. This does not make it any easier to classify practices that do not conform to a fixed hetero/homosexual meaning. Sometimes acts performed in the zone are outside the confines of a gendered event. "Talk," for instance, as a sexual practice may or may not include utterances that verbally reproduce a gendered fantasy or subject. The practice, regardless of the subjects involved, may not always include any description of a human body as part of the materialization of an erotic performance. In other incidences, transgendered, as well as female, prostitutes described practices that required commodified objects to be involved in the sexual act, such as the client wanting to caress a leg while it leans on the steering wheel of a car; or, client request to have the sex worker beat them with an harmless symbolic object, anally penetrating the client with the heel of a shoe or other practices that involve bodily fluids or "cutting" of the client. What do these reenactments mean when they are commodified and ritualized repeatedly? Does the gender identity of the actor drain out from the notion of performativity? As in the case of both drag and the sexual act, perhaps such practices will be taken with a bit of levity, transforming the production of gender and commercial sexual practice in the process.

I also examine ways symbolic capital[2] (Bourdieu and Passeron, 1990; Margolis, 1999) is conferred at different locations as a way to reinforce a habitus[3] (Bourdieu, 1990; Pinto, 1999), in which sex workers and other agents struggle to accumulate money, commercial space, and status. In this section common beliefs attached to streetwalking zones, perceived as low status and dangerous sites, are challenged. Contesting this label are the collective voices of streetwalkers who resist this stigmatization by identifying economic and social benefits they gain from working in an unregulated streetwalking space. Their perspectives also challenge what are commonly held views about the symbolic value ascribed to standardized commercial venues.

"IN THE ZONE"

Streetwalking zones[4] are designated prostitution sites in numerous Dutch cities. Over ten years, various areas around Den Apelhaven[5] have been designated and then relocated for unregulated streetwalking. Similar to unregulated prostitution sites in other urban areas, those early locations grew out of spontaneous demands around harbor docks or waterways rich with heavy commercial transportation activity. In the zone's previous location, the area ran along a busy road in full view of area hotels, promising hourly rentals that lengthened time spent with each client and increased payment for services. When the city's mayor decided to "clean up" the city, the zone moved to its current location. This meant greater distances from hotels that were no longer available to them. Residential development meant new neighborhoods did not want prostitution in their backyard, thus giving further motive to push prostitution into liminal, industrial areas. As in the case of Den Apelhaven, the site condensed in size, making sidewalk space competitive, and shrouding the industrial area in a mystique of danger.[6]

Over the years stigmatizing associations have attached to the zone. The space and its vicinity to public transportation bring a large number of drug-addicted prostitutes there to turn enough tricks to get their next fix. There are also rumors of a high incidence of HIV transmission circulating around, but assumed to be contained in the drug-addicted female population. Of course, this practice says nothing of the potential for clients to cross over and transmit to other populations working in the zone. Those other groups include migrant, transgendered, transvestite, transsexual and non-addicted female prostitutes.

When I gained access to the Den Apelhaven center (also called the Living Room) in my eagerness to arrange my visits I didn't take into account my lack of prior knowledge of that city. In addition to my unfamiliarity with the city landscape, I was equally naïve about the informal rules that governed the surrounding area around the zone. What I discovered was that the last stop on the tram route was in Kronigenplein, at the precipice of low-income housing occupied by Arabs and Surinamese residents. This required me to walk about fifteen minutes to Luvweg where the center was located. During the first trip to the zone, I asked a transit worker for directions to Luvweg. The man behind the booth carefully studied my face—I suppose searching for signs of heroin use—and then left his station to point out with a gesture of his hand the direction to the Living Room. My arriving on foot wearing baggy clothing and carrying a backpack made me a suspect. I was nervous crossing the multiple lanes of traffic, bike paths, and train tracks, checking to see if anyone had followed me, before veering down a major roadway. The streets were empty but for male cruisers heading toward the zone.

Summers in the Netherlands meant light would grace us until after 10:30pm. The time was nearing 6pm as I moved toward my destination. When I returned to observe that winter season, darkness struck at 4pm. On my way to the Living Room for the first time, I passed from behind a short hedge where a strung-out woman was trying to provoke a reaction from a drunken man seated on a bench. The pub may be a common place frequented by workers during their lunch hour but at this time appeared empty. Passing a wholesale outdoor pool store I encountered an androgynous female walking in the same direction. We acknowledged each other. She said her name was Samia and she was originally from Tunisia, then she told me that I looked Middle Eastern. I said was Albanian-American.

I asked if she were on anything (drugs) to which she replied "yes," and then said that she was hungry. I stopped for a moment, feeling vulnerable from gawking men driving passed, and grabbed a sandwich from my bag. When I handed it to her she thanked me, pointing me toward the cinderblock structure before she headed off through the closed off area where one or two prostitutes stood. I passed strung-out men standing on the periphery of the area as I came upon the functional square building. There were no police in sight, but pedestrians never bothered to cross the gate intended to keep them out.

As I made my way up a wheel chair ramp, I entered another world. Some "girls" -as they were called- were pushing each other trying to make room in front of the make-up mirror. The main room was decorated with couches and dimly lit candles. Other "girls" with an ID[7] stood in a line to access an in-house drug dealer and to use smoke and needle rooms where they could consume crack or shoot up heroin after their purchase[8]. Off that main room was a shower facility generating all kinds of activity. Women with wet tangled hair emerged sometimes in their underwear or a towel. Needle marks, acne, and the ravages of heroin identified who partook in what types of drugs.

Plastered on a glass wall hung a pencil composite of a suspect in the murder of a prostitute. Later I would learn of the local streetwalker whose dismembered body had been found in another part of the country. The face of the man in the sketch had a taunting serenity about it. This rendering of the suspect portrayed a man with soft brown tones recollected by a prostitute-witness who described his features under the guide of hypnosis. The killer could be out there at that moment, as I learned about a pattern of unsolved prostitute murders dating back years. This week, a major soccer event was taking place across the nation, making the zone relatively quiet[9]. By nightfall cars flanked in Turkish flags paraded through the area, blaring their horns for their national win in the first round of the games.

The facility was divided into two sections. Each section was designated to segregate the two dominant groups working on the street. The larger of the two rooms accommodated drug-addicted females, and the smaller space was the transgendered dressing room, furnished with a few stools, two bare tables, and a harsh fluorescent light. The only person present in the latter space was a Dutch transsexual prostitute named Nadine. She found so little business waiting for her outside that she had returned to the center. Most of the transgendered sex workers were not expected to make an appearance until after dark. In the meantime, Nadine was eager to talk to me after I identified myself as a graduate student studying Dutch prostitution.

Nadine wore a big blonde wig with an early 1960s dip, a micro baby blue dress exposing flesh from her buttocks, high white boots, a small white cotton sweat jacket, and gold hoop earrings. The look had the staged appeal of Jane Mansfield or a satirical John Waters film, appealing to a type of clientele hungry for campy nostalgia. Her blue eyes detracted from a surgical scar on her neck and decay around her front tooth. Nadine told me she was twenty-seven years of age and had been working as a prostitute since she was seventeen. Streetwalking was an evening job that she pursued a few times a week, sometimes only a few times a month. Her day job was as a nurse's aid at a nursing home.

In and out of the foster care system since her parents divorce at age ten (her father left her mother for a neighbor), Nadine told me she was finally happily engaged to be married to a man completely accepting of her and providing stability driving a rig for a piping business. Only later did she tell me how they met when her fiancé and his brother-in-law made a trip to the zone. It was love at first sight. Nadine and her fiancé spent nights talking on the phone and formally dating for two weeks before consummating their relationship. The big dream was to marry and leave the business for good. Six months later when I returned to the Living Room for my follow-up observation, Nadine was still there working on the street having postponed her wedding date due her fiancé's involvement in a truck accident.[10]

CROSSING THE STREET

In the streetwalking zone, the gender identities of streetwalkers are labeled according to how local human service agencies mapped out the area. The enforcement of gender labels determined where streetwalkers stood on the curb. This arrangement, in many ways, reified the binary between groups considered transgendered and female. *Travesti* and transvestite prostitutes stood on one side of the street while women and transsexuals worked on the more visible side of the strip (this situation is explained in greater detail later in this chapter). Most streetwalkers I spoke to identified themselves according to how they were physically situated in the organization of the zone. For this reason, Nadine's position as a transsexual was significant within the context of gender definitions demarcating of the area. Over the course of the previous year Nadine's gender status changed as a result of a sex reassignment, requiring her to move her commercial operation from the transgendered side of the zone to across the street on the women's side of the strip.

Nadine stretched over the windowsill in the transgendered dressing room, peering out at traffic movement into the zone, where I first encountered pimps and junkies hanging out at the entrance. As she leaned unselfconsciously forward her buttocks slipped out of her mini dress. Unfazed, Nadine continued on about how she had never experienced any kind of aggression or negative reaction from clients. As a standard rule, before entering an automobile, she always informed the client that she was a transsexual.

The weather turned to rain, but Nadine needed to return to the women's side of the sidewalk, making a run for a metal overhang. I moved into the station used by staff that joined the drug-addicted women's section to the transgendered dressing room. Just then an onslaught of "girls" requested toiletries and snacks, throwing me into the role of volunteer. I passed out free condoms (four each), sold packs of tissues used after every exchange, served sugar water to heroin addicts. Cigarette lighters were a popular item sold in large volumes because many drug-addicted women often misplaced their lighter. Mostly, I prepared sandwiches (called *tostis* in Dutch) and retrieved custard desserts from a stock in the refrigerator. Each item costs between 1 and 2 guilders, and was often the only meal some drug-addicted women would eat in an entire day. Everyone addressed me in English after I explained my lack of understanding in Dutch.

As dusk descended upon the zone, the transgendered dressing room started filling with sex workers getting ready to work a long night. Activity on the streets also picked up with a steady stream of automobiles. A staff member surmised that the soccer match must have been over. Who would have guessed that the summer season was considered the least profitable time of the year in the zone?[11]

THE INTERIOR LAYOUT

Transgendered streetwalkers shared their dressing room with many non-drug addicted females who found the chaos of the "girls"[12] side a source of aggravation. There were two small mirrors and a single sink, but the room had a quietude not found in the space designated for drug-addicted women. Technically, the drug addicted female streetwalkers were not permitted to use the transgendered dressing room. And no matter how busy the room became, a "girl" could be found sneaking in to use the toilet. Sometimes tensions mounted when one of the females nodded off on the toilet. Other times, girls tried consuming hard drugs in the closet space, or simply were seeking private space since there was none in their section. Mostly, the girls were responsible for clogging the toilet. One or two transgendered sex workers usually took responsibility for spraying the toilet closet with air freshener and disinfectant after such an episode, and often made the effort to clean up after the first round of coffee breaks cluttered the room with cigarette butts and empty plastic coffee cups.

A fight broke out between two "girls," requiring staff to intervene and placing entry restrictions on the female who instigated the fight. I was witnessing one of many rules staff had to enforce. Because many drug-addicted females were too doped up or too aggressive to control some were ordered to leave the premises for a one-month period of time. Meanwhile, in an attempt to diminish the rate of theft and potential fights among drug-addicted females, the center provided lockers in which they could deposit their belongings for locker numbers. Most of the in-house tensions remained confined to the drug-addicted section.

Inside the Center, streetwalkers using the facility could be observed from the employees' station. Management of streetwalkers' activities was possible as a result of glass partitions dividing each room. Staff could easily survey whether a fight was breaking out or a boyfriend, client, or male drug-addict was trying to enter the building. Since the latter was prohibited, they could quickly escort unwelcome guests out. This layout of the space put staff at an advantage and allowed for them to control the environment.

CHANGES IN THE CENTER

During my follow-up observational fieldwork, in January 2001, numerous new rules had been enforced in the *huiskamer*. The most obvious change appeared to be a lack of tension between many drug-addicted females, who the previous summer had aggressively sought to purchase hard-drugs from an in-house dealer. The city government decided to remove the in-house drug dealer, forcing drug-addicted women to seek purchases outside the center. The frenzy to score or bring portions of crack or heroin out to pimps and boyfriends had all but disappeared. Additionally, the interior of the facility had been redesigned to give greater surveillance power to staff watching the needle and smoke rooms. In the process, the transgendered dressing room lost floor space and still needed renovation.

Other changes had affected the culture of the space as well. There was a new rule requiring sex workers to ask for toilet paper from the staff. The task of staff to roll wads of toilet paper was another in the long list of responsibilities already required of them. Each person received four small pieces upon request. Having to request toilet paper placed the bodily functions of prostitutes under scrutiny, creating an infantile sort of relationship with staff who had control of the paper. Understandably feelings of indignation among sex workers lingered, as these restrictions were likely the result of a drug-addicted female's misuse of the facility. For some sex workers, this rule represented an invasive piece of information not unlike commercial bodily practices that were queried by public health officials.

The toilet closet held social meaning to sex workers in other ways, besides providing a moment of quiet from a cacophony in the dressing rooms. That intimate little space was the first stop for most transgendered and transsexual sex workers who required the use of lubricant before venturing onto the street. Time spent waiting for an available toilet could be upwards to thirty minutes, as drug-addicted females tried to consume drugs or nodded off in it. This delay had economic consequences for transgendered sex workers.

Between the magic hours of 10pm and midnight, the atmosphere in the transgendered dressing room became buoyant. Usually before anyone exited the Living Room there were social moments between sex workers sharing humor, gossip, cosmetics, and meals. Many Latinas took this time to sit together for a communal dinner. On more than one occasion I saw them hovering together over a Tupperware container for rice and pork warm from the microwave.

SELF-REGULATION OF THE ZONE

Michel Foucault's writings focus on the regulatory structures of the penal system, development of medicine and psychiatry, and regimes of sexuality, each contributing to a complex definition of power-knowledge, and consequent resistance by which agency may occur (Weedon, 1987: 107; Smart,

1985: 27). Regimes of sexuality, which on the appearance of self-regulation and sexual identity politics bring practices that were once hidden to the mainstream as a form of "normality," in turn require institutions to devise greater forms of covert control and new forms of regulation. Framing sex work within a public health model, as the British government attempted to do in during the Victorian era (Walkowitz, 1982), or how many contemporary European agencies tend to organize their research with a similar framework (TAMPEP, 1996, 1997), in the latter case enforcing sexual practices under the guise of "safe sex," constitutes modes of regulation of sexuality through self-regulation.

Self-regulation, therefore, can be defined as a means through which sex workers reinforce their own social role in society. Every aspect of their commercial enterprise, from the geography or the actual performance, is bound to assign meaning that (re)inscribes their social position as sex workers. Forms of self-regulation manifest in daily modes of commercial operation in the zone, such as requiring streetwalkers to stand on a closed block negotiating with clients before entering their automobile. Notions of a set cost for services should require little negotiation between informed clients and sex workers because of assumed standardization of practices. This was not always the case as some migrants and low-earning Dutch sex workers undercut standard prices and shift the expectations of the client base. Other standard practices conform to expectations and role-playing, particularly after a client agrees to service charges and sexual services are then provided inside the front seat of the client's car after parking behind a metal overhang where most streetwalkers stand. The transaction usually is regimented, almost choreographed, taking no longer then fifteen minutes from first contact to when the sex worker exited the automobile.

Competition among sex workers for sidewalk space has tightened over the last ten years because the area designated by the city of Den Apelhaven has diminished in square footage. As a result, sex workers must stand side-by-side with little personal space demarcating one prostitute from the person next to her. New prostitutes are discouraged from entering the area. During my first series of observations, an incident occurred when two Bulgarian prostitutes "just showed up one day."[13] Victoria, a senior member of the streetwalking community, was instrumental in pushing the women out of the area. However, given that other undocumented prostitutes worked in the zone with impunity, the Bulgarians called Victoria's bluff when they refused to leave.

This was not the last time Victoria and the others saw the Bulgarian women, or the first time self-regulation turned violent. The Bulgarian women, coerced by their pimp watching from an area just outside designated streetwalking area, returned on two separate occasions intending to become a tolerated fixture in the space. Each time the women returned, they were met with violence from Victoria and the other women, out of view of surveillance.

When the Bulgarian women returned a fourth time, they sought the assistance of police. This attempt to engage law enforcement suggests the Bulgarian women believed they had a right to work in an "unregulated" setting just like other undocumented workers. They also assumed that the police were more interested in regulating conduct than enforcing informal prohibitive measures keeping new prostitutes from working in the strip. In the end the Bulgarian women gained access to sidewalk space as the police, rather than enforcing rules around who could use the strip, threatened Victoria and a few others with expulsion from the area.

Many documented sex workers kept score of when the police sided with them and when the police chose to enforce the rules or to provide assistance to undocumented workers. Police relations largely depend upon what department the police team represents because of the diversity of departments and the degree to which they enforce. Not all departments present in the zone were there to interrogate undocumented workers. Thus relations between sex workers and police are tenuous at best. Documented sex workers reported, however, this was not the first time they "could not rely on the police" to enforce rules or protect them. Migrant sex workers, meanwhile, had an implicit fear of the police, even though only "immigration" police could request passports and working papers. Consequently, both documented and undocumented streetwalkers took it upon themselves to monitor the street.[14]

Whoever enforces informal rules, whether they are sex workers, the police, or *huiskamer* staff members, they have done so with a degree of success and failure. Forbidding new sex workers from entering the zone has been highly effective at keeping large numbers of Eastern European women from moving into the area. And, as long as Dutch and Latina women continue protecting this small strip of space, they will prevent other ethnic groups from relocating to the area in large numbers.

The notion of self-regulation of the zone left one unanswered question about the changing ethnic groups that worked in the space. How were other ethnic, undocumented populations able to secure space on the strip? "Why," I asked, "didn't you kick out Latinas when they started arriving in large numbers?" After all, Ecuadorians, who now outnumber other ethnic groups, like Dominicans and Columbians before them, are undocumented, speak only Spanish in some cases, and are believed to be driving down prices for sexual services.

When I posed this question to Victoria, she struggled to respond because she had not witnessed the arrival of many workers from Latin America, having been "out of the business" and not working as a prostitute during that period.[15] Whoever was working in the zone at the time failed to adequately protect their turf, allowing an onslaught of undocumented streetwalkers to establish themselves as mainstay there. There was another probable explanation to consider. As I suspect, many Latin Americans[16] who arrived in migratory waves utilized preexisting familial or congenial relations already established on the street to gain entry there. Hence, if established sex workers allowed two Bulgarian women to set up shop, a domino effect would occur and more Bulgarians were certain to follow.

CULTURAL INTERMEDIARIES

The streetwalking zones provided financial and social opportunities for some migrants who thrived economically or who found social meaning in the social organization of the environment. These members functioned as cultural intermediaries bridging the social gap between undocumented and EU sex workers. Pamela's position represents such a role. Whenever Pamela, a Brazilian transvestite, arrived in the dressing room carrying her gym bag and dressed as a "boy," her colleagues stopped whatever they were doing and greeted her with rounds of kissing and hugging. Very few sex workers were too absorbed in their eyeliner application not to glance up and greet Pamela. Of course, not everyone earned this kind of response.

In contrast to Pamela's social position in the Living Room, Veronica, an Ecuadorian transsexual,[17] made a less notable entrance, receiving a tepid response from other sex workers whenever she arrived at the Living Room intending to work. Veronica made it known to all that she was well read, coifed for a high-end market, conversant in English, and had her rightful place on the "women's side" of the street. Most streetwalkers simply tolerated her personality. I, on the other hand, was always aware of her ability to turn other people's statements around for the sake of holding an adversarial position. Veronica could create a swirl of distrust between the streetwalkers with the wand of gossip at her disposal. I felt her power to manipulate relationships, and I was not above being directly affected by her. With one thread of gossip Veronica could tamper my relationships with other informants. To most streetwalkers, though, she was identified as having an antagonistic personality. This made her an untrustworthy member of the street, but I moved around her with trepidation. Veronica's "mood" was compounded by her status in the Netherlands. She was in immigration limbo after she broke up with her Dutch boyfriend for three years. This meant she was now ineligible for a residency card.[18] Consequently, after a long absence from the zone, Veronica's sudden appearance in the transgendered dressing room was a surprise to everyone. Only later did Veronica reveal that she had been (illegally) working in a window in another city.

Unlike Veronica, Pamela held a special position in the Living Room. She had a reputation for working seven days a week, ten hours a night, accumulating sizable savings. Her serious entrepreneurial drive drew respect from Dutch prostitutes and migrants alike. Her fluency in English, Dutch, Spanish, and Portuguese meant she acquired knowledge around how the zone, immigration, and commercial relations operated. Moreover, her long-term relationship with a Dutch national gave her the privilege of possessing a Dutch passport and EU citizenship. Pamela's successful navigation through the system and dominant Dutch culture require swift acclimation and acceptance of those values and language. But her acculturation into dominant Dutch society did not stop her from helping migrants out when they were in legal trouble, which meant her knowledge of the immigration system proved invaluable to many South Americans staying close to their ethnic community. Consequently, the social position Pamela held with Latin Americans and Dutch nationals translated into single handedly bridging relations between Spanish speaking migrants and Dutch prostitutes.

Dissimilar to the concerns of Magdalena or some other sex workers who protect themselves against the petty jealousies of colleagues, the fruits of Pamela's labor were celebrated in the context of the zone. With her bodily labor, Pamela rebuilt a life for her family back in Brazil. On one occasion Pamela brought me photos of a piece of land and a villa she built for herself and her family back in Brazil. These luxuries were hardly something she could enjoy as she worked ten months out of the year, all the while concealing her employment and her sexuality from her family.[19]

On a busy night the room was charged with a creative energy. Sex workers were transforming themselves from unassuming pedestrian into eye-catching streetwalker. Most streetwalkers prepared for up to an hour applying make up, spraying and styling their hair, and determining whether each other's wardrobe and footwear would have drawing power. During the preparation period it was also evident which prostitutes spent hundreds of dollars on their wardrobe. Some sex workers brought in their gym bag alternating costumes to suit the mood of the street.

On numerous occasions, I watched Nadine or Veronica change into more than one costume during the course of a single evening. Sometimes they transformed into a different type of fantasy–changing their hairstyle, color theme, boots, and even wigs for dramatic affect. On occasion, Veronica, who created a streamlined appearance with her coifed hair and designer clothes, found that her work attire was often too "sophisticated" for her clientele and sometimes resulted in a loss in business earnings. As a practical measure, she would change her costume, conforming to the standard attire clients have come to expect of streetwalkers. Of course, not everyone reinvented herself on the street. Prostitutes such as Pamela and Victoria marked themselves with a signature outfit night after night, claiming that by wearing the same clothes each night, clients could identify them from other streetwalkers.

The contrast in cultural styles and business practices converged in the transgendered dressing room of the *huiskamer*. Many sex workers relish the social interaction and discussions that would break out in groups of three and four. This is an amicable time spent smoking cigarettes and buying each other coffee, and reflecting on other aspects of their lives. The real drama remained outside, but inside the dressing room, it felt like the "backstage" at a theater. The strip of sidewalk represented their stage as they exited for the street, transformed in high boots and black latex tucking away bulges or pushing flesh outward to attract clientele.

On occasion, a cocaine-addicted prostitute scurried through the room selling pairs of black leather boots or knit sweaters stolen in bulk. Transgendered sex workers usually bought their goods just to help out. Sometimes sex workers shared their tools of the trade: hair spray, nail polish, pantyhose, and even shoes.

On average, depending on the weather and flow of traffic, streetwalkers spent around an hour outside soliciting clients before coming in for a coffee break. During the colder weather, many Latinas lingered inside sharing meals and cigarettes, or choosing to forgo making money altogether because of the cold. Many EU prostitutes noticed this behavior, interpreting what they saw as excessive fraternizing spent in the zone as a waste of productive time and a lack of discipline.

Perhaps there were other places some sex workers would rather have been than hanging out with friends in the Living Room. Negative feelings about the space or productivity levels did not divide along migrant and EU worker lines. Many migrant prostitutes worked for the duration of the twelve-hour shift without complaint sending all their earnings to family back in Latin America or Africa. Numerous ambitious Nigerian sex workers returned night after night after experiencing repeated windfalls on the streets. This kind of economic drive perplexed a few Dutch prostitutes who would have taken their earnings and disappeared for weeks at a time or until necessity forced them to return to the streets.

CLIENTELE RELATIONS AND DESIRES

An invisible partition in the street defines the biology of one set of sex workers from the other, and ultimately the type of services they perform. Transgendered sex workers reported that many of their clients were men who defined themselves as heterosexual. As a means of protecting their heterosexist status, many clients of transgendered sex workers attempted to conceal their pursuit of their desires in a number of ways. Automobiles looping more than a few times past female sex workers often exposed the driver's intention of seeking services from a transgendered prostitute. Not by accident, these same customers engaged in their pursuit after dark. "Crossing over" after nightfall had a direct effect on transgendered streetwalkers' labor practices. This occurrence motivated streetwalkers to begin their daily operations long after dark, sometimes hours after the zone was opened. This practice, I believe, influenced their earnings and required an intensification of street working in the condensed time afforded them.

During this type of transaction client relations are complex. Client and sex provider hold mutable social positions based on their individual interests and identity claims. This is particularly the case if the client needs to conceal his desires behind a "heterosexual" identity. This kind of concealment can lead to potential manipulation on the part of the sex provider. In particular, some transgendered sex workers described similar client relations that gave them a more favorable position from which to negotiate in the commercial exchange. In order to assume any disruption of the social order of prostitution relations on the part of transgendered sex workers, the influence of desire fulfillment, the social meaning attached to sexual practices by the participants, and any identity concealment on the part of "heterosexual" clients must be considered. Likewise, imbedded in this scenario are other social determinants intersecting social relations between client and sex worker. For instance, if a sex worker holds Dutch or EU citizenship, she will probably be able to negotiate better in Dutch or English. This language barrier for undocumented workers dramatically affects their ability to negotiate. It should also be said that this is not to assume that all clients are Dutch or Dutch speaking. Quite possibly an inexperienced or non-English speaking client would struggle to communicate during this stage of the exchange.

Consider the following scenario I witnessed: On the morning I rode a train with Pamela, I witnessed her encountering one of her regular clients. After purchasing our tickets, we boarded the train, moving through a chain of coaches as we searched for a seat. Pamela/Fernando signaled for me to keep walking as she made a conscious effort to keep her head turned down under a baseball cap. When we found an empty coach, she told me to turn and take a glance at the professional looking man seated in the coach we had just passed through. I turned noting a well-dressed Dutch man, in his early 50s, reading his morning paper and most likely traveling to work. As I returned my attention to Pamela, she explained how the man was a regular customer of hers and had sought her services early the previous evening. The regular client, Pamela said, was married and middle class.

In that moment, by not acknowledging the former client in public, Pamela protected both her clientele base and the client's privacy. Of course, it was quite possible that the client had not recognized her in her male street clothes. But by virtue of his concealed sexual practices, he had more to lose socially than she. Understanding her social power in that context, Pamela continued to distance herself from the client, and, in effect, afforded herself total anonymity. For this reason, perhaps the greatest advantage transvestite sex work could have is the mutability of gender and identity, especially for prostitutes who want to establish boundaries around their private lives.

SYMBOLIC CAPITAL

Sex workers (as well as advocates involved in prostitution issues) held the belief that different types of prostitution sites conferred varying degrees of symbolic capital to those who worked there. Their reading of sexualized spaces facilitated a hierarchy among prostitutes. Citing a number of spatial factors signified the social rank of any commercial venue. This includes the physical conditions of surrounding commercial property, luxury items found in a window interior, fluxes of human traffic, social exclusivity assigned to a site, degree of visibility of sex workers, whether solicitation occurred indoors or outdoors, and if an exchange transpired in an automobile, hotel, or window. Conditions at streetwalking zones were described to me as having lower social value when compared to other sexualized spaces.

Unlike the regulation of windows where a prostitute generates a taxable income, and pays a weekly rental fee, streetwalking zones remain a bastion of unregulated prostitution in the Netherlands. Often these sites carry a stigma stemming from a number of sources. First, there is the presence of drug-addicted prostitutes and their boyfriends and pimps selling and consuming hard drugs that negatively affect the symbolic value of the area. Second, most sexual exchanges occur in the front seat of the client's car rather than on a bed found in a window space. Furthermore, there is the presence of undocumented prostitutes from Latin America, Africa, and Eastern Europe who are believed to lower standards and prices. In this instance, the zone can be the only commercial place accessible for undocumented segments of the population, since window rentals require documentation of residency. Not all streetwalkers, however, are drug-addicted or undocumented. There is also a large community of transgendered prostitutes. This last group remains distant from hard drug culture and collectively describes the work location as favorable.

Like any field[20] (Bourdieu, 1990; Butler, 1999), the "zone" operates in a dynamic way as agents strategize to accumulate economic and cultural capital[21] (Bourdieu and Passeron, 1990; Margolis, 1999). A social order is established and dismantled depending upon the space and who occupies it. Whether the agents are clients, boyfriends, drug-addicts, public health workers, immigration police, or the sex workers, capital interests are involved.

What symbolic status is conferred to sex workers in the zone depends on material relations such as sex workers' commercial rate of success; whether services are provided at an established rate; what types of clients they attract[22]; the conditions under which personal relations are developed and maintained; and how a sex worker articulates her habitus through gestures, attire, and movement. Symbolic capital can also be conferred if a commercial transaction occurs outside the designated zone, such as in a hotel room. Refusing to adhere to spatially mediated rules can also cost sex workers their social standing among their peers. A loss of status can include how sex workers respond to the customers of other sex workers, disrespecting physical parameters between streetwalkers, or simply arriving in the zone uninvited to work for the first time.

The following example supports how spatial relations mediate symbolic capital in the zone, and what can occur when social rules are broken. During the summer of 2000, during my observation, three never-before-seen Polish prostitutes appeared in the zone. Most likely they assumed that because the zone was "unregulated" they could enter the area without any negative recourse. But streetwalkers coping with physically cramped sidewalk conditions responded violently to their arrival. To magnify the tension, the women arrived dressed in high-fashion outfits, breaking the street dress code, and instantly garnered attention from consumers who responded favorably to their youthful and exotic presence. To ensure a piece of the market share, the women opted to sell their services for under the standardized prices, boldly undercutting other workers, and went the extra effort to provide full nudity and kissing[23] to their repertoire of services. Within a short period of time, senior members on the street physically attacked the women and eventually pushed the newcomers out of the space. During this incident police units were forced to intervene. When the

Polish women sought refuge in the center, staff told them to vacate the area because they were not following the price rules, were "marked" differently in their attire, and were rumored to have broken codes of contact with costumers.

SEX WORKERS PREFERENCE OF PROSTITUTION SITES

Each prostitution site[24] has its benefits and drawbacks as a location for erotic labor. Prostitutes' preference for particular types of sexualized spaces varied depending on the type of services they provided and what symbolic or material benefits they assumed the prostitution site offered. For instance, transgendered window prostitutes,[25] who at some point in their career worked on the streets, claimed the window sites provide added personal comfort and a degree of employment stability. They found having food and toiletries delivered to their window an added advantage of working at this site. Conversely, they described working outdoors exposed to the elements, with the vulnerability of entering an automobile, a procedure typical of streetwalking, as an undesirable low-status activity.[26] This partiality illustrates only some of the elements that make a location preferable or undesirable.

Not all transgendered streetwalkers, however, would agree with this construction of streetwalking. Repeatedly transgendered and female streetwalkers[27] reported a preference for the zone because of the various ways the site represented commercial autonomy not found in windows or in the clubs. First, the windows constrained their physical mobility. Window prostitution limited access to clients confining sex workers to the parameters of a small (about 50 square feet) room rather than creating flexibility about where and when commercial sex could occur. Another criticism of window prostitution concerned a financial commitment required for the duration of an eight-hour shift, five to seven days per week. Window prostitutes pay upwards of 150 to 200 guilders ($75 to $100 or 100 Euro) per shift, averaging 1,200 guilders per week ($600 or 600 Euro). Streetwalking zones provided a flexible work cycle. Should business slow down or other obligations require their attention, there would be no "lost earnings" from rental overhead nor negative recourse because on the streets there is no landlord taking notice of their absence.

In the windows, bodily display has become a performative expectation for all who work there. This requirement was framed as unacceptable for streetwalkers. Many streetwalkers expressed feelings of compromise when discussing bodily exhibition notably initiated in window prostitution and clubs. Contrastingly, as a standard practice on the street, streetwalkers stand and wait for cars to pass using minimal nonverbal communication with would-be clients. Streetwalkers are not expected to partially disrobe for "inspection" or perform before would-be clients, as sometimes happens in the windows. This additional effort requires window prostitutes to attract attention to draw costumers into a negotiation and is unnecessary for streetwalkers to carry out. As a Dutch transsexual streetwalker, Victoria, explained, "if a client [standing outside a window] wants me to turn around while I'm standing there, I'd tell him no way, I'm not a piece of flesh."

The activities of the Red Light District in Amsterdam including commercial erotic operations, prostitutes inhabiting windows, and interactions with clients, all contribute to shape social arrangements and the meaning of the surrounding area. Whether down narrow alleyways or along major canals making up the area, prostitutes are accessible to gaze upon like a commodity or an advertisement in any enterprising window. The bodies of prostitutes are visibly inscribed with hues of red and ultra-violet fluorescent light and marked by performative coding that pulls even a fleeting spectator into the sex theatre. Regardless of the season or time of the day/night, they sit or stand clad in a scant bra and panty posing in their role for the purpose of drawing the attention of potential customers.

Unlike the windows, zones designated for streetwalking have parameters around their commercial usage. The local government dictates this site location and has the power to close it down, relocate it, or increase police enforcement at will. Nightly activity is relegated only to desolate industrial areas, away from residential communities, and within a fenced off cul-de-sac. A curfew from 6AM to 6PM standardizes streetwalking; afterwards, the area is closed off with a locked gate, and "normal" commercial activity resumes during regular working hours. Automobiles and bicycles are permitted to drive through the area. Streetwalkers stand on two sides of a sidewalk, under a metal overhang, and wait to negotiate with clients who pull up to the curb. If an agreement is reached, the streetwalker enters the front seat of the car and they pull around to the other side of the overhang where parking spots are marked. Streetwalkers wear clothing that accentuates their bodily form but dress according to the seasons. The spatial make up of each site influences how commercial relations are arranged between sex workers, their clients, and other actors. Sex workers expressed their preferences for working in a particular type of erotic venue based on a number of factors. Many informants correlated their earning power to their favored work site. Others expressed a relationship between their chosen site and how they felt about themselves in that space, the type of services they performed, the type of clients they attracted, and their degree of interaction with other sex workers. Status conferred at a particular site also swayed their partiality for a place. Despite all the spatial differences between windows and zones in location, parameters, scale, types of sexual services provided, and the codes that organize those sexualized spaces, a common struggle for earnings mediated through sex and commercial relations ignite these domains.

CONCLUSION

Poststructuralism contests the notion of the social agent as an "autonomous being" but rather as the product of social and historical relations in which he or she is entrenched. In turn, this entrenchment shapes the direction of collective consciousness about social reality (Namaste, 1996). The impact of which determines where "subjects can appear and in what capacity" (Namaste, 1996; 195). Social regulation and institutionalization becomes a by-product of these controlling forces. Foucault identified ways in which the "homosexual" was an invention of the historical forces dictating the classifications of sexual identities during the Victorian era (Namaste, 1996). With the same breath of awareness, it is possible to consider how the construction of transgendered and female sex workers in the context of Dutch prostitution is a product of regulatory forces, language, and the designation of sexualized spaces in which they work.

The streetwalking zones represent the last bastion of unregulated sex work. In this respect, understanding commercial relations in this setting tells us about how "informal" conditions affect commercial relations inside a nation with ample legal venues. As pointed out, among window prostitutes there is the perception that streetwalking is a site of low status prostitution. However, much of this perception is based on the predominance of drug-addicted sex workers working in the area, attaching "risk" to the site. Streetwalkers in the zone reject this construction transforming the social meaning attached to where they work.

The streetwalking zone is also an example of what Bourdieu considers to be a field in which group relations among prostitutes are naturalized and played out as every day activities. This environment and the social action of members in it are the result of internalized habitus reinforced through shared rules, knowledge, and values (Margolis, 1999; Thompson, 1999). And while this social world appears to be regulated and controlled by the social agents who operate within it, commercialized sexualized spaces are by-products of macro-level social forces. At the center of this organization are streetwalkers vying for different forms of capital. Among streetwalkers there were members who held dominant positions and at time imposed their will on fellow cohorts. Two examples of Dutch streetwalkers protecting space against the entry of new migrant groups were evident of such a social order. This is not, however, to suggest that all migrants held the same social position. As I described with the story of Pamela, some "migrants" gained access to privileges, earnings and social clout, making the site a dynamic place to observe.

The zone proved to be an interesting case in point of ways the dominant society imposes "disciplinary" control over streetwalkers. Public health measures made a concerted effort to teach streetwalkers about high-risk behavior and exposure to STDs and HIV. As an incentive to regulate the gynecological health of drug addicted women, the center only permitted use of their smoke and drug rooms to women who had registered with their on-site physician. In another instance, a *travestí* migrant from Ecuador mistook me for a medical doctor and in broken English tried to "confess" of her recent contraction of an STD. In effect, these public health agencies control the bodily activities of streetwalkers, as well as other prostitutes in the Netherlands, through internalized "preventive measures." As a result of these public health campaigns, streetwalkers became more self-regulating in terms of their sexual behavior.

The surface of a commercial sexual exchange, one might argue, does not always tell what relations are transpiring. Whether the sexual exchange takes place on a bed behind a drawn curtain of a window operation, in a car, inside a hotel room, or in the home of a sex provider, each environment is partly self-regulated by the occupants working there. But to assume that all social arrangements begin and end with the exchange, neglects to consider how other players, such as spectators, police, and nurses also produce meaning on Dutch prostitution. Unquestionably the State plays an instrumental role as an agent in the transformation of sexual space from sites of criminality to site of production, suggesting to readers and researchers something about the way sexualized space is organized in many western societies.

Chapter Six

Victoria van der Way

INTRODUCTION

The life story of Victoria van der Way[1] can be understood as a contribution to a growing body of transsexual narratives told from the point of view of the subject (Bogdan, 1974; Albuquerque and Jannelli, 1994; Bornstein, 1994; Wilchins, 1997). However, Victoria's daily experiences as a transsexual also embody many other social roles and knowledges that are not always represented in the life histories of transsexuals or prostitutes. The intersection of Victoria's multiple social roles include working in prostitution for twenty years, possessing Dutch citizenship, training as a geriatrics nurse, comprehending taxation laws as a property owner, and holding a transsexual identity. Her understanding of her material and cultural conditions has been informed by the multiple positions she holds. Whether these identity claims overlap or produce cultural discontinuities, reconstructing the life story of Victoria brings into focus questions about agency and gender migration in prostitution.

Understanding Victoria van der Way's life story requires recognizing how the state sanctifies, legitimates, and supports the individual in Dutch society. She is a product of the state's laws, benefits, and rights. The state has intervened in Victoria's adult life, codifying her as a productive citizen. Her gender migration was authorized, as she was qualified as a viable candidate for a sex reassignment, and all the expenses for her to become a transsexual were covered. The state was instrumental, again, when framing prostitution and Victoria as a prostitute. Because of legalized prostitution in the Netherlands, Victoria has never been incarcerated for selling erotic labor. Lastly, Victoria is also a nurse, who returned to school when the state offered to reeducate her. In the context of the Netherlands, Victoria is economically and socially productive and represents a "success" story in many aspects of her life. It is for this reason that Victoria's life story and perspective are so significant to the literature on prostitution narratives.

Victoria's story is also about her interpretation of prostitution as a business. Besides articulating her material needs, she informs us of how sex workers participate in the cycle of production and consumption. Part of her understanding of these material processes includes her recognition of the exhaustibility of her own participation in this market. Because her own bodily services will cease to generate a source of income in the near future, she rationalizes an intensification of her current work cycle.

The ongoing relationship that developed between informant and researcher serves as a backdrop for the reconstruction of Victoria's story telling.[2] In structuring this life story as text, I chose a "conversational" tone for a number of reasons. First, I wanted to entrust the reader with my engagement with this subject. Through use of a "personal" stance rather then a distant, authoritative mode of writing, I remind readers that these are living people with whom I developed a relationship. Second, I want to capture the evolution of my relationship with Victoria. Introducing the development of trust between informant and researcher demonstrates how, in a particular case, reciprocity unfolded, how relations are not just one-way flows of information, and required renegotiation of our respective roles. As stated in the chapter on methodology, I did not have the luxury of recording with an electronic device, which would have permitted me to cut and paste Victoria's cadence and rhythm of speech into the text. Thus reconstructing her personality and rhythm of speech required choosing this mode of writing.

This life story is told from the point of view of the subject alone. Victoria dominates the telling of her life story through a succession of tales and self-interpretations of her experiences. Secondary informants who could substantiate her reconstructions are absent. Having known Victoria for over three and a half years, I am confident of how I am reconstructing her story. I introduce Victoria as I met her in the zone during my field observation in January 2000. I recount her life in prostitution as it relates to her material opportunities, history of the zone, intimate relationships, and her social positions as a Dutch transsexual. During the course of this life story, I reconstruct fragmented memories of her childhood in Den Apelhaven, growing up with a female gender identity, and how she adjusted to her sex reassignment. Other aspects of her professional life include her experiences as a nurse.

ON THE STREETS

"The state will not be my pimp, *the state will not be my pimp*," Victoria stresses for a second time as she contemplates the benefits of not declaring income on her taxes when street working in a "zone" designated for street-walking. She pauses a moment to take a long drag on her cigarette, and without losing momentum exhales, "I use my body to make this money, *they* will not have any of it." Victoria stands over six-feet-six-inches towering over most sex workers. This physical attribute, as well as her majestic presence, is a factor that enhances her material success in the zone. As the "Grand Dame" of the streetworkers, she undermines the conventional image of what a streetwalker is supposed to look like as she stands in an industrialized cul-de-sac flooded with fluorescent street lamps and passing cars. Victoria appears composed under a corrugated metal shelter where streetwalkers stand protected from the elements. During most winter months working conditions make Den Apelhaven[3] inhospitable, however unfettered by the climate Victoria's coifed red hair holds tightly in a French twist, her faux fur coat reveals little indication of what lies underneath but for a glimpse of cleavage.

If there are any signs giving clue to the evening's exchanges in and out of client cars or an occasional hotel room, the markers will be transformed or concealed by the time Victoria ends her shift. Keeping alternate articles of clothing available somewhere in her automobile, she sits in the driver's seat of her sports car, slipping over a long black skirt to conceal her work clothes and changing into a flat-heeled shoe tucked under the floor of the backseat. Only after this costume change occurs is she prepared to enter her penthouse apartment on the other side of the City. Tonight was a good night yielding 700 Dutch guilders ($300), but that money pales compared to earnings in years' past. After twenty years working in windows and various streetwalking zones, saving for her car and her house, now she distinguishes between "black money," as she calls it, made on the streets and income earned from her day job as a geriatrics nurse.

LIFE NARRATIVE

Victoria's longevity in the sex trade made her an invaluable source while I was gathering data in the field. Since our first conversation her scope of knowledge of sex work in the Netherlands has taught me a great deal as she chronicled the history of area prostitution through her own life narrative. Over the past twenty years, dramatic social and legal changes in Den Apelhaven's sex trade have paralleled her career in prostitution. Victoria's account of those transformations are reflected in her experiences working in the windows and clubs in Den Apelhaven and in neighboring Breburg,[4] and at various streetwalking zones designated by city government.

In addition to moving her business to numerous street walking zone relocations, Victoria also witnessed changes in the ethnic make-up of area prostitutes. In the last fifteen years, "new immigrants have changed the way prostitutes must do business here," she said. "Now we must 'suck *and* fuck' for 50 guilders [around 20 Euro before the convergence of currencies in the European Union], before it was 'suck *or* fuck.'... They've ruined the business." That change was brought on first by the migration of Dominican and Columbian prostitutes to the Netherlands, and then once they were established, next came other Latin Americans, Southeast Asians, Africans, and finally an influx of Eastern Europeans. We both recalled an incident from the previous summer in which three youthful Eastern European women showed up in the zone trying to sell a "suck *and* fuck" for fl 25 ($11). The women were pushed out by the local prostitutes and eventually told to leave by police. During their last bid to stay in the area a fight ensued forcing the women to retreat to the Living Room. Staff told the women that they should leave the premises or risk bodily harm from those already stationed on the strip.

At the time of our initial conversation,[5] four months had passed since stricter regulatory laws were supposed to have been enforced in all streetwalking areas across the country. Victoria had not noted any changes on the streets or any unusual deportation of undocumented workers who dominated the space. But even though she represented a minority of Dutch citizens still working in the zone, she was a strong proponent of streetwalking over other sexualized commercial spaces.

Streetwalking provided Victoria with the opportunity to amass untaxed income, or "black money," as she called it. It also offered economic and social advantages over regulated windows or clubs. All the money generated on the street afforded her perishable and nonperishable commodities – though inhibiting her from purchasing a high-end item such as an automobile. Moreover, this work site provided spatial mobility and flexibility around her work cycle producing a discretionary power regarding her choice of clients and what kinds of services she performed.

These early conversations with Victoria focused on money and her use of it in the acquisition of material objects. Earnings from formal means lead her to purchase a house, and with the profit of its sale, she purchased her current penthouse apartment. Meeting the criteria for a mortgage required having good credit standing and resources from her taxable income as a nurse.[6] Only later did she explain that sex workers are largely excluded from this benefit. In spite of improved working conditions and elevated social status conferred on sex work as a "legitimate" taxable activity in the Netherlands, prostitutes were often systematically denied home mortgages and insurance. Thus without her earnings as a nurse, working in an unregulated zone could mean complete exclusion from services provided by banking institutions.

Victoria expressed pride in and put emphasis on her material accomplishments. She described her apartment as a beautiful place where few members from the zone had ventured. Valeria, a tough female Dutch prostitute, 23, was the exception, and spoke with admiration as she described the ambience of Victoria's apartment decorated in Asian lacquer furniture and antique Buddhist statues. Each object bought with untaxed income transformed Victoria's bodily labor into acquired high-end items. Underlying this depiction of her material comforts, however, was a pressing fear of having her home and personal objects confiscated by the government. In effect, this concern motivated her to become self-educated about tax laws and to purchase only furnishings, clothes, and food items with her unreported income.

As a senior member on the street, Victoria must compete with younger members working in the zone. They, however, do not pose a financial threat to her livelihood. This is the result of Victoria maintaining a healthy clientele dating back ten years. She attributes it to her knowledge of how to "tend to their needs." Like most people in the customer services sector, she follows her own rules of always being "courteous," as she "would never tell them to 'hurry up,' as so many of the younger prostitutes do." Most importantly she revealed, leaning closer to me as she dropped to a whisper, "clients are vulnerable in that state and might need time." We both smiled with amusement. "Vulnerability" was rarely a term used when speaking of male sexual "purchasing power," however Victoria expressed control of her own enterprise and client relations. Her way of looking at client relations dismantles dominant paradigms often used to portray disparate power relations between sex worker and client.

Victoria could rationally diminish the social value of "younger" competition, but no one, not even she, could ignore the influence of Latina, Eastern European, and West African migrant sex workers on the street. They had collectively shifted practices performed by prostitutes intensifying commercial standards previously set by Western European sex workers. Nor could she ignore how "new" standards of services were forcing her and everyone else to adapt to a new sexual-affective "model" requiring "sucking and fucking" rather than providing one or the other erotic service. In spite of these changes, she claimed no matter how much money was involved there were "things" she would never perform. The line, she said, was drawn around demands for "anal sex." When customers requested the service, she told them "maybe next time," smiling graciously. Other popularized requests she refused to service included "cutting and stitching" and anything to do with feces. But the fact remains that over the course of the last ten years, mainstream customers were increasingly requesting "customized" or exoticized practices now perceived as "standard services."

Victoria sat at a table with a calendar hanging behind her from the wall. Many of the regulars who frequented the Living Room had their birth date listed on that calendar for a monthly gift collection. At the beginning of every month, Valeria collected donations to purchase gifts for whoever celebrated a birthday during a particular month. Some of those same participants also contributed to a weekly drawing managed by Valeria to financially benefit a different sex worker each week. Money collected and redistributed was upwards to fl 1,500 ($700), the equivalent of one good night's pay. The drawing served two purposes: it alleviated working so hard for each person who contributed and received a payment; the camaraderie produced was beneficial to the overall mood on the street, assuaging feelings of competition produced by disparate nightly flows of clients.

Victoria told me that she was born under the sign of "Leo" then asked what I thought her ascendant might be. From my childhood interest, I studied her pointed brow and judging from the power of her gaze, uttered "you look like a Scorpio rising." My interpretation impressed her as she yelled out "yes." Suddenly our conversation expanded to other esoteric interests. Victoria turned to me and asked about my birth date. "My birthday is today," I replied. "You're a Capricorn, just like my mother," she said. She asked about other details such as my ascendant that made her smile because she said her beloved grandmother was born under that same sign. Clearly, our roles - as sex worker/informant answering questions of the researcher - shifted in a matter of minutes. What unfolded was a rapport richer than any pre-interview contact had it been born under formal interviewing conditions. My participation in this conversation about metaphysical interests was neither a prop nor ploy to manipulate a false or accelerated intimacy with my contact. Instead, out of our shared interpretations and experiences grew feelings of trust and a mutual affinity. This was a heart-felt rapport deeply touching my life.

Chaos of another kind swirled around us during our first informal conversation. In the transgendered dressing room a cocaine-addicted woman, Clara, entered. In her mid-forties, Clara left her native Yugoslavia twenty years ago to work and live in the Netherlands. During the previous summer we had held numerous, albeit brief, lucid conversations, but in the subsequent six months her condition had worsened. Clara's frame appeared pared down from sleep deprivation and a lack of appetite. Wound up to the point of incoherency, she talked incessantly, moving in a dervish swirl, bouncing off of the personal spaces that she crossed. The clamor snapped us back into real time.

Under "normal" conditions Clara's appearance in the transgendered room would have warranted a staff member to request her to use the appropriate space in the adjacent room. In reality, though, on any given evening, "girls," who otherwise would be occupying space designated for "drug-addicted" prostitutes, slipped into the transgendered space to use the toilet, mirrors, or to sell articles of clothing. Transgendered sex workers vigilantly keep order in the space, and while there were fewer amenities in the transgendered room, the sparse room was cleaner than the "girls" side. In the facility, drug-addicted women were the dominant group, cramming before mirrors difficult to gain access to because other dazed addicted women applied and reapplied eyeliner and lips sometimes for hours before embarking on the street or entering the drug usage room.

Our first conversation took on other spontaneous shifts around shared personal exchanges, esoteric phenomenon, and the sex trade. Victoria's face expanded in an unguarded expression as she described her work with Alzheimer's patients. She derived great satisfaction bringing them comfort, laughter, and care. I then reflected on my experiences working in nursing homes as a teenager, and later disclosed having coped with the condition of a family member afflicted with the disease. Victoria held my gaze and told me how she liked the way I shared parts of myself with her rather than simply asking one-sided questions.[7]

Anke joined Victoria and me at the table, and the discussion shifted to the role of intuition in connection to their encounters with clients on the streets. Victoria believed that she possessed an "instinct" that gave her insight into whether she should enter a stranger's car or should refuse an offer. Anke also used a similar technique. Both, however, could recall past difficulties with potential clients. Victoria systematically "looked into the eyes of the client and could tell," whether there was danger. On one occasion, however, when her "defenses were down" after a break-up with a lover, she entered a car without using her built-in antennae. At a stoplight, on the way to a hotel, she felt the need to exit the car immediately. Only as she departed did she catch a glimpse of a second male on the floor of the backseat. This was Victoria's closest encounter with "real danger" on the street.

The conversation shifted to other dangers. Victoria qualified how intimate relations in her private life proved more hazardous to her well-being than any risks she might have taken at work. Alone for over two years, she gave "everything" in her heart to a man whom she called her "husband." Sebastian, she said, was Indonesian-Dutch, seven years her junior, whom

Victoria met as a would-be client. During that first exchange, they "talked and talked" spending hours together. The courtship blossomed and grew into a period of harmony for Victoria. "I loved him like a son, father, brother, friend," she said, but after two and a half years Sebastian claimed that he had fallen in love with another woman.

As Victoria understood her circumstances, the reason behind their break-up had more to do with protecting Sebastian's highborn status and his golden career armed with an MBA than simply falling out of love. She suspected he feared that his family would eventually find out about Victoria's sex reassignment. After the breakup, Victoria, who was raised a Catholic, said "I lost my faith after that and removed all religious icons and religious figures from my house." There was a sunken feeling between us and my eyes became moist reflecting the change in emotions. At that very moment Victoria shifted out of our shared experience to observe my reaction. Only days and months later would she relay this observation that sealed a trust between us.

Fluorescent lighting in the transgendered dressing room glared down on the stark tables littered with ashtrays made of recycled soup can lids. Victoria vowed to smoke only one more cigarette before going out in the cold night to earn more money. We had been talking there for over two hours.

For all of her successes, during our first conversation Victoria also recalled hardships from growing up "different" as she put it. Long before her sex reassignment "operation," she framed her identity as part of a larger mythology beginning with her mother's pregnancy during which she carried twins. As Victoria told me, her twin died in the womb leaving Victoria with both a sense of loss from before birth and an instant embodiment of "two souls." Thus she was born both man and woman making holidays such as Queen's Day an early justification for dressing as a female. By her estimation, most family and friends suspected that she was really a female-minded person in a male body, however there was tremendous resistance from male members of her family. Her father posed the greatest amount of resistance to her identity as he expressed disbelief in how she could not remain a "certain way" in her ascribed gender role. Once her sex reassignment process began, her father was the person who drove her across the country to a hospital for hormone injections. But this part of her life history was a long time ago, and part of an identity struggle before Victoria's twenty-first birthday.

The cigarette burned out, and Victoria suggested meeting again to talk during her break, or later that week when we could spend the day at her apartment.

As Victoria was about to stand up to return outdoors to the street, she turned to me and said, "I can see you starting a center like the Living Room...because your heart is in the right place. You have what it takes because you have an open heart." Victoria's words struck me as I wondered aloud where could I possibly start such a center given the judicial climate towards prostitution in the United States. "You could start it out of your car, with a box of condoms and some hot coffee to pass out," she said. The idea crystallized.

The following night, I rode the subway escalator up to a tram station past a group of young males hanging around the entrance. As I passed swiftly into the darkness, I tripped and fell on the ground. In that moment I knew that onlookers perceived me as just another junkie heading to the *huiskamer* because there was no way of distinguishing me from the other women carrying backpacks and heavy winter garb. Quickly, I regained my composure and headed across the train tracks, passing the empty storage buildings. Out of nowhere a man in a white Opel drove directly at me, missing me but for a few inches. This was just one of the nightly dangers of being a female pedestrian in the spatial vicinity of the zone. Each night as I approached the Living Room, my identity melded to a community of junkies heading in the same direction. This was not the first time a car sped by dangerously close or slowed down long enough to exchange eye contact. As Desiree later explained, some of these drivers were former clients who had been robbed by drug-addicted prostitutes during an exchange. I had a sense of relief that evening spotting Victoria's sports car parked out front. Victoria had arrived early that evening to work.

Within minutes of arriving at the Living Room, Victoria came in from the winter chill to warm up over a cup of coffee waving her astrological chart in hand. We sat for a long time discussing the themes of the chart. I was able to address the issue of material security in her life in the context of what astrological elements were "absent" in the document. Shaking her head in agreement, "I must have luxuries, I must have luxuries" she blurted out. This would not be the last time she would tell me of her need for "luxuries." Victoria then explained why she worked both jobs, divulging how she devised "a plan" to work for five more years. The "plan" included payment for another facelift - her first undergone at the age of 36- a desire to go to South America to have laser work done, cheek implants, a nose job, and then there was the possible exploration of Indonesia.[8]

As we sat in the dressing room, Latinas squeezed into their work clothes, sprayed their hair, while others applied their make-up. Staff popped their heads through the door now and then. Meanwhile, Victoria mentioned that psychics and other clairvoyants had suggested extensive travel in her lifetime, even as she insisted on staying close to her parents. "I think of moving to Indonesia a lot," she said. The image of travel led Victoria to describe how she entered the sex trade after a trip to India.

Victoria traveled to India with her Hindu boyfriend Verag. When she arrived, his family hardly acknowledged her presence. For four months she "sat looking out a window" completely ignored by her boyfriend's sisters. When these women were not ignoring her they played mind games behaving cruelly towards her. Meanwhile, Verag was supporting a woman with whom he fathered a child but refused to marry. The emotional strain led Victoria to finally leave India feeling devastated by the relationship. Upon her return to the Netherlands she went on "social security" (welfare) having "no money for clothes, and had to shoplift [her] meats at the grocery store." Finally, she decided to work. Some transsexual friends had been making good money as prostitutes, so she thought, "why not." Victoria entered the business after renting a room in the Chinese quarter of the City.

When Verag returned from India, he wanted to borrow 1,700 Dutch guilders ($750) from Victoria for the purpose of gambling. Such a request insulted Victoria to the core of her being because using and potentially losing her money for such a frivolous reason in some way denigrated all the physical labor that went into generating her earnings. In addition, there was the social meaning attached to how Verag planned to use Victoria's money. Since the end product of her labor afforded Victoria a dignified life with high-end material items, the manner in which it was accumulated became somehow exalted. The social meaning attached to Verag's intention, however, degraded both the money and social implications attached to how the money was earned.

Victoria finished her cigarette and decided after an hour or two had passed that she should try to earn more money. As she exited, I returned to the staff station where a staff worker, who was trained as a nurse, watched Victoria exit the building for the street. Out of earshot the nurse called Victoria's actions and choice to continue working on the street as "stupid" and that what was at stake was "a job, house, and car that she could lose for what?...more money?....stupid....stupid," the woman repeated. I remained silent.

The staff member's judgment was loaded with meaning and complex social relations between sex worker and advocate. First, Victoria was professionally at par with most nurses working in the *huiskamer*, and may have out-ranked some of the staff that no longer regularly performed medical procedures for which they were trained. Reasons why Victoria would remain in prostitution after having "graduated" to professional ranks undermined any conventional construction of who works on the streets and what motivates them to be there.

Meanwhile, staff had to reconcile with their own authority as they had the power to exert some control over the behavior of prostitutes and enforce rules on anyone who entered the center. Their role as rule enforcers shifted relations with some prostitutes, such as Victoria, who operated with an air of autonomy. Perhaps, in the case of this staff member, there were underlying feelings of contempt for what services prostitutes provided as a means for making a living. How then could staff protect their own social status while one of their professional peers performed sexual services? Ultimately, Victoria's presence wore down educational and class barriers between medical staff and street workers.

The issue of material value placed on one's labor added to the already complex relations between staff and sex workers. In reality, many successful sex workers, including Victoria, earned in a day what staff earned in a month. As a result material realities produced tense social relations between staff and someone, like Victoria, who held multiple social positions.

During the winter months many Latinas congregated in the transgendered room spending a good part of the evening standing by the window looking out onto the zone rather than working outside. This night was a particularly cold January night, and some Latina *travestís* found themselves inside because of inclement weather. At the same table where Victoria and I sat earlier, a bleached blonde, stout Ecuadorian *travestí*, Bibiana, sat alone. Bibiana's bountifully silicone injected buttocks and hips baffled numerous Northern European prostitutes whose aesthetic "sensibilities" were deeply rooted in Northern European modes of femininity believed desirable on the street. Bibiana opened her wallet to count her money then pulled out pictures of her six nieces and nephews who were receiving financial support from her. This evening she had one customer.

An hour passed before Victoria returned to warm up over some coffee. A Latina followed in behind her calling out to her colleagues, "*Nada, nada, nada.*" No one was making money tonight, including Victoria. I brought her a cup of coffee, smiling she lit up a cigarette. Keeping her fauxfur coat on for warmth, we picked up the conversation exactly where we left off.

We returned to a pattern of tensions between her working on the street and having an intimate life. The emotional complications translate into a life long pattern for Victoria, who systematically left prostitution whenever she became engaged in a serious relationship. And after giving up streetworking for the duration of a relationship she often found refuge in prostitution after a break-up. One ex-boyfriend stalked her while she worked on the street. He would compulsively drive pass Victoria as she negotiated with customers or as she stood alone on the strip. When the two made eye contact the ex-boyfriend motioned the cutting of her throat with his freehand. Other times he would call her on the phone accusing her of kissing customers. "It drove him crazy," she said, when she returned to the street and regained her autonomy.

Before she called it a night, we agreed to meet Friday morning at 10:30AM. She drove me to my hostel where she would pick me up the following morning.

VICTORIA'S SANCTUARY

Outside in the chilly morning rain Victoria sat waiting in her car with the engine running fifteen minutes ahead of schedule. Our drive across the City led us to a residential section of elegant apartments. After parking the car outside and greeting a few neighbors, we walked through a labyrinth of locked halls and elevators to her apartment. We entered a long hallway surrounded by sepia tinted mirrors that produced an illusion of greater depth and size. Piet, her collie, timidly greeted us. He was Victoria's second collie. In the foyer, a Chinese wooden chest, an antique Victorian-era doll, and Asian artifacts began to appear as we headed down a gray tiled hall to the living room. The apartment was decorated in black Asian lacquer furniture with statues of Buddhist deities lining one wall, and Bonsai plants populating the porch and living space. Victoria asked whether I would like tea or coffee, and so we started with green tea and an Indonesian pastry she prepared with palm and coconut mash rolled in a green wrap. Piet sat on the couch with Victoria as she lit up a cigarette and waited for the water to boil.

Victoria mentioned having a great-grandmother of Indonesian ancestry. And although Victoria grew up in a deeply Dutch Catholic household, over the years she came to identify with Indonesian culture and cuisine. Her kitchen cabinets were packed with aromatic spices purchased at the local Asian market, making Indonesian cuisine a mainstay of Victoria's everyday life.

REMEMBERING CHILDHOOD

Our conversation drifts to Victoria's childhood. Growing up, as she shared during our first dialogue, Victoria *knew* she was different. Spaniards whom she encountered while living in her family's lodging knew "'this is not a boy,'" though her parents couldn't quite accept such observations. Victoria recalled how when she wanted a gender neutral "puppet," as she called it, as a gift for her birthday, her parents were horrified making her return the present. Victoria played with girls and "only liked females and never liked males." As she explained she never had attractions to women but experienced a comfortable feeling in their presence. In school, "children can feel when a child is different," she says. They were very hard on her. Boys gave her a woman's name. They teased. Victoria "swallowed [her] anger" until she exploded by beating up three boys.

Her maternal grandmother's love gave her "shelter." Grandmother was like a mother to her, and her mother like a sister. Here, too, Victoria attributes tolerance to a family tale. She relayed how although her grandmother came from a Catholic family with fourteen children, she had a progressive way of accepting others living outside the tenets of Catholicism. Had *Oma*, as she was called, lived to see her working as a prostitute, Victoria believed that her grandmother would have been more tolerant than other family members. She attributes this belief to one of her grandmother's brothers having "disgraced the family" when he married a prostitute. Only *Oma* refused to shun her brother and his family.

After school, Victoria would run to her grandmother's house, sometimes being greeted by an awkward grandfather who didn't know quite how to relate to his grandchild. Victoria suspected her grandfather was jealous of her relationship with her grandmother because the child always wanted *Oma*'s attention. The reoccurring memory of Queen's Day and dressing in her mother's high heels and dresses to resemble the Queen affirmed Victoria's early gender identity. By the age of ten, Victoria's life changed when her grandmother suddenly died, and thereafter she experienced the "worst time in [her] life."

"I always felt alone amongst my family," she says. Victoria interprets this familial disjunction through Chinese astrology that exposes how her father and brother were born in the year of the Tiger; her mother was born in the year of the Dragon; and only she and her grandmother were born in the year of the Sheep. As kindred spirits the presence of *Oma* continues to linger in her life.

Oma was already gone by the time Victoria reached puberty, and tensions were mounting at home. To rebel against her father's authority, she dropped out of school at the age of fourteen, taking a job at the post office. By then, she said, she had "breasts that were covered over in a boy's shirt and pants." This changing reality of her corporeal being was still nameless in her own plan on how to proceed with her life since she was without any role models to guide her.

Equally confusing to a young person coming of age thirty years ago were the identity politics of the early seventies. This meant systematically

having to adopt or being labeled a "homosexual" if she were not a partici-
pating member of heterosexist society. Not until Victoria was working as a
waitress did she encounter a person who was in transition as a "pre-operative" transsexual.[9] A "bright light went on inside" Victoria's head about
who she was and what she had to do to become that part of herself. Without any hesitation, Victoria began her gender migration quite early in adult
life. The hormone ingestion and feminine attire facilitated a dramatic
change in her identity, transforming her entire appearance at a stage when
most of her teenage peers were struggling with their own changing bodies.
A new waitress position where customers and employers assumed she was
a female made her transition easier without peers surveying her changes.

ENTRY INTO PROSTITUTION

Victoria's entry into prostitution illustrates how she, as a subject, is a product of the regulation of commercial sex. Victoria recalled how the mayor of
Den Apelhaven initiated the closing of all windows providing commercial
sex in the early 1980s. In effect, this change in the landscape required Victoria to find sex work in neighboring Breburg where she rented a window
from 7PM to 5AM. Performing erotic labor was "hard for my friend" -the
Indian boyfriend - who by then had returned to the Netherlands to their
floundering relationship. They fought daily over her right to work as a
prostitute. As a last effort to shame Victoria out of the business, Verag
threatened to tell her mother. "He told my parents and everyone that I did
prostitution," she said. Victoria never responded to the accusation. Over
the years, she developed tactics such as "when someone hurts me, I don't
talk to them."

  During this period, after Victoria's break-up with Verag, she returned
to her parents' house to live and told them that she worked the night shift
at a hotel as a temp-worker. Not long after returning home, her mother
found "too much money" in Victoria's purse. Her mother knew instantly
that Victoria must have been working in prostitution. Victoria's response to
her mother's prying set all future personal parameters when she stated to
her mother that "you have your life," while, "I do this my way, I do prostitution." Her mother threatened to throw Victoria out of the house, retort-
ing "'if you do this work, I will never talk to you again.'" Not long
afterwards the elder welcomed her daughter back home.

  Victoria's mother communicated her acceptance of her daughter's
profession by expressing an unusual interest in traveling to Breburg to
watch her work in the windows. Although her mother never followed
through with her request, through time she came to terms with Victoria

working as a prostitute "in a doorway" on Lemmerdreg in Den Apelhaven for five or six months. That juncture between parent and child came after her mother learned of the high number of heroin addicts present in the area, and inquired about the dangers involved in working under such conditions. Today, as a gesture of her acceptance of the material fruits of Victoria's entrepreneurial efforts, her mother cleans her house.

Back in the 1980s, on a good night Victoria could earn around 700 guilders ($300). She paid 50 guilders per day for a room working there from 9am to 4pm five days per week. Because window rentals required an inflexible schedule she opted for street prostitution, "when you work on the street, you are *free*, you can come whenever you want and go whenever you want."[10]

In the years following the closing of the windows in Den Apelhaven, "many men asked if I wanted to work in clubs. I refused to do floor shows." The situation in the clubs is considered undesirable to many autonomous streetwalkers. Prostitutes in the clubs are required to drink alcohol and "go upstairs [with the client] for 30 minutes" at a time. "Girls sit around half-naked, plus half goes to the boss......I work with my body, so all the money is for me. When I am working, I'm all business, no money, no honey," she smiles and lights another cigarette.

ADULT RELATIONSHIPS

Memories of her "early days" recollect different intimate relationships that developed in tandem with her customer relations. At seventeen, before "the operation,"[11] "I had my first [sexual] experience...I didn't like it." During that period, Victoria frequented "Greek bars" that catered to naval and cargo ships coming into a neighboring port. Before her sex-reassignment, there were numerous one-night stands but no long-term relations.

A traditional heterosexual model dominates the ruling codes of behavior and role-playing in Victoria's long-term relationships. "Rules" by which romantic relationships develop outside of Victoria's work as a prostitute also apply to relations that began as a commercial transaction. "Don't lie to me; don't beat me; and don't go out with another woman" set the parameters of engagement for Victoria. The last requirement of monogamy has singed relations with a degree of suspicion, especially when the relationship began between client and sex worker. On four separate occasions she formed long-term relationships with former clients. Of course, attractions happen with clients, but the idiom of "once a client, always a client" proved more consistent, especially when fellow prostitutes are quick to relay sightings of a lover discovered cruising in another city.

The first time Victoria fell in love with a client she was twenty-eight years old and her paramour was twenty-two. Hank was a mechanic. In the beginning of their relationship, Hank's mother - who still sends Victoria a Christmas card each year - accused her of being a prostitute. Victoria quipped back that her son had been her client. The information silenced the woman. The relationship lasted two and a half years. "He was a nice man [who] worked hard...We had a nice relationship but he was too young to handle me. I was the Boss. Sometimes they compete with me," she said implying that a power struggle ensued after Victoria agreed to stop working on the streets.

The dramatic loss of income changed her lifestyle forcing her to sell her Pontiac Firebird. When Victoria's savings dried up Hank complained about how much of *his* money she was spending. To communicate her opposition to his economic dictates, Victoria stopped purchasing name brand food products, and instead began preparing the "cheapest items" she could find. Eating baloney sandwiches two times a day, she surmised, was the lowest point of the relationship. When Hank and Victoria came to a critical impasse the issue was over food after he made a snide comment about her cooking. Victoria concluded that "[it's] difficult to hurt me. I have big walls, but you criticize my food, you hurt me, I don't talk to you."[12]

The relationship hurt Victoria in other ways too. She tried to accommodate her lover's need for her to be at home, but this decision meant forfeiting her financial autonomy. "I earn my money with my cunt (she spreads her legs symbolically)...I always must have money in my life. Sitting without it, the walls close [in]." The apartment was in her name, but eventually she had to move out leaving all the furniture that had special value. "The furniture, I worked for it. But when you work in prostitution,...with your body. It's very important [what you purchase with that money]. Furniture is emotional."

After their break-up, Victoria worked overtime on the streets in part to emotionally distract herself but also to make up for lost savings. "I go to work again, and he said he would kill himself. He was really sad. He was drunk. I thought he might kill himself." Hank's self-destructive gesture could be interpreted as manipulative, but for many prostitutes his demand could be read as a sign of care and fidelity. "I am alone [now], but when a man has no problem with [his girlfriend] doing this business, he doesn't love her." How sex workers interpret their companions' degree of "care" is subjective.

Shortly after discussing Victoria's tactics in balancing intimate relations with prostitution, I was invited to join an impromptu conversation that arose between five sex workers[13] sitting at one of the transgendered dressing room tables. A debate erupted around the unspoken rules of professional engagement as they affected their personal lives. Each sex worker had her own ideas around financial autonomy and emotional management of erotic labor practices. There was, however, a consensus that sex workers should not have to work in prostitution during pregnancy. One prostitute's story crystallized the meaning of this violation as it relates to the role of the partner involved. Apparently the husband of a sex worker in Breburg not only battered the woman but he also forced her to work on the streets throughout each of her three pregnancies. The situation culminated with the woman's water breaking while in a client's car. To the sex workers sitting at the table, the husband's actions were deserving of violent retribution for his callous disregard for his wife.[14]

Many sex workers interpreted a serious personal relationship as an arrangement quite separate from their commercial activities. The decision to continue working on the streets was left up to them rather than their partner. For others, money they generated on the streets was a primary source of income for their households. Retiring from sex work while in a relationship was not an option in this case.

Victoria's relationship with her first Indonesian boyfriend occurred back in 1989. He, too, had been a client. Once the relationship deepened, Victoria, again, ceased to work in prostitution. In the beginning, relations were good, but because Lan had a child with another woman, he had other distracting commitments beside Victoria. Only later as their communication deteriorated were there sign of Lan's manipulation and obsession with Victoria.

Lan never lashed out with physical abuse, however he used emotional taunting to control their relationship. After Victoria's sex-reassignment operation, having sexual relations was painful. There was also Victoria's concern that her vagina was too small. Lan, she says, took advantage of this insecurity and made many hurtful comments regarding Victoria's ability to have sex with him. After they broke up, Lan's behavior became more obsessive as he would "taunt me [showing up on the street] to work wearing a wig as a transvestite across the street from where I stood at night." Victoria and Lan would engage in shouting matches in which Victoria would have the final word: "go to your fucking wife!"

After several years alone, Victoria met Sebastian during an evening in the zone. "I was completely myself," she said. After initiating a commercial exchange they talked in the car for an hour and a half. Sebastian asked Victoria for her number, and then the following week, she had him over to her house for an Indonesian dinner that she prepared. "He brought flowers and wine." Two weeks into the relationship, Victoria stopped working on the street, again. Sebastian never pressed her to quit, and told her that if she wanted to continue to work, she should continue. At this stage of their relationship, he had no notion of Victoria as a transsexual. The day of personal disclosure came gradually.

Victoria had him over because she "has to tell him something." "We have some wine then some French coffee, and I tell him I was operated. He goes and gets champagne." It was that easy. She shakes her head flashing back to the memory, "I spoiled him. He put his arms around me and I wept."

The insecurity around her vaginal reconstruction followed her. Afraid to lose Sebastian because of a shallow vagina, Victoria decided to have it enlarged. The issue of size and depth was never a problem for Sebastian, however Victoria wanted to be able to have deeper sexual intercourse. She had two options: a skin graft from her stomach or her thigh. At this moment she stood up and raised her loose three-piece black rayon pants set to show markings of the graft on her stomach. This was a difficult period for her. When she entered the hospital one of her breasts shrunk. Meanwhile, her hospital roommate lay in bed screaming from her recent operation. It was a moment of great anxiety going into surgery, however the reconstructive surgery was a success. Victoria had to keep a metal tube inserted in her vagina to prevent it from collapsing and she feared "my pussy might get closed again."

After her physician cut the stitches, oil had to be used to loosen the metal object that had shaped the interior of her new vagina. Walking was made difficult, as the object remained lodged in her body. "Oh this is nice," Victoria said with a sarcastic playfulness. When the tube was eventually removed Victoria still found it impossible to have sex. Consequently each day for four to five weeks, she was required to use a vibrator to keep her new vagina open.

Not long after the relationship went through this major event, Victoria thought to herself, "this is it, this is for the rest of my life." For the first time, Victoria gave of herself completely, "He really broke me...He was my grandmother, mother, father, child."

Two years into their relationship, Sebastian declared he was in love with another woman. While he took a business trip to Boston, Victoria gave him three weeks to decide whether to continue on together or not. Still undecided, upon his return, he pleaded to leave his belongings at her house but she insisted that he remove everything. The entire break-up was civil. There was no yelling, but Victoria's parting words were, "I will never let you go." Victoria held Sebastian in her arms as he wept like a child. He wrote her a long note trying to explain what had occurred, but Victoria responded only with politeness because "I knew how far I could go with him, I'm never a big mouth with him."

The cycle of working on the street for over twenty years, of course, has been broken by serial relationships that intensified and then broke off. "I'd meet somebody nice, and stop, [then] work [again, then] stop." A resounding pattern appears in each of Victoria's stories about her intimate relations. Each time Victoria entered a heterosexual arrangement, she resumed a traditional role that, in the end, had damaging economic effect on her fiscal mobility. Whether Victoria found herself quitting her erotic labor enterprise as a way of proving her sexual loyalty or whether she simply assumed a "traditional" gender role much like other single-income households in which the male is the breadwinner, is difficult to interpret.

The irony of these stories rests in that four of those relationships, including her most recent break-up with a Pakistani man, entered an emotional pact with the foreknowledge - as her former clients - that Victoria made her livelihood with her body. Understanding the nature of her commercial work, one might think that a clear emotional parameter and respect for her bodily production would have permitted her to continue working on the streets but this was not the case.

SEXUAL GRATIFICATION

Over twenty-five years ago Victoria underwent her first vaginal plasty. She assumed the sex reassignment would instantly transform her life. "Now I'm a woman," she thought of herself, "but it doesn't change. I wasn't complete." With a "new kind of pussy, I was afraid [to have sex]. It was like the first time," Victoria said describing having sex shortly after the surgery. More important than experiencing sexual gratification as a woman, Victoria became preoccupied with the reproductive limitations of her sex reassignment. Her insecurities were driven by the fact that regardless of whether a lover wanted children, he always had the option of starting a family with a born woman. Until four or five years ago she was unable to talk about "the operation," but has since disclosed her transsexual identity to her lovers. Customers, however, are never informed because most clients assume they are with an anatomically born female rather than a transsexual.

Unlike the self-doubts that followed her in her personal life, workings on the street proved to be easy because she always held her client's penis in her hand at the edge of her vagina and rarely, if ever, did it require "rough sex." With customers, she said, she "turns everything off. I feel nothing. You don't have feelings for the customer. If they lick me, last time two years ago, maybe it feels good, but the main thing is the money." At twenty-nine years of age, Victoria can recall a single customer who caressed her neck and then aroused her. This encounter was the only time she felt a bodily reaction to a client. Nonetheless, she "never fakes her groans."

In reality, Victoria has never experienced sexual gratification in her adult life. To date, Victoria has never experienced an orgasm neither while working nor in a personal relationship. Only in a sleeping state does she experience sexual gratification, "I have them when I dream." Even in her youth, before her surgery, Victoria experienced sexual frustration, never enjoying sex, and absolutely deploring even the idea of having anal intercourse. Although other forms of oral contact produced pleasure, in her private life, the sensation has never produced an orgasm.

SUCCESS ON THE STREET

"Everything is work, money is the money," Victoria says about what she derives from her work as a streetwalker.

What skills are required to be a successful prostitute? Victoria lights up another cigarette as Piet curls around her on the couch. "First," she said, "I hear from the customers that I am sensual. I'm [also] very tall." When would-be clients drive by the zone, they often see a cluster of women of the same height, however "when they see me, I stand out." As for her appearance, "I wear expensive perfume, my hair and make-up are nice...they don't see you as a common hooker."

Victoria emphasized how particular she was about whom she would service. As for the customers, they "must always be clean," and in response, she customarily must "be nice to the customer," and "when the car stops and opens, I say, 'Good evening, it is 50 guilders,'" always smiling. After a customer agrees to her charge, she enters the car, spreads out a napkin on the front passenger's seat, and then puts on a condom before asking the client whether to "start with a fuck or a suck"? She then "plays a little" with the client's genitals. Since 1980, condoms have systematically been worn on the job, "although occasionally clients request 'blow-jobs' without them." Thus as part of her opening performance, Victoria communicates, "always with a condom" before the transaction begins.

Her former lover, Sebastian, transformed her social life, and as a result Victoria no longer wears short skirts, or other items commonly worn on the streets. "[My ex-boyfriend] changed my life. I became very educated. I'm more educated so some of my clients are more high-class people."

In the zone, mingling among the female prostitutes are drug-addicted females looking to purchase crack or heroin after a commercial exchange with a client. I asked why she thought some clients sought out the drug-addicted women. As if surprised by my naive question, "clients," she said, "know that the drug-addicted girls will do anything, and some without a condom." But, the biggest draw she suspected was that some clients liked the risk of being with someone from whom they could contract HIV.

Customers love inquiring about who Victoria is, and sometimes ask whether she was married or had a family. On most occasions she learned more about them than they would learn about her. Of her fifteen to eighteen regular customers, only one is married. He often talks about his children or wife, who has cancer. But during most sessions they asked her about her other job, and in disbelief that she works two. "'Why do you work," they would inquire, "you're so beautiful?" to which Victoria replied, "Why not!"

Occasionally, a customer would ask pointed questions about her identity. When a client asked, "You are an operated woman?" Victoria quipped, "You shut up and you fuck." Sometimes, Victoria said, there were male clients who specifically preferred women like herself. She described this type of client as having "His 'problem,'" because "he likes women like me," then surmises that perhaps in "[the client's] mind, maybe they're bi-sexual. Or, maybe they like the idea that you were once a man."

The doorbell rang and Victoria's father enters to take Piet out for her afternoon walk.[15] When he left, we resumed our conversation about her experiences on the streets. Not unlike the demographic changes in the Netherlands, Victoria's daily practices on the streets reflect her conformity to changes in client expectations. For instance, twenty years ago Victoria only accepted Dutch customers, however now she receives clients who are Turkish. She still refuses, however, to service African clients because, as she puts it, "when I say my price they try to bring it down, I don't like this." On numerous occasions she recounted her verbal sparring with a would-be Turkish client who said to her, "'I have ten guilders,'" to which she replied "You take your ten guilders and fuck your mother." When the Turkish man replied, "'don't say that about my mother again,'" Victoria quipped, "your mother, your mother, your mother." Each time the tale of the Turkish client was told, it produced the same amusing self-empowering charge for Victoria. What this story also reveals is the origins of why some Dutch prostitutes refuse to service clients from the Middle East and North Africa. As described in the chapter on "Sexualized Space," Magdalena identified the same culture practice of haggling for goods and services as a source of nuisance for many prostitutes. Unlike Middle Eastern cultures, which encourage haggling, Dutch society is more prone to accept standardized prices for goods and services.

Levity is also part of the retelling of commercial exchanges she recounts. Whether her tales involve an elderly client that long awaited an encounter with her after months of saving coins in a Kodak film roll container; a graphic simulation of accommodating an obese client requiring her to stretch her limbs wider than usual; or performing oral sex during a trip around the drive-through at Mc Donald's restaurant; each client vignette possess humor and satire in the individual details. There is no emotional compromise because Victoria is using her body to procure capital in these scenarios. From her perspective, the client has a need and she provides a service, having the final word whether the client's fantasy will be fulfilled.

Satisfying a client's fantasy entails a believable theatrical performance. The material rewards are significant, when she agrees to perform an S&M role. Victoria could recall countless tales of playing out the dominant role to fulfill a sexual fantasy of the client. In some instances she was paid to taunt, humiliate, beat, or urinate on clients. The rewards, however, were generous and usually did not require performing genital or oral sex. Instead, a successful performance required a command of strong language and use of inflection. Simply immersing the client in his own fantasy required skill, creativity and a sense of knowing her own bodily and emotional parameters.

During an S&M session, when a performance necessitates high theatrics, Victoria impersonates different personas that might appeal to the client. On occasion the client "wants me to humiliate him while talking, and then he jacks off." Other times, hard drugs might be involved. She described one customer who needed to be high on cocaine before requesting that she completely undress and press herself against his body. Without any form of sexual penetration, the client climaxed as Victoria told him what he couldn't have from her, or what was he was being denied him in terms of sexual contact. This particular performance required quite a bit of imagination, as she would conjure up new dialogue scenarios while driving to the client's home. "You get exhausted from it, just yesterday, [one client] wanted to put sun-lotion on my buttocks, he talks a lot too, and [that kind of client behavior] takes all the energy out of you." After such an event Victoria usually does not feel like working.

Most commonly requested are S&M performances during which the first time client and sex worker discuss the specific roles the customer wants to play out. "I have to tell a different story [each time we meet], in the hotel something [such as a scenario] comes to me. This he likes: At a stop light, with cars around, he addresses me and I tell him to call me 'Mistress' then I'd strike him." In this instance, other motorists would become spectators to the client's fantasy and humiliation thereby facilitating his arousal.

But, she says, "Most of the time, when you have a short time (ten minutes), the customer has his needs. Sometimes the customer wants me to have a nice time, this is difficult. They get too close,...this, when they ask what I want. I'm working for the man's pleasure, not mine. Then, it's difficult to stay in the role of the prostitute."

"Only once, long time ago, two men [approached]. He said he liked 'crazy things' and 'wanted a knife in his ass.'" He was willing to pay 500 guilders but had 1,000 in his pocket. Victoria agreed to stick a stiletto heel in his rectum for the additional 500 guilders, with the expectation that there would be other sexual services exchanged. She thought this client was "crazy," and then convinced him to go outside and look for his friend, while she went looking for him in another direction, Victoria made off with 1,000 guilders that night.

Victoria, however, didn't consider such practices as "normal." Other acts of submission such as licking balls was an unacceptable request. "It's dirty," she said.

A large part of the game requires inflating the value of the role-playing because the sex worker holds all the labor power. Because of customized consumer habits and the labor it requires to fulfill them, a client who enters negotiation to have his fetish or fantasy scenario performed is, in effect, captive to his own need. Most sex workers are aware of the advantage they hold in this scenario, and certainly Victoria was one to articulate what her labor power should dictate in terms of material returns for her services.

"I'm a business person, I'm in charge." But it was impossible to make a living working as a dominatrix, without actually providing sexual intercourse. Over the years, maybe she had made a good 10,000 guilders from clients who just wanted to lick her shoes. But, that's not enough to live on. "I do lots of things, but there is a limit. I never [allow people to] dominate me. I like money but not to be humiliated."

Who has the *power* in the exchange? I asked. "I always have the power. I control everything. You have a customer in their car, I put on the condom, I say when we do a blow job, we do it."

But this portrayal is only part of the picture. As Victoria's life story reveals, the history of Den Apelhaven's streetwalking zone has changed over the years. One night while driving me to my hostel, Victoria drove past the previously designated zone that occupied a busy intersection. That story was as much about the changing identities of the ethnic groups who worked the zone as it is about the site itself. After working in a window in the Chinese section of the city, Victoria moved to the streets. "[When] the Colombians [arrived,] they ruined prices." Later, women arrived from Thailand, then Ecuador. In the last two years, she said, the latter group has begun to talk to the Dutch prostitutes. Tensions have diminished partly because they are "nice" but mostly because the Ecuadorians agreed to "go for the same price" and because "the street is small, we don't need new women." But the overriding feeling is that "one day one arrives, next day more, then they ruin business."

The influx of migrant sex workers has produced fluctuations in Victoria's earning over the last twenty years. On a bad night, she could leave the zone with nothing or between fl 150 to 250 ($70 – 120); normally though, she said, she made between fl 300 to 500; on a good night she could expect between fl 600 and 800 guilders; on a very good night, fl 1,100 to 1,200.

These figures are relative to inflation, new sex workers on the street, and a plethora of normalized services now commonly requested of sex workers. Twenty years ago, fl 400 to 500 guilders was considered a bad night. Of course, there were exceptions: the single paying customer who offered fl 800, or another who paid fl 900, then another fl 750 in a single night distorts what it means to have a "normal" night.

In this economy, earning fl 900 ($400) from a single customer requires performing an all night event however rarely it might happen. Recalling such times, Victoria described it as easy, you "talk a little, then sit, go to their home, have a drink." The client will then request that she put on a particular dress and bra. They touch a bit, and then later she will enter the client's bed. For the most part, "the physical work is only ten or fifteen minutes," the rest is ambiance, mood, and decent company.

When asked how she determined whether a customer had a lot of money, she replied this way: "You can 'feel' when you're with a customer with money, then you have to figure out how to get more money out of them. When they want something different, you see it, feel it." When asked where she went with these high-paying clients, she said, "sometimes in the car, sometimes, if I want to go, to their house. When I feel it's good, some of my customers come to my house." This costs more, and starts at 200 guilders. There are other guidelines. The client must call before 5PM on her cell phone that is used only for customers. The younger ones, around 35-36, try to become "private" and want to go out for dinner, but Victoria charges for dinner on an hourly basis.

PRIVILEGES OF DUTCH CITIZENSHIP AND SENIORITY ON THE STREETS

Throughout this chapter and those that follow, I describe how social relations have transformed on the streets, forcing new members to struggle for money and space. Despite these changes, subjects such as Victoria continue to hold privileged social positions because of their identity. In particular, her status as a Dutch citizen combined with her senior membership on the streets affords Victoria an authority when dealing with other streetwalkers, the police, clients, and staff at the Living Room. Moreover, because of her medical background and understanding of tax laws, Victoria vocalizes her civil rights when violation of their privacy occurs, thus permitting her confrontations without reprisal when addressing authorities.

Sometimes Victoria asserts her position for the common good of the streetwalkers who work in the zone. Other times self-interest is involved. Recently Dutch law enforcement attempted to gain greater regulatory control on the streets by enforcing the use of an ID system intended to keep track of the reported income of streetwalkers. Victoria came forward contesting this regulatory obligation, arguing that other actors in the zone - pimps, drug-dealers and clients – did not have to pay taxes there, therefore why should the prostitutes? She won that argument with the police.[16]

Victoria was also a vocal agent when public health workers gathered sex workers together to determine how to convert services from the Dutch guilder to the Euro in December 2001. When public health workers suggested raising a standard "suck and fuck" to 30 Euro, Victoria expressed concern that the increase, which converts to an fl 10 increase from their standard fl 50, was more than what clients would be willing to pay. In the end, sex workers agreed upon 25 Euro as a fair commercial exchange, raising standard services only fl 5 in fifteen years.

Victoria's authority in the zone as one of the "regulating" forces has translated into dominance and violence on occasion. During the incident involving two undocumented Bulgarian prostitutes Victoria demanded to see their passports. When the Bulgarian women could not produce papers to work in the area, Victoria demanded they leave the site. When the women contested her authority to throw them out, a fight ensued. This kind of exchange occurred three or four times before the women finally left and the police threatened Victoria and a few others with banishment from the zone.

NURSING SCHOOL

From early on in her career as a prostitute, Victoria realized her longevity in the business would be dictated by aging and changes in the erotic labor market. By her early thirties, she began planning for an alternative career. The state education system allowed her to pick up where she dropped out at the age of fourteen. In October 1991, Victoria completed a three-year program, including pre-nursing school, in two and a half years. Before being assigned her day shift, she worked evenings. Conveniently, she worked at the nursing home until 11pm and then spent a few hours working on the street. Now that she works on an Alzheimer's disease ward, her schedule involves getting up at 5AM for her 7:30AM shift and working until after 3PM. Usually she would take a quick nap before driving over to the zone. Sometimes she works two nursing shifts or forgoes streetwalking for long periods of time altogether. At the nursing home she described to me how "she gave something of [herself]", "I'm different with the patients, I can see myself."

The two worlds of nursing and streetwalking are parallel sectors that never intersect. Whatever risk there might be of losing her nursing job while working on the street, she flatly replies, "I do with my private life whatever I will. Suppose my colleague sees me, it's their word against my word." However legalization might have changed the right to provide sexual services this self-protective strategy exposes a longstanding social stigma still attached to sex work. Victoria went on to say that her colleagues were "afraid of [her], because I speak with a knife." This candor that is so much a part of her streetwalking world jeopardized her relationships with some authority figures at the nursing home.

Contrastingly, on the streets "if the girls don't like you, they tell you," but at the nursing home she described her colleagues as "sneaky." Because of the honesty found on the street, Victoria identified with prostitutes more than with her nursing colleagues. "With the girls on Sarphatiweg,[17] I feel more with my heart with the girls. Many of the girls have had a hard life. We have serious conversations, I like helping them."

Victoria continues to have clashes with nurse administrators who are disarmed by Victoria's vocalization and her criticism of how the facility is run at the expense of quality care for their patients. Victoria's troubles with authority occurred when she noticed the deteriorating condition of her former head nurse who became a patient after suffering a stroke. Victoria began keeping notes on patients' condition until a team leader sensed she was under professional scrutiny and tried to turn the roles around. This administrator tried to "catch me," as Victoria put it, but she refused to sign any kind of document admitting to negligence or wrongdoing. When Victoria threatened to "get a lawyer, go to the union, and go to the newspaper" because of many medical wrong doings, the head nurse backed off.

Sitting in Victoria's living room, the phone rings breaking the momentum of our conversation. Victoria's mother calls to inform her that her father planned to walk the dog at 3PM. When Victoria mentions our interview, she frames the exchange as part of her Registered Nursing program. After they hung up, Victoria relays this conversation in English explaining that her entire family knows of her work on the streets.

This interruption drifted the conversation to her familial relations. Victoria and her only brother both live in the same apartment building, however rarely see each other. To date, they gather at Christmas time for her mother's sake but remain distant. Her brother never approved of her work, but when her brother moved to a new house, he willingly accepted Victoria's monetary gift. Coming to her defense, her father was quick to ask her brother "'why do you take her money [if you disapprove of her lifestyle]?'"

Yet, for all the tensions over Victoria's work as a prostitute, her brother, sister-in-law, mother and father were there at the hospital to see Victoria after her sex reassignment. And when a lover struck Victoria, -"if I had stayed he would have killed me" –her father and brother were there to tell the man he had to leave.

FINDING MEANING

As Victoria prepares our Indonesian dinner, and darkness falls, she describes her experiences as a nurse on a geriatrics ward and how she helps her patients through the death and dying process. In that context, she finds great meaning in her life's work as a caregiver. In particular, she described becoming close to a withdrawn Hindustan woman who felt abandoned by her children living in London and across Europe. When Victoria went into the woman's room to care for her, she said a few sentences in Hindi to which the woman responded. "She was an Aries, very stubborn and strong," she said describing the woman with a sense of nostalgia for her combative nature. The relationship between nurse and patient wasn't easygoing. The irascible woman fought even as her health declined. In the end, Victoria stood by her because "I don't want them to die alone." After the woman passed away, Victoria was the one who bathed the body and dressed her in an appropriate sari.

She told other stories of patients who found great comfort in her humor and strength, and although her spiritual "faith" was destroyed with her romantic break-up, she was there, again, beside people, holding their hand as they faced death. "I love them and care for them, and they feel it."

Over dinner, seated with Piet by her side, with her own spoon Victoria slipped the dog mouthfuls of Indonesian beef. She fed the dog alternating who would eat the next mouthful from her utensil. The hostess relayed how people warned her that she would get germs from the dog but she insisted that it never happened.

As she drank a glass of wine, her mood became more somber. Pain welled up as she told me how "hard life had been." She couldn't understand why she had to endure certain pain. She glanced to my right and had a vision of an elderly woman dressed in black. I suspected she was seeing my paternal grandmother's spirit. While I washed the dishes, Victoria admitted to sleeping with the lights on so she can see the spirits that appeared all around us.

After dinner we returned to the living room and resumed our conversation about prostitution. It was an awkward transition, but Victoria found a favorite expression to pull her back into a story telling mode. "Once a prostitute, always a prostitute. I don't have bad feelings about prostitution. My heart hardened from my relationships with men, not prostitution. The money you give me, I spend very nicely."

Then she recalled an example of how that idiom might apply to her overriding ability to convert even a casual encounter into an economic opportunity. Once coming out of the grocery store, she recalled a former client recognizing her. He begged her for her services. After putting her groceries in the trunk, she agreed to meet him at a particular site. The exchange generated was a "quick 100 guilders" and Victoria rationalized this disruption to her daily routine as having just paid for the groceries that awaited her in her car. Commercial sex is not limited to a space or time in the day. It is a spontaneous and highly opportunistic endeavor.

In another instance, while involved with Sebastian, another former client rang her doorbell. She told him, "I'm in a relationship, can't do it." The would-be client begged, "'oh, please,'" but she said "no" then closed the door thinking, "Oh, 300 guilders, but then I would have had to tell Sebastian." While this tale exemplifies her devotion to her relationship, and her ability to remain outside the commercial sexual realm, it is also a story of missed material opportunity that she shall remember for her entire life.

I wondered what this lifestyle afforded her, and inquired whether she could be satisfied with her lifestyle were she to stop working on the streets? Counting all of her income, Victoria made fl 30,000 (about $12,900) on the street last year, and another fl 35, 000 ($15,000) were earned as a nurse. She had a five-year plan, but if a significant person were to come into her life, she would forgo her retirement savings and remain out of the business. Then she told me that she was still waiting for Sebastian to return. Without him, it is unlikely that she would allow anyone to get close, and therefore would remain in the business.

I mentioned wanting to return to the *huiskamer* by 8:30PM, therefore Victoria had to weigh her own emotional mood after a day of disclosing pieces of the past. She decided to take a shower then work for a few hours on the street. Feeling lighter, though vulnerable, she concluded that before we left she would have to "put [her] mask back on." When she returned from the shower, wearing a silk floral robe, she mentioned how she had purchased an extra perfume bottle, then she handed me my birthday gift, a bottle of Samsara perfume.

We entered Victoria's sports car and she turned to me and said that she felt like "50 percent a prostitute." She was emotionally exhausted from our ten-hour conversation about her life in and out of prostitution. Now, she was suddenly exposed, entering an environment that required her full attention and savvy. After we pulled into the area and parked the car, she changed her shoes and skirt while in the car.

Back at the *huiskamer*, I encountered Veronica who was short of cash and needed to buy lubricant on loan. Because the center's rules did not permit "lending" out items, I agreed to purchase a tube of lubricant for the Ecuadorian transsexual, who without it could not work on the street. Later, while Victoria and I were sitting together drinking coffee, Veronica returned and paid me back for the lubricant. Victoria, herself, had also returned for a coffee after an exchange with the elderly man who paid her in coins contained in five separate Kodak film rolls.

We caught a glimpse of a silhouette in black lycra and long blonde wig out in the hallway. Steluta had arrived and once she came through the doorway, made a point to kiss each of us before she joined our little table. She was eager to share the news of her new job as a nurse's aide. After struggling for years on the street, Steluta finally received her green card, but now turned to Victoria to learn of the educational opportunities before her. Steluta expressed concern about her ability to comprehend the Dutch language, "It's not because I'm stupid, I just have difficulty with the Dutch language." Both Victoria and Steluta agreed that her working eight hours in a Dutch environment would strengthen Steluta's language skills.

During her conversation with Steluta, Victoria carried the role of advocate. She, like Steluta, was first placed in a position as a nurses' aide before entering a nursing program. Victoria recommended that Steluta should stick with this low-paying post on the geriatrics ward because once she completed the two-year contract, the nursing education would be state funded. Once Steluta adjusted in her new place of employment, Victoria promised she would recommend the right nursing program to pursue.

The conversation drifted back to the immediate surroundings and Steluta proclaimed that she was here to "better [her] life," thus determined to stay the night until earning fl 200 to pay her bills. Both Victoria and Steluta glanced over at a group of Latinas who had spent most of the evening inside the transgendered dressing room. Out of nowhere Steluta recollected her lost opportunities to purchase a building in Bucharest when she was earning enough money on the street and property was cheap. She pondered what could have been her own little shop. The thought of purchasing property triggered Victoria to remind Steluta of the important lesson of always generating a source of "legal money" to disguise purchases made with "black money." With that Steluta turned to me to describe her "education" as a painfully difficult process, but that Victoria's presence had become an emblem of perseverance and success for her.

Again, the conversation drifted from the monetary to the psychic realm, and Steluta disclosed having frequented the House of the Seventh Ray in Den Apelhaven for a psychic reading knowing full well the place was a scam. Whenever she returned to Romania, she visited the village psychic who forewarned Steluta that she would journey abroad and suffer many hardships before prevailing in her personal life.

Valeria joined in to disclose her many encounters with the spirit world and how her mother's "gypsy" status evoked that connection. Valeria proudly told me that she spoke Dutch, English, Spanish, Turkish, Russian, and Berber, and communicated with her Moroccan boyfriend in Arabic dialect. Over the years, she had many violent encounters with prostitutes, police and antagonistic would-be clients, but tonight she was sharing her encounters with her dead grandmother who had not forgiven her for a transgression before the woman's death.

The time was after 11pm, and Victoria needed to rise early to work the 7AM shift at the nursing home. As she walked to her car two young men in business suits approached to comment that she was the oldest and most elegant sex worker there. She thanked them, waiting for me in her car as I passed them on the wheelchair ramp. When we sped off into the night, Victoria noticed in the rear view mirror that the men were behind us and were gaining speed. They flashed their lights and sped passed us. Whether this was another lost commercial opportunity for Victoria, I will never know. She drove me to the door of my youth hostel, regenerated from having played the game on the streets for a few hours and then we parted.

IN THE TIME SINCE

In the three years that have passed since our initial series of interviews Victoria and I remained in contact via e-mail, with an eight-hour visit to her in her home in January 2002, and a follow-up visit to my home in the spring of 2002. During this passage of time, Victoria has stayed on course with regard to her life goals. She spent most of her time working on the street and in the nursing home, in addition to returning to school to complete another nursing certification. In the meantime, she has also begun and ended a brief tumultuous relationship with a Pakistani man who stole her sports car and is presumed to be in hiding from the police and Victoria.

CONCLUSION

In this chapter the narrative is structured to parallel the development of my relationship with the informant. Through the use of a conversational mode of writing, thematic stories are reconstructed to flow closely with the tone and manner in which they were communicated during multiple interviews. The end result invites readers into an intimate perspective, shedding light on Victoria's personality, and drawing out complex ways in which she negotiates her multiple social positions. Unlike existing representations found in many "prostitution narratives," Victoria's story undermines a fixed social location often assumed of sex workers.

Victoria's narrative is dominated by how she participates in economic and social processes inside and outside of prostitution. The material implications of her participation illustrate how money is understood, recycled, and consumed by her. As an agent, she maneuvers in the zone and in the nursing profession for money, power, and space. This participation touches upon a diversity of strategies used in Victoria's economic life, revealing how bodily performative productions are rationalized in this framework.

Victoria's story is significant in other ways. She holds multiple social positions as a prostitute in the Netherlands. Whether as a streetwalker, transsexual, geriatrics nurse, advocate, or middle-class Dutch citizen, each role facilitates cultural production evoking disjunctures and continuity in her daily social interactions. Therefore, the intersection of these social roles –as streetwalker, transsexual, and nurse- challenge commonly held notions about gender identity, age, and sex work. [18]

In conclusion, Victoria's life story illustrates a perspective of prostitution where individuals can produce optimal material returns under conditions providing rights and benefits to them. When sex workers can operate autonomously from "middle management" or fear of arrest from authorities, they can negotiate with clients in a more favorable way. Although legalization of prostitution does not eliminate the social stigma attached to it, in some sectors of the sex industry workers can go about their professional and private lives with a sense of personal dignity and openness. Victoria's case study is a living example of a successful "freelance" prostitute who holds multiple social positions inside and outside of the Dutch system.

Chapter Seven

Coping Strategies for Economic, Physical, and Emotional Survival on the Streets and in the Windows

INTRODUCTION

Traditional concepts of community have arguably been organized around entirely isolated, coherent, and monolithic entities. As post-modern life would have it, most of us happen to belong to multiple "spatially dispersed" groups based on shared interests. Their manifestations are communicated in everyday enactments of membership through a plethora of learned practices. Sociability in prostitution communities requires reassessing the fundamental nature of community itself. Real life community building has historically been based on closed, tight networks, however with a multiple, and at times transient, social groups working in the zone and in the windows, in the construction of new forms communities they are operating around codes of behavior, interests, and maintenance of the social order. This chapter explores how female and transgendered sex workers utilize different personal and collective strategies to optimize economic, social, and/or emotional benefits from their working conditions and living arrangements.

These accounts represent the complexity and diversity of experiences found in the professional and intimate lives of sex workers. Through different cases and tactical themes, I argue that sex workers approach prostitution with many individualized and collective approaches, challenged by ongoing social and regulatory shifts in the sex industry and giving some semblance of community for sex workers. Knowing about the ways sex workers understand their own professional practices, a term that I call "coping strategies," gives some indication of how they are adapting to challenging, and often inequitable, conditions. The secondary purpose of this chapter is to illustrate how communities, in this case prostitution communities, organize around shared interests. Through story telling and daily rituals on the streets and in the windows, each technique informs my research of how sex workers produce their own sense of well-being and commercial viability.

This chapter begins with the case of forty-four year old Anke, a female Dutch citizen, who reconstructs her professional and personal experiences streetwalking in Den Apelhaven.[1] Anke lives on social welfare, and subsidizes her benefits with prostitution in an unregulated streetwalking zone. Anke faces health related problems, and her personal life, meanwhile, has been marred by emotional stress from having cared for drug addicted heterosexual partners who depleted all of her resources and left her in debt.

Anke's twenty-eight years in prostitution gives her a subjective understanding of her working conditions. This perspective influences her streetwalking "codes" devised for running her commercial operations with the least amount of personal compromise or effort and repeated acts of resistance to changing conditions and commercial relations there. Anke rebuffs numerous clients who express expectations of more intensified sexual services at the same cost. Her most economically consequential acts of defiance involve her repeated refusal to conform to professional aesthetic standards enforced by most streetwalkers, resulting in poor economic returns on the streets and strained relations with her cohorts.

Despite these shortcomings, Anke reassigns status to her whiteness when dealing with her African and Middle Eastern clients, focusing on other aspects of her bodily performance clients find desirable, and deriving esteem from refusing to perform certain sexual acts which she makes publicly known to other streetwalkers. The trials of her intimate life, meanwhile, have given Anke illuminating hindsight. She now gives priority and value to her autonomy and unencumbered status living alone. I suggest that Anke's narrative should not be understood as a simplistic representation of an economically unsuccessful prostitute, but as an agent of cultural production in her life and the life of the streetwalking zone.

In the section "To migrate across the street," informants discuss economic and social implications of gender migration. I present their different approaches to a post-operative transsexual identity in the context of a personal strategy. Commercial implications of a gender reassignment vary depending upon informants' interpretation of their clients' needs, competition with other sex workers, and the value they place on a technologically reconstructed female anatomy. Informants express additional concern for the institutionalization of surgical procedures that they believe has robbed them of control over their body.

The next section, "Tricks of the trade," is devoted to a litany of sexual performative techniques deployed by transgendered and female prostitutes when providing services to their clients. Informants including Anke, Victoria, Nadine, Desiree, Veronica, Magdalena, Agnese, and Ramona all described using some or all of these techniques as part of their daily routine on the streets and in the windows. Many of these practices are intended to earn sex workers the most earnings for the least amount of effort, but they also function as a guarantee of their physical or emotional safety when exchanging services with clients. These practices are more than forms of physical manipulation or masquerade on the part of informants. Instead, they suggest that all acts of sexual simulation are part of a performative regime, and therefore understanding these methods as modes of coping to counter taxing conditions under which many prostitutes work clarifies their intentions.

There are many innovative ways in which sex workers guard against potential dangers on the streets and in the windows. The fourth section "Safety Measures" is divided into four parts. In the first part, I detail how the streetwalking zone in Den Apelhaven has moved to various industrial locations over the last fifteen years, each time relocating further away from the city center. Because of the physical space in which the commercial exchange takes place, either in an automobile or in an area hotel, issues around safety require female and transgendered streetwalkers to use their surrounding to ensure their security. In "Staying in the Zone" streetwalkers suggest measures taken to ensure their safety as they provide sexual services in the front seat of automobiles, opting to remain under video surveillance rather than venturing out of the area where their security becomes less certain.

In the second part, "Getting the Money First," Ramona, an Ecuadorian *travestí* working in the windows of Amsterdam, gives a brief history of lessons she has learned, resulting in her establishing firm rules of engagement with clients. After experiencing random violence, Ramona now operates her business in a manner that guarantees her well-being. These measures include collecting payments for services before performing a sexual exchange, wearing a condom, and refusing to kiss clients or becoming emotionally involved with them.

In the third part, "Staying out of the system," I consider the role of social agencies in the lives of streetwalkers. Giving two case examples, I illustrate the disparate relationship each streetwalker perceives herself to have with public health agencies. Steluta, a Rumanian transvestite, and Valeria, a Dutch female prostitute, describe their disparate understandings of being in the system. While Steluta welcomes entry into the social services that provide Dutch languages classes and employment in the health profession; Valerie describes how she has made herself "disappear" from the census records and public health surveys as a way to maintain her autonomy.

Lastly, I describe the role of the private realm in the intimate lives of some of my informants. In "Caring for the Self," the physical and emotional demands of sex work frame the structure of intimacy for many sex workers. I suggest how some sex workers blur the line between commercial relations and their private lives, and in other instances chose to remain outside of any committed relationship altogether. In this section, I establish the benefits from having a state recognized "permanent partnership" for transgendered and migrant prostitutes.

ANKE'S STORY

Anke and I are the only two people standing in the transvestite changing room on a cold January night. Peering out through a window onto the street where she works, Anke turns to me and says, "I never work when I menstruate. Working while having my period makes me feel dirty. It's dirty." At forty-four years of age, a Dutch female, she caresses her breasts and then gives me a directive glance motioning me to look at her chest concealed beneath her black spandex dress. "I can feel my breasts are getting swollen," she says. Suddenly Anke perks up as she recognizes the automobile of a former client driving into the area.

Anke complains of producing meager results that evening on the street. Her total earnings are thirty-five guilders ($17 or 17 Euro). Implicit in her disclosure of fl 35 is a more significant admission. At that moment Anke declared having performed oral sex or maybe a "quick fuck" for under the going rate of fl 50 ($20). Sensing my understanding of her discrepancy of 15 guilders, Anke went into an explanation of her actions claiming that "people talk but they know that I'm alone, I don't have a boyfriend to take care of me, . . . So I say, paaaah. . . . If I charge fl 35 instead of fl50. . . . I have to eat, you know." She obviously felt there was no need for an apology for charging under the standardized price if survival was at the root of her strategy. Even so, an unspoken rule of 50 guilders (20 Euro or $20) for a "suck and fuck" was still the going rate on the streets and her fellow streetwalkers took note of who was undercutting. Despite Anke's undercutting of prices for erotic services, she and other Dutch prostitutes believed that they couldn't make a living on the streets because undocumented "immigrants" were bringing the prices down.

The social strategies exercised by Anke, not unlike those shared among sex workers, reflect how prostitutes make sense of their professional realm on a daily basis. A boundary upheld around the maintenance of the body, such as in Anke's example of not streetwalking while menstruating, expresses ways Anke negotiates her needs with the commercial demands of her work. In addition to guaranteeing her survival, her codes of self-management facilitate a de facto regulation of prostitution sites in which Anke and others work.

Over the last twenty years many changes have occurred in the cultural production of prostitution sites. The arrival of many migrant sex workers has produced a disruption of social arrangements in the sex trade. These cultural discontinuities and adaptations have been ongoing and largely the result of an influx of ethnic groups from Latin America, Africa, and Eastern Europe. As many EU sex workers and Dutch prostitution advocates attest, migrants as an umbrella of ethnic groups have transformed both the representation of sex workers as well as modes of operation at prostitution sites. Thus embedded in the perception and professional tactics shared by Anke and other EU sex workers is a focus on the negative impact "immigrants" have on the sex trade in the Netherlands. Central to this belief is the assumption that migrants are solely responsible for a breach in protocol around observed standardized prices for services.[2] While the streets have become more competitive in terms of cultural diversity and services provided in the sexual marketplace, notions about undercutting, as a practice of migrants alone, are exaggerated. As in the case of Anke, and rumored of others, undercutting is a practice used by many migrant and EU streetwalkers alike.

As Anke's former client drives by in the darkness she comments, "he always shows up around when my period is about to start, he knows that I won't work if I am menstruating." What regular client is obligated, if at all, to frequent the same sex worker night after night? Anke's preoccupation with the would-be client was a way to vent a greater concern for she had not earned enough disposable income before starting her menstrual cycle. Based on her scant earnings, whatever unreported income she could generate would not get her through to the end of her menstrual cycle.

The Dutch social welfare system is considered to be one of the most generous in all of Western Europe. Anke, however, cannot manage her living expenses on her monthly subsidies. She supplements her social welfare check of about 1,200 guilders ($550) per month with streetwalking, but after rent, her benefits amounted to 860 guilders ($400) per month for any other amenities. Anke elaborated on the impossibility of surviving on either income source alone. On the previous Friday night, a night considered busy by most prostitutes, Anke made a meager 75 guilders ($35). This money earned on the streets she said would be used for purchasing clothes.

There were other anxieties weighing on Anke. Equally as pressing as her economic situation was the condition of her hair. A widow's peak on Anke's forehead marked a receding hairline of frizzy, brittle brown hair. Although I hadn't noticed much of a change since we last conversed the previous summer she expressed a growing anxiety around her hair loss as a result of diabetes medication. Around my follow-up to the *huiskamer* in January 2000, Anke was scheduled to have blood tests after noticing dramatic hair loss from increased dosage of her diabetes medication. Anke decided to cut back her dose to two capsules of insulin without medical supervision.

Around the *huiskamer* there was much talk about hair loss of other prostitutes. In particular, a Moroccan crack user named Sumia experienced hair loss as a result of syphilis (and scabies) that was later diagnosed when a nurse, another crack-addicted female prostitute, and myself, accompanied her to the emergency room of a local hospital. The diagnosis was an acute case of constipation from crack-cocaine use. Perhaps in an attempt to control rumors of her condition, Anke established that her hair loss was the result of diabetes medication.[3] Some staff members interpreted her health condition as a direct result of stresses caused from working on the streets; others would attribute it to Anke's self-created life of poverty and held her responsible for her life choices that produced her position. In spite of a "generous" welfare system and free health care in the Netherlands, it seemed that her social role was assigned to the economic and social margins with little dignity bestowed upon her.

During our multiple conversations, Anke's narrative moved in a non-linear structure between her experiences in the past and her life in the present. When talking about her life growing up, Anke defined herself as the "black sheep" of her family. She was estranged from her father, an auto mechanic, until his death. This estrangement was due to "something very bad" that he committed against her. She never forgave him, expressing her long-standing derision by refusing to attend his funeral. This decision caused a tension with her mother, with whom she is no longer on speaking terms. She also mentioned how her mother disapproved of Anke's early stint as a prostitute. Her mother is unaware of Anke's involvement in prostitution during the last ten years.

At fourteen years of age Anke left home and dropped out of high school. For eight years she worked as a cashier in a grocery store, taking pride in memorizing prices before the advent of scanners simplified the process. At the height of her combined incomes of prostitution, social welfare, and an unreported job at a hotel, she earned fl 6,000 per month, of which fl 4,000 were unreported income. In subsequent years social welfare agencies tried to assist Anke's reentry into the formal labor market. She expressed a favorable response to work in the service sector.[4] However Anke described herself as "too old," to work in the formal sector because "no one would hire [her]." After twenty years on social welfare she could not understand why the state was attempting to retrain people over forty years of age.

Just then Anke lit up a cigarette. Staring at the cigarette, she said, "I no longer drink and my only vice is smoking because it's too late to stop." Anke started smoking cigarettes at eleven; gave up an alcohol addiction at the age of eighteen; and began working as a prostitute at seventeen. "It was easy, I took customers from the bar where I worked. I was young then. They would give me fl 100."

Intimate relations also played a dramatic role in shaping Anke's life. She was married to a French man for five months. After that marriage ended in divorce, she was married to a Moroccan heroin-addict, whose name is tattooed on her forearms. However intolerable the situation may have been she was proud of never having become a "junkie" herself during their eighteen years together. The dealers, she said, respected her for never succumbing to addiction. Narcotic drug dealers used to slip her money for purchasing groceries after her husband spent all of their income for hard drugs. When reflecting on that period she said, "He took everything from me," leaving her to inherit his debt of fl 18,000 ($8,000).

There were two other significant relationships in Anke's life. She had a two-year relationship with a Ghanaian man who taught her English before he was deported back to his country of origin. Later Anke spent six years in a relationship with a Portuguese man who was violent toward her. She escaped the violence, though he later tracked her down and broke into her home, stealing all of her things. Not until the authorities caught up with this man was he eventually deported and removed from her life. With her history behind her, Anke prefers living alone, "since men, in particular junkies, take all your energy away."

In the context of those past relationships, Anke revealed an unfulfilled longing. She expressed a "love of children" however resigned herself to remain childless because she was without a long-term partner or the financial means to support a family. Wanting to give her child "everything," her economic circumstances gave her little opportunity to do so.

One winter evening in the *huiskamer,* while taking a break over a cup of coffee and a cigarette, Anke declared she could no longer make enough money from prostitution and therefore wanted to get out of the business. During this pronouncement there were numerous shifts in how Anke positioned herself in relation to sex work and her intimate relations. As Anke reflected on her poor material returns, she reassigned herself as a "victim" of sorts. In the context of past intimate relationships she explained how economic circumstances necessitated her streetwalking. However the "flexibility" of street prostitution allowed her to recoup monetary losses.[5]

During that conversation and subsequent others, Anke would pick up wherever we last left our dialogue. Dealing with male companions, she reported, had become easier ever since she began "keeping them around only for the weekend." This reference of "keeping them around" garnered her greater control when reconstructing her personal life. They treated her better, she said with an air of autonomy in her tone. Suddenly, Anke was no longer a "victim" of her intimate heterosexual relations.

Anke described an endearing South African friend who invited her to go with him on his last trip to Africa. They met on the street, not while she was streetwalking. Although this man doesn't call her with regularity, when he cooks for Anke, he always tells her to eat more because she is a "very important person." Anke did not expect the relationship to develop further because the lover was not that accessible since he exports used cars to Nigeria. In the reconstruction of this tale, sex was not central to the relationship. In fact, when Anke described being together with her lover, it was about "holding each other through the night," reporting that *he* "only wanted to have sex once per night," which often translated to having "sex only once per month."

Commercial consequences of resisting normative aesthetic rituals

On any given night Anke arrived at the *huiskamer* wearing one of her latest finds from the area street markets. Sometimes she walked in wearing a denim overall-style dress, loose cotton pants, or a pair of sneakers that became the central object of her conversation as she begrudgingly prepared for her street performance. Anke made it known to her colleagues how she disliked devoting time to ritualized aesthetic practices that now consisted of wearing a standard black spandex tube dress that concealed her protruding belly and wearing a pair of patent-leather platform boots that rode to her thigh to showcase her legs—her "best feature" as she referred to them. In the evening, much like during the day, Anke preferred wearing little make-up and no jewelry. Therefore, the extent to which Anke partook in any ritualized, cosmetic procedure consisted of a quick application of black eyeliner on her upper eyelids and a swab of red lipstick on her thin lips. She justified going without blush or make-up foundation because her complexion was already flushed from a mild case of eczema.

Anke's refusal to conform to many aesthetic street practices affected her economic circumstances and also aroused a negative reaction from many of her cohorts. One might assume that Anke's lack of desirability on the street benefited these same streetwalkers however this was not the source of their frustration. Instead, Anke's behavior was understood as a lack of self-initiative to improve her own economic value. In effect, fellow streetwalkers were tired of Anke's chronic complaining about a lack of customers and saw her appearance as a sign of Anke's inability to grasp aesthetic demands of the competitive market.

Whether Anke's physical presence diminished the symbolic value of the zone or whether she facilitated a financial boom for other streetwalkers is hard to tell. Countering these accusations about her lack of effort, Anke's legs were always "featured" with French fishnet stockings and knee high black suede boots. In the summer she wore straps with gold heels appealing to clients with a foot and shoe fetish. For instance, one client requested that she rest her shoes on the steering wheel as he stroked her legs and masturbated. Another paid her to walk across the street towards his car just so he could watch her walk. Anke suspected that he enjoyed looking at her legs in her short skirt. Customarily she wore a mini skirt, "because men like my legs." This articulated understanding leads me to believe that Anke knew well what her symbolic worth was on the street, however drew a parameter around how much aesthetic production she would invest in her street performance. Night after night, while taking a drag on her cigarette, Anke reproduced her appearance based on *her* normalized standard.

A commonly held belief on the streets is that customers prefer "younger" prostitutes to middle-aged ones. And while youth is commodified, Anke's clientele base remains mostly men between eighteen and twenty-one years of age. Most of these same clients are of African or Middle Eastern origins. After a few hours on the strip, Anke returned to the *huiskamer* reporting that a "small black male wanted services." After she agreed the potential client's "tall friend appeared" out of nowhere. Based on the latter man's size, Anke determined that she could not provide adequate sexual services because, as she put it, she was "too small" physically to perform genital contact.[6] Later Anke admitted that she had a "hard time keeping customers," because, "they say that I look 'angry' [while having sex]." That same evening Anke acknowledged that she had serviced only a single customer, however needed one more exchange before permitting herself to leave the zone. Her goal, she explained, was to earn enough money to purchase a pair of boots she had spotted at the open market. The overall denim dress she wore into the *huiskamer* that evening was an item purchased with work money made the night before, and now she wanted to return to the market for a pair of boots. Having turned down the two potential clients earlier in the evening, the night proved futile for

Anke, in bleak contrast to some of the high earners who were already on their way home.

As if to shift Anke's focus away from her disappointment, I inquired about a female Dutch prostitute named Betty who paired up with Anke throughout the previous summer. Anke's face lightened as she told me of Betty's pregnancy and how she was living with the father, an East African drug dealer who used to sell inside the *huiskamer*. Betty, she reported, was no longer working on the street. Whether Betty's companionship on the streets facilitated a more promising economic impact on Anke's business or whether time had exhausted Anke's profitability in the zone was an unanswerable thought kept to myself.

Anke's sexual parameters

During another field observation, Anke and a Surinamese woman sat together with me at a table. As Sumita applied makeup and worked on her hairpiece, Anke described the futility of her evening on the street: "My first possible client wanted a blow job without a condom; my second wanted the same; the third one didn't want to pay the amount and same with the fourth one." Even though Anke ended up with no earnings she had not acquiesced to unacceptable demands of potential clients. Both women commiserated over how many clients wanted sex or oral sex without a condom. These same men, we all agreed, returned to their wives at night. As another example they recalled a Pakistani man who frequented the zone, and whom they said should "know better" because he worked in a hospital. Another would-be client went as far as to claim, "His doctor told him he could have sex without a condom." With this comment, we all burst out into laughter at the rationalization. Anke added, " I eat with this mouth, I don't want that in my mouth . . . I make my boyfriend always wear one, too" The women surrounding the table all nodded in agreement as an African woman at the other end of the table joined in to say, "it's all in their head thinking the condom will make them go limp."

Anke didn't earn any money that evening, however while streetwalking she bumped into some of her regulars looking for a "little variety." She reported how some of her customers "crossed over" seeking services from transvestites. Their search for a variety of sexual practices left Anke wondering whether her customers wanted sexual services from a prostitute willing to perform anal sex. As for Anke, she made it known to all her peers that she thought this part of her body was "for [the purpose of] going to the bathroom." Although Anke refused to perform anal sex, she permitted, and even welcomed, her customers to fantasize about the sexual practice. One customer, she reported, orgasmed within seconds after he *imagined* that he was in her anus. When she finally revealed to him that he wasn't in her anus, she suggested that he "pretend" to have the experience.

Anke's parameters around refusing to perform anal sex represented status elevation for her and many female prostitutes as a way to distinguishing "common" prostitutes from those who would perform any sexual act for money. Retelling Anke's story of "pretending" to perform anal sex was a way of clarifying to her peers that she did not provide such services and ensured her status among her cohorts.

Anke also placed a time constraint on her clients. She was also not above communicating to customers that they should "hurry up" if they took longer than the standard ten minutes to complete a sexual exchange. She did not, however, charge more if an exchange exceeded more than ten minutes. On most occasions she performed a "standard service," straddled on top of larger clients. She reported that if clients enter her from behind, they ejaculated within seconds. On occasion, she said, clients requested her to orgasm to which she conveyed that since she was "here to work" the exchange should be about their experience, not hers.

Anke communicates with her customers quite clearly what other sexual roles she is willing or unwilling to perform. One customer who liked Anke for her legs told her he would never seek out her services again because, as she put it, she was "incapable of playing the dominant role because I can't shout at someone." Meanwhile, one elderly client, a single man who lived with his older sister told her "he felt 'peace' when he was with me because I don't talk much, I'm quiet and soft-spoken."

Sex on the streets and sex in Anke's personal life overlap partly because current boyfriends were once customers whom she met on the street. Enjoying sexual satisfaction with these same boyfriends has been elusive. Since Anke was seventeen years of age, around the same time she entered prostitution, experiencing an orgasm has been impossible. Anke took pleasure in being desired, and described how black men found her attractive. Understanding her desirability and market value, Anke described her very pale skin as highly attractive to some African and Arab men. In this instance, Anke constructs herself as exotic from the point of view of outsiders in the Netherlands.

During our conversation regarding the commercial appeal of whiteness, a tall African woman by the name of Lina entered the dressing room. During the previous night Lina and another woman from Sierra Leone accompanying her earned over fl. 700 ($325) and fl 1,100 ($500), respectively. The two undocumented women were back to work another informal shift in the zone. In utter disbelief at their reappearance, Anke threw out the rhetorical question of why they had come back that evening. She then turned to me and retorted, "I would have stayed home after making that much money."

Anke perceived the industrious work ethics favored by many migrants as a form of material insatiability. Rooted in this judgment is a deep cultural disjuncture between many EU and migrant sex workers around perceptions of work flexibility and accumulation of money. Besides the dominant group dictating what is an appropriate amount of earnings before retreating from the zone, this misconception overlooks how Anke and others ignore their own privilege as Dutch citizens. Unlike Dutch sex workers who have legal rights to reside, work, and even transgress the law with degrees of impunity, many African and Latin American prostitutes face conditions that lead to an intensification of work because of the temporary nature of their immigration status. Working underground and supporting dependents in their country of origin motivate migrant sex workers to work continuously through a workweek. At any moment migrant sex workers could be threatened with deportation by enforcement of immigration laws, as was the case of a few migrants in the zone after fellow EU sex workers revealed their illegal status to Dutch authorities.

And yet this very same competition between EU and migrant prostitutes has taken its toll on Anke who touches strands of her hair that effortlessly fall into her hands. Added to the competition and stress on the streets are the daily physical dangers. Earlier in that same evening she showed me a seven-inch knife that she carries and mentioned keeping a pair of scissors in her possession. She then recounted how four Moroccan boys once tried to jump her but how they ran off after she pulled her knife out. The economics of her daily life, however, presented the greatest strain, "I go out there, cars pass, other girls get customers but I don't. I wonder what is wrong with me. *What's wrong with me?*" Her voice cracks as she repeats her words.

Theorizing why Anke was such a marginalized member of the zone requires considering the intersection of her identity, community participation, and individual streetwalking tactics. Based on how privilege and social power is constructed in the Netherlands, Anke's Dutch citizenship and her knowledge of the Dutch social system might have provided her with material advantages on the streets. Despite her social locations, and her Northern European appearance, she rarely thrived in the market. Age, bodily morphology, personality, strategy tactics, and social class determined her ability to accumulate a large clientele base. Another setback for Anke was how she presented her professional persona to her peers. Couching her own narrative as part of a sweeping victimology running through her life did not sit well with many of cohorts who saw a direct relationship between Anke's codes of behavior and her social and economic predicament. In effect, her peers did not respect her streetwalking tactics or her choices in self-destructive intimate partners, and therefore were less inclined to show sympathy for her, or for that matter, look out for her.

But Anke is not a one-dimensional representation of personal failure and gendered subjugation. Even under increasing intensification of services and competition on the streets, and a lack of material success, Anke's account is resilient and thoughtful as an example of a person who is engaged with the struggles that are before her. In the face of economic and social marginality, her role in the zone also denotes an active participation in the making of a streetwalking culture. Cultural overlaps and disjunctures between her occupation and personal life illustrated Anke's membership in a prostitution community. Despite Anke's internalization of some of the more negative associations with "prostitution life," her approach to sex work functions as a historical artifact meshing and tugging cultural meanings and changes around Dutch sex work.

TO MIGRATE ACROSS THE STREET

During my first observation at the *huiskamer*, a staff member gave me a copy of a rubric pathologizing different transgendered identities and their corresponding sexual practices. Out of curiosity, I studied the graph in attempt to understand how the Dutch public health agencies might categorize the different groups present in the zone. I was uninhibited about showing this interpretation of sexual and gender identities with transgendered streetwalkers. Veronica was the first to dismiss these definitions as a way to control and monitor the community. The labels were wrong and didn't accurately represent the sexual practices of the groups that were mentioned. Other transgendered members clarified how these definitions and conceptualizations were limited to how heterosexuals saw transgendered people. At this stage in my exposure to the transgendered community, I was just beginning to learn about firsthand the diversity of gender and sexual identities in the zone.

As explained in an earlier chapter, the street walking zone is split in half in terms of the types of prostitutes working there, in effect enforcing an ideology of sexuality and gender onto the streets and the people who work there. Female and transsexual prostitutes stand on one side of the street and transgendered, including *travestíes* and transvestites, work on the other side. If a transgendered person has a sex reassignment, then she is expected to work on the "female" side of the street. Some transgendered prostitutes interviewed for this project were in the preoperative stages of a gender reassignment. Each person ascribed different meaning to a permanent gender migration[7] and how post-operative "tools" would impact her economic life.

This segment addresses concerns shared by transgendered sex workers before considering a "permanent" identity migration. The section illustrates how they frame transsexualism as a material and social reality in their professional lives. Both in terms of their identity claims and commercial services they provide, the implications have direct economic consequences for them. As a result of material factors that come into play when a transgendered sex worker considers a sex reassignment, embedded in this decision are tactics to ensure their economic and social survival on the streets and in the windows.

Each sex worker, regardless of what stage she was at in her gender migration, approached her identity claims and client relations differently. In the cases of Nadine, Veronica, and Victoria, each informant expressed emotional satisfaction with their transsexual identities and reported positive client relations. When communicating an understanding of her gender migration, Nadine, in particular, expressed a transparency around her recent transsexual identity. For the most part, she experienced no harmful response when disclosing her new sexual identity to her clients and no downward economic shift providing services as a transsexual. Unlike Nadine, Victoria chose not to disclose her transsexual identity with customers.

Unlike some sex workers who work in prostitution in a pre and post-operative state, Magdalena, a transgendered Brazilian, expressed a commercial need for maintaining her "intersexed" body parts.[8] This informant described the vital role of her male genitals as part of her success as an "exoticized" prostitute providing unique sexual performances. For this informant her penis remained an appendage used for labor purposes, but without much erotic function or meaning in her personal life. Not until Magdalena retires from prostitution will she consider an operative reassignment. In this instance, an operative gender migration was described as a sacred ritual waiting to be traversed, in which genital reconfiguration will not be for commercial use.

Some sex workers anticipated a transsexual migration as a fulfilling process, while for others, the course appeared wrought with emotional fear and material uncertainty. Still, for some sex workers the notion of a "migration" as a physical act seemed an unnecessary process to achieve a gendered identity. The responses were highly subjective and depended on how a sex worker felt about her "marketability" on the street. For one transgendered sex worker, a physical transformation held no significance to her material viability in prostitution, however for others a sex reassignment did not translate into economic fortuity. "Angst" describes the dominant emotion shared by numerous sex workers who are contemplating an invasive and total gender migration.

A Dutch transgendered informant, Desiree,[9] embodies such fears around a sex reassignment. The removal of her Adam's apple left a scar across her throat as an emblem of her first steps toward a migration. However after five years of unmonitored hormone ingestion she has spent another five years taking hormones regulated by a physician. The hormones, she says, "played tricks on her head," giving her the feeling of never knowing where she was at any given moment. Desiree's thoughts on a sex reassignment and then having to make her livelihood on the street as a transsexual feel uncertain for her. She expects that when she follows through with her sex-reassignment operation, "I will lose all my customers [because] they love that I look like a woman but have the (pointing to her genitals) male gear."[10]

Not everyone on the cusp of a sex reassignment anticipates the same dire economic predictions as Desiree. Agnese, a transgendered Ecuadorian in her late 30s, faces other concerns about making a gender identity transition. Shortly after I met Agnese, she revealed her unaltered, flattened chest to me. Although she had cosmetic surgery to her nose, she declared having permanently postponed breast augmentation.[11] Dressed in a conservative dark blue suit and jacket, she resembled a schoolteacher, an occupation she dreamed of pursuing since she was a child. The mistreatment of gays in Ecuador, she said, had prevented her from finishing her studies, however later she attended hairdressing school. During that period in her life, Agnese lived as a gay man in Quito. The idea of living as a woman or a transgendered person, or contemplation of taking female hormones and silicone injections had not been conceived until she moved to the Netherlands.

After illegally migrating to there, she began a new life as a transgendered person. In the nine years that followed since settling there, she had become fluent in English, had entered a stable seven-year relationship with a Dutch man that provided her legal residency, financially supported her mother and family in Ecuador, and maintained two properties in the Netherlands and Latin America. "*Travestí*s are treated differently now [in Ecuador]," she says, "We have power because we have money and everything." Hence being identified as a "*travestí*" rather than as a gay man elevated her status in Ecuador. Adding to the sense of belonging in the Netherlands, she says, "*travestí*s are treated with respect."

Agnese described contemplating "the operation" after having already delayed the procedure once before, when surgeons wanted to simultaneously augment her breasts and build her a vagina. Despite medical recommendations to complete the sex reassignment in this way, Agnese had other ideas about how the operative sequence should follow for her. She preferred having her breasts augmented first, and then once adjusted to the change, having her genitals reconstructed. She was particularly distressed over the institutionalization of the sex reassignment procedure because she could not control the invasive process to which her body would be subjected. The fact that a medical board had to approve her candidacy for a gender migration only made matters worse for her. To date, Agnese's insurance has covered laser surgery for facial hair removal (a procedure that costs over fl 8,000 or $3,500), but the ultimate decision for initiating procedures is in the hands of psychiatrists determining who is an appropriate candidate and when they are "ready."

Unlike Desiree, Agnese expressed confidence that her clients would remain with her after the operation. When asked whether her clients sought her out for her penis or anal sex, a practice customers might be less inclined to seek out from a female, she declared that all of her clients were Dutch, and that Dutch men are just "sexual" and "don't care who they are with [because on] one day they go with a transgendered and the next to a woman. Mostly I suck. Sometimes they suck me. But usually they are surprised when they see my penis."

Lastly, a few transgendered sex workers expressed the view that operative modification in the construction of a gender identity was irrelevant to how they viewed themselves or their material well-being. Kasmira, a transgendered Rumanian who received political asylum in the early 1990s, and Steluta, a Rumanian transvestite,[12] expressed how they could not find a justifiable reason for "having to be a woman only [by] wearing a particular item or having the surgery."[13] Regardless of their opinion about sex reassignments, both informants sought some external modification to serve their transgendered and transvestite niche markets. In the case of Kasmira, she appeared to have had breast augmentation and facial cosmetic surgery. Steluta admitted to having shaved her entire body to appear hairless. Both expressed "that [body modification] won't make you happy, but it can be achieved by just accepting who you are in that moment."[14]

The previously described narratives on gender migration represent individualized and collective examples of the fluid definition of gender and suggest how such configurations have the potential to shift outside of a "continuum" that flanks the Western ideology of gender. They express more than a climate of accessibility through medical intervention. It would also be limiting to assume such gender migrations as simply a matter of "personal choice" informed by the market place where subjects sell services based solely on their gender configuration or that it is a consequence of consumer practices in which expressions of life-style is the central focus of one's existence without mentioning how the gender and sexual identities identified were social produced. In this case, it is fair to consider the role of the state. Because of the increasing normalization of this gender migration process, a few subjects mentioned in passing that what was taking place could only have occurred with a degree of ease under the favorable social climate of the Netherlands.

Dutch policy facilitates such options, albeit under heavy medical supervision when determining who is a proper candidate for a gender reassignment and how that sequence should take place. Nonetheless, the state and its public health policy support of gender reassignment plays a key role in the formations of multiple gender identities and what genders are designated as a medical possibility. This is not to suggest that all gender migrations and configurations are simply the end result of the state's terms of agreement. Some of the narratives presented around gender migration are also the products of highly repressive cultural conditions; in particular, many Rumanian and Latin American transgendered people endured horrific violence and discrimination for their gender and sexual identities in their countries of origins. Those same repressive conditions produced forms of resistance and expressions of dissent through gender performances. Hence, the results of which have had a direct impact on how transgendering manifests and evolves in those same people who are now living in the Netherlands.

TRICKS OF THE TRADE

Each sex worker uses a variety of performative techniques as part of her daily routine on the streets. Besides providing the standard 15-minute "suck & fuck" for 25 Euro, sex workers delve into other commercial practices when exchanging services with clients. These tactics are often forms of simulation, or mediated through technology, space, and identity politics. Often performative tactics used by anatomically born females, transsexuals or transgendered informants are not exclusive to any one or all of the groups mentioned. Sometimes transgendered sex workers influenced tactics and sexual practices of "female-born" streetwalkers and vice versa. Victoria, Nadine, Magdalena, Desiree, and Agnese, all transgendered, helped to link these practices to their economic returns as well as find value in their function as physical or emotional safety measures. Rather than interpreting these practices as forms of manipulation, I suggest reading these sexual performance techniques of simulation as "coping" methods used to economize their efforts and as a way to counter taxing working condition.

Cost Invention

Seven years ago, the streetwalking zone was located closer to the center of Den Apelhaven. The former location had many conveniences economically benefiting sex workers. Easily accessible from the main road into the City on foot, by tram, or automobile, the site afforded streetwalkers a provision of services they could offer at neighboring hotels. Evidently, the site also had its risks as a less controllable, porous space with no formal parameters keeping drug users at bay. But those were also the days when a streetwalker could actually stand under a real streetlight or sit on the hood of her car, and without notice vacate the area. This situation changed when the new mayor of Den Apelhaven decided to move street prostitution to a less visible site in a remote industrial area.

The advantages of the old streetwalking location were implicit in the services arranged between sex worker and client. As it happened, most sexual services were easily transferred to a nearby hotel room. This tactical strategy not only moved the sexual exchange from the prostitution site to the private sphere but also transformed the exchange into an anticipated and costly event. Tacked on to the relocation were costs including rental of a hotel room on a per hourly basis and costs for the time it took to reach that location. The simple sexual exchange therefore became an anticipated performative act costing over hundreds of Dutch guilders.

In the subsequent years a new site was designated, transforming commercial relations. For instance, convincing a client to move a sexual transaction to a hotel has now amounted to a creative effort difficult to arrange and execute. If a transaction transfers to a hotel then sex workers should expect to perform more elaborate performances than a standard ten-minute "suck 'n fuck." This adjustment in the commercial arrangements could amount to committing a few hours to a single client or fulfilling an elaborate role dictated by a client's whimsical fantasy. The impact on the sex worker's time and effort with a single client are intensified.

Less accessible satellite streetwalking locations, therefore, force prostitutes to find inventive ways of using the space afforded them. Today, as a result of the existing streetwalking zone, most sexual exchanges are relegated to the confines of the front seat of a car unless the client agrees otherwise. In the instance where the transaction remains in an automobile within the zone, the main object of negotiation becomes maintenance of standard prices rather than the tacking on of costs or performing a fantasy.

"Finishing Up"

Most sex workers understand their job as a service where they provide sexual satisfaction to the client. The focus of the transaction is clearly on fulfilling the client's sexual needs. Only on rare occasions does this exchange arouse sexual desires for the sex worker.[15] Simulation of sexual reciprocity, however, exists during most exchanges. When a client requests for a sex worker to experience erotic satisfaction, the visual representation of the sex worker climaxing translates to a performance for additional cost.[16] Framing the sex workers' role in this way allows them an economy of effort when dealing with a high volume of clientele and enforces emotional and physical barriers between "authentic" sexual desires experienced in their intimate lives and their professional work.

The term "finishing up," is a common colloquialism on the streets for orgasm. When clients desire for the sex worker to "finish up," a performance from sex workers requires a number of techniques to simulate an orgasm. In the instance of transsexual and female sex workers, extra lubricant is used as "evidence" that their desires for the client are reciprocal. After which, in a theatrical climax, most sex workers fabricate a physical experience through muscle contractions, simulating a vaginal spasm for the sake of meeting a client's need for "physical evidence."

"Speeding Up"

Most standard sexual transactions take, on average, about ten minutes to complete. On occasions when sex workers have experienced a labor-intensive shift, have personal health conditions that hinder their physical stamina, or they have a need to complete an exchange promptly, accelerating a commercial procedure with a client can become a necessity. "Speeding up" of the sexual transaction is another technique used by transgendered and female sex workers to guarantee earnings on a per hourly basis without them having to follow-through with an agreed upon service. This standard technique requires clients to pay for services before hand, and then involves the prostitute to "accidentally" over stimulate the client's genitals, effectively causing premature ejaculation. This stroking method abruptly puts a halt to additional services while focusing on the client's "lack of control." Since the client has already paid for the services, and achieved an orgasm in the process, the sex worker can expect to keep all money charged at the onset of the agreement.

Phantom Penetration

Some transgendered and female sex workers use another technique involving "phantom" genital contact when providing services to their client. In this instance, prostitutes simulate sexual acts without the client's knowledge. Meanwhile, clients believe they are experiencing anal or genital penetration when, in fact, no such event is occurring. Numerous prostitutes described how they held the client's penis in such a way that there was no genital entry or contact. In most instances, the sex worker can sense that the client was completely unaware of what was not being performed. Given the risks of STDs, and the physical exhaustion that can occur when a sex worker has an active night, this technique of a phantom penetration makes the exchange less physically taxing on her body.

Hands on

Lastly, Victoria and others described systematically holding the client's testicles in their hands during all commercial exchanges. This tactic ensures that sex workers have some control over their immediate environment, and are able to disable the client should he behave inappropriately. Victoria recalled the following story that required using this technique. Shortly after the murder of a local streetwalker, during a commercial exchange a client fixated on the details of the murder trying to evoke fear in her. The client went as far as to put his hands around Victoria's neck as he spoke. Recognizing the potential danger surrounding her, Victoria squeezed the client's testicles with enough force to completely diminish whatever potential threat this client might have been to her.

The debates that overly eroticize power take many forms in and outside of compulsory heterosexuality, and as mentioned in the Introduction, radical feminism. The previous examples described in "tricks of the trade" could be qualified as individual tactics, however they should also be designated as acts of dissent to undermine the existing sexual order. Whether or not these tactics were performed by "transgressive or progressive" sexual outlaws, both the sexual acts and the people performing them possess a taken for granted "sexual license," whereby they are conducting themselves from a privileged position (Jackson, 1996: 19). Sex workers collective awareness of these "tricks of the trade" and deployment of them raises other questions regarding the discourse on the act of phallo-penetration. Phallo-penetration encodes all bodily protrusions as crafted as a symbolic form of male power (Jackson, 1996: 29). The previous commercial tactics might also suggest that it is possible to contest the "power of the penis" or resignify it as it encounters new genders and sexual practices. It further challenges why all material power that men disproportionately possess must relate to their penis and its whereabouts.

SAFETY MEASURES

Staying in the zone

The physical place where the sexual exchange takes place certainly evokes great concern when considering issues of safety. A composite of a murder suspect hangs on the glass window of "The Living Room" as a reminder of the risks prostitutes take each time they enter a client's automobile. To some extent a need for self-protection regulates how sex work is exchanged and restricted in public and commercial space. Traveling from the zone to a hotel promises material gains, however once a streetwalker leaves the zone in a client's automobile, she is no longer surveyed by her other colleagues or video cameras on the main street. Despite facing this potential threat, sex workers continue working outside the zone. Many prostitutes manage meeting clients outside of the designated area or, in some instances, inviting regular clientele into their homes. Usually crossing this threshold into their personal space is only advisable after meeting a client numerous times and establishing a mutual understanding.

The business has changed since twenty years ago when working as a prostitute was impossible without a pimp. Today most window and drug-free streetwalkers operate on their own. Legalization of the industry and clustering of prostitutes creates a self-regulating atmosphere in the zone. With the exception of drug-addicted females and some Eastern European women, the pimp as a "safety enforcer" has become obsolete because of police presence and social workers who now function as de facto guardians of prostitution sites.

The question remains whether sex workers in the windows and in the streetwalking zone have found autonomy resulting from standardization. For the window prostitutes to whom I spoke, there was a sense of comfort and assurance in the windows. The police, of course, could not be everywhere at all times nor could friends in neighboring windows. Ramona, an Ecuadorian *travestí*, attested that she has never had a problem working in the windows and neither has Magdalena, although she articulated concerns of a "Serbian mob" that might come by and take her papers. There are layers to the types of prostitution that exist, some of which are concealed under the guise of window leasing, "boyfriends" and contactors who encourage friends and family to immigrate. In theory, the window, as an entrepreneurial establishment, operates in close proximity to other windows and other economies that warrant a degree of conformity in densely populated areas, however there are elements that are underground and invisible to advocates and police.

Learning the hard way: Cash first, please, and knowing when to cut your losses

Ramona's history in prostitution has changed since she began working in the windows of Amsterdam during the 10am to 7 pm shift. At thirty years of age, Ramona, a *travestí*, has been in the sex trade for over four years. When she arrived from Ecuador by way of Paris, she had ample rules to govern her enterprise. The rules included always wearing a condom, never kissing, and taking the money before an exchange. Even when the parameters were set in place, these rules were subject to change because of clients who behaved aggressively towards her.

While in Paris, Ramona worked on the streets in the area around Sacre Coeur Church. She spent one year there working under unsafe and "wild" conditions. There she also witnessed some violence. One time, someone stole her bag and she lost everything. Then, Ramona described how a client lured her into a hotel without paying her first. As a result of this exchange, she always takes the money first. The most dramatic and potentially life-threatening experience occurred when she entered an automobile not noticing that there were men sitting in the back. They demanded sex without a condom and without pay. Ramona, thinking fast, convinced them to use a condom. This situation, by any standard, was a nonconsensual exchange constituting as a form of rape, however Ramona never defined the experience as such. In the end, there was the added humiliation and violence of being thrown out of a car after the sexual assault. Ramona is grateful that she escaped alive and relatively unharmed, chalking it up as a hazard on the street and for her lack of experience.

Because of safety issues, Ramona finally left Paris on a travel visa. This occurred after being thrown out of the country on two separate occasions. She worked for a time streetwalking in another part of the Netherlands before moving to Brussels, Belgium where she was forced into a "business arrangement" with a pimp. As an example of his power, the pimp asserted his position by beating up another prostitute who had refused to pay him. This display of attempted domination frightened Ramona and became the deciding factor for returning to the Netherlands.

Even in the windows, she still faces the occasional grievance largely due to her feminine facial structure. Most of her clients are "heterosexual" men who are tourists, however some customers are Dutch. If the client does not know she has male genitals, hiding them becomes a challenge for her. She can usually tell when the client doesn't know because they are more "gentle, easy, show me respect, sometimes they ask about my children, whether I have any." Yes, even with regular customers, Ramona asked aloud, "How can they not know? I think they are stupid." She then comments that some of her customers are "more like women, more like five women combined."

On a few occasions where a client doesn't know of her transgendered identity there is the risk of the client expressing anger. In this instance, the client usually demands that Ramona "give [them their] money back," In order not to have problems, Ramona returns their money. Overall, the working conditions of the windows suit her in a number of ways: a. they were safe; b. the space felt like her home; c. she could order food; d. she could wash after each client; e. the windows maintained a sense of routine to her day.

ENTERING OR AVOIDING SOCIAL SERVICE AGENCIES

As explored in an earlier chapter, prostitution locations are regulated by numerous social service agencies. Every individual who comes in contact with agencies involved in regulation of prostitution sites becomes a quantifiable object under surveillance. The end results are "objectifying knowledges" produced to control STDs and HIV transmission, educate on safe sex procedures, understand the vitals of who is working in the industry, and determine how policy best fits the different forms of erotic labor that exists in the Netherlands. As a result of this intrusiveness, staying out of the "system" by sheer avoidance or refusing to give honest information to public health workers, social welfare services, the city police, immigration police, the residency registration, and the Ministry of Finance translates into a strategy of resistance from being "absorbed" into their data. Not surprisingly, migrants have an easier time remaining undetected by these controlling institutions than Dutch nationals who are a registered entity with the national bureaucracy since the time of their birth. Of course, once a migrant begins the residency process, she, too, enters an elaborate multi-tiered state and local system designed to exclude some candidates and award rights and responsibilities to others.

Similar to Foucault's "disciplinary discourses," Dorothy Smith also identifies "objectified knowledges"—medical records, prisons, and other institutions—as central to the maintenance of power. Such classifications rob individuals of their everyday life occurrences, and instead replace them with mass interpretation of the dominant society. Concealed within clinical texts and public health models that gather statistical data on sex workers is a gendered bias with abstractions and truth claims (Seidman, 1994: 307). This conceptualization of the (disorderly) gendered body marks every piece of knowledge produced whether inside the academy or in the form of scientific objectivism. Such claims are then positioned and presumed as "universal" (Seidman, 1994: 309).

In the instance of the medical establishment, psychiatry, and prisons, individuals become further abstracted in the process of being categorized for statistical purposes. Lived experiences are then reduced to classifications of symptoms and labeling, the later set a standard of normative conditions and behavior. However even with a plethora of parameters around behavior and the public/mental health model there are gaps through which sex workers and transgendered people can evade these constructing labels (Seidman, 1994: 310).

Many sex workers perceive these social service agencies and the intrusion of social workers entering the Living Room for the purpose of gathering data on their lives as an annoying if not ineffectual part of their professional lives. Most sex workers simply accept their intrusive presence, while acknowledging that they are pawns in the political agendas of each agency. A part of that perception is directed at who or what group is made a priority to these agencies. It is common belief that agencies prioritize some ethnic groups' needs while neglecting others. To support this perception about who gets pushed to the margins and who is a "social concern" or "social problem" for Dutch agencies, Valeria vocalized her hypothesis that if she, as a Dutch citizen, and Steluta, a Rumanian transvestite wanting residency status, were both to walk into a social service agency at the same time, she believed social workers would help Steluta before they would assist her. As a working-class Dutch citizen, Valeria felt utter contempt for the role of public health workers whom she believed marginalized many Dutch nationals who worked in prostitution by denying them services and respect.

In the case of Steluta, a Rumanian transvestite, Valeria's hypothesis holds some currency. For Steluta, prostitution in the Netherlands has led indirectly to residency and transitioning out of the industry. She described her experience on the streets of Den Apelhaven as her "education" and a painful process because she was never "meant for this kind of work" as a self-described "soft and open" person in a competitive market. With the assistance of staff at the *huiskamer*, Steluta began filling out employment forms given to her at a local social service agency. She was surprised that when disclosing to social workers "that I'm a homosexual, and I do prostitution," "they didn't laugh," or act differently toward her. As a result, the agency has paid for Steluta's Dutch language course, access to health care, and employment at a geriatrics hospital. In effect, Steluta is now integrating into mainstream Dutch society and benefiting from being in the system.

Steluta's case may be rare, because often migrant "invisibility' amounts to not having some services available to them, outside of the free STD or HIV testing that they provide. For Dutch citizens, however, having services available doesn't always translate into privileges. Mandatory STD and HIV testing is a public health measure that requires constant vigilance to avoid. Valeria is an example of someone who has never paid taxes, and never sought public assistance. The police do not know her real name, and she likes that arrangement. Her sentiment is that once in the system, agencies will ask with an air of judgment and suspicion, "'why are you looking for aid now, and how were you supporting yourself before?'" This authoritative presence of social agencies in the lives of most prostitutes leads a few EU sex workers to regain their autonomy in less than conventional ways. It is a matter of "no longer existing" for Valeria and another female Dutch friend who have "disappeared" since city and state registries no longer know where they live or whether they "contribute to the state [through income taxes]." If asked, Valeria's mother knows to inform them that her daughter lives in Thailand.

What does this anonymity afford Valeria? A few years back she was involved in a stabbing of a would-be client who harassed her and made insulting remarks about her mother. Valeria disappeared but another sex worker, who resembled her, was arrested. Her double snitched on Valeria, a rule not to be broken on the street, but nothing came of the incident because Valeria simply no longer "existed" in the social system.

Around the time Valeria disclosed her "invisibility" to me, a pair of social workers were spotted entering the zone and heading for the Living room. As we watched two confident and well-suited women enter the building, Valeria commented that the social workers "act like they know what it's like to be a prostitute but they can't because they have never been through the experience." Implicit in her comments was an overt contempt for their very presence. As for the police, Valeria said, "they do nothing. They're never here to protect us." Which, I might add, was the consensus of many streetwalkers.

CARING FOR THE SELF

How sex workers organize their intimate relations can also involve a strategy for indirectly handling their work. As a coping device, some sex workers refuse to allow commercial relations to enter their personal lives, while others desire to retreat from intimate relations altogether. Among some sex workers, the distinction between commercial relations and their private sphere blurs, as high numbers of them engage in personal relationships with their former clients. Whether positive status is conferred onto the relationship largely depends on the behavior of the boyfriend/former client. In the case where client relations are transformed into the "personal" realm they are legitimated in new and meaningful ways. However, because client/prostitute relations function as an "architectural apparatus" in which the state regulates the behavior of clients, these relations can be understood as a controlling force inside the private sphere.

Long-term relationships with EU citizens benefit transgendered and transvestite sex workers in a number of ways. These relationships provide emotional and economic stability, and make it possible to obtain residency visas when one party is not an E.U. citizen. Such an arrangement can lead to a state recognized partnership, cultural assimilation, and permanent Dutch residency. This status for migrants, therefore, is contingent on the Dutch government's acknowledgement of long-term, monogamous "same-sex" relationships.

After a twelve-hour shift, just before dawn, Pamela and I took a train home together. As the train pulled out and exhaustion set in under her skin, Pamela longed to wash off the night's sweat and fluids, and most of all to fall asleep. She anticipated seeing her companion only for a few minutes before her partner would depart for his civil servant post. She described her relationship as convenient and stable, but lacking the kind of emotional intensity someone younger and more idealistic might expect of a relationship.

Pamela's long-term relationship benefited her in a number of ways. Pamela was now a Dutch resident with the option of becoming a citizen. Cultural integration into Dutch society meant she had learned the Dutch language and understood how Dutch bureaucracies operate in this society. Her two-income household provided her with economic stability, and also afforded Pamela yearly two-month vacations during which she returned to Brazil to oversee the construction of her home. The Dutch government's recognition of long-term gay partnerships made Pamela's mobility and status possible.

While we rode across the Dutch countryside, Pamela described her first gay relationship in Brazil. The relationship was marked with a passion and illicitness partly because of the minor status of her lover and partly because homophobia underlies Brazilian culture. That relationship was a risk capable of socially destroying Pamela had her family discovered the liaison. In the end, there were other more important obligations for Pamela, such as her father's lost cannery operation and the need to regain the family's social standing. The devaluation of the Brazilian currency was partially responsible for forcing Pamela to forego her passion and assume a sense of responsibility to regain the family "fortune" through prostitution. She was in the Netherlands, therefore, to make money with no time for reckless relationships. As the train pulled into the outskirts of the City, Pamela pointed out an elegant high-rise apartment where she lives with her companion.

Choosing a solitary life without a principal companion can function as a strategy for some sex workers. During a follow-up visit to the Netherlands, one year after my initial interviews with Victoria, she was just coming out of another tumultuous relationship. Through e-mail correspondence, I learned many of the details that led up to her Pakistani boyfriend stealing her fabled sports car. The former lover was now on the lam from Victoria and the police, but during the course of that year, this companion disrupted her life and took advantage of her material worth. When Victoria finally "kicked him out of [her] life," the sports car and the ownership papers had already been stolen and resold but she was free of him.

Now, in his place, a two hundred pound statue of the Buddha sits in the corner of her living room. Each evening, Victoria playfully sits in her English leather chair and holds the hand of her tranquil Buddha. "He," she said, "is the only man in my life" from now on. Victoria has resigned herself to a solitary path after a succession of relationships that didn't work out. With additional schooling to become a nurse practitioner, she cannot afford distraction from a destructive lover.

Another example is Chandra. Now in her mid forties, Chandra came from Suriname to the Netherlands at the age of nine. She began presenting herself as transgendered very early in her life. She is nostalgic for the old days of working as a streetwalker; the work she said used to be enjoyable, but those days are now long gone. She recalled, too, when the *huiskamer* was on an open street near the center of Den Apelhaven. During those times she made good money. There was also a stint in window prostitution until she entered a relationship and, like Victoria, stopped working while emotionally involved with someone. Now, after seven years in one relationship, one and half in another, Chandra prefers her arrangement of being alone.

Unlike Victoria or Chandra, Ramona described the emotional toll sex work has had on her relationships. Recently, she went back to Ecuador to formally break up a five-year relationship with her boyfriend who is now married to a woman and fathered two children. Another brief relationship with a Dutch man proved to be too wide a cultural divide for them to sustain a commitment. When she finally met someone for whom she felt love, the feelings were not reciprocal. They never consummated the relationship, however Ramona did disclose her professional position as a sex worker. As she put it, her daytime job "works on the brain of boyfriends." Her work has taken its toll on relationships, and although she dreams of love, between falling for the "wrong man" and the demands of sex work, relationships become "harder and harder to develop."

Embedded in Estrella's standard rule never to kiss a client is the declaration "never to fall in love." An Ecuadorian transvestite in the zone, she is another who has grown tired of the emotional maintenance of relationship as she balances erotic labor with her personal life. Sometimes Estrella finds sexual gratification with customers, whom she desires, however she flatly refuses to allow anyone into her private life because she "doesn't believe in love."

CONCLUSION

This chapter is an ambitious attempt at linking many individualized practices, and at times incongruous themes, to how sex workers cope with the
demands of their work and its impact on their personal lives. It is ambitious
because of the effort it takes to grasp nuances that are "praxis," for
instance, in the life of Anke. Fleshing out her strategies is inseparable from
her narrative and relationship to other sex workers, therefore making her
strategies necessary to write about them as part of her professional and personal life. At the same time, framing a sex reassignment as a "coping strategy" or survival tactic may seem out of place here. However when
reframing debates about gender migration as having a social and economic
impact on transsexuals and inter-sexed people, a "strategy" evolves out
from the decision to have a sex reassignment or not. Considering, too, how
sex workers respond to the invasive presence of social workers and nurses
can also develop into a response that is closely tied to their well-being and
survival. Valeria's decision to remain outside of the system is as justifiable
as Steluta's decision to gain access to benefits as an "immigrant." Here the
micro-practices and responses of Valeria and Steluta are in direct reaction
to sweeping immigration and employment policies as much as they are
about public health initiatives and "being in the system." As a result, a coping strategy often develops around sex workers' intimate lives and what
impact it will have on their civil rights, in the case of monogamous transgendered people. By now it's fair to say that none of these findings are in a
social vacuum. The practices described in this chapter are directly shaped
by the environment and regulation of sex work as much as they are the
product of public attitudes and expectations of clients. Hence, the formation of sex worker communities is the results of many social forces at play
on their interests. By framing these tactics as forms of "coping," it draws to
the surface the material and emotional conditions under which sex workers
work and how their response affects the quality of their lives.

Chapter Eight
Conclusion

My research explores how the everyday quality of life for most prostitutes is influenced when the state grants social and economic rights to sex workers. Of the twenty-two sex workers whom I interviewed, seventeen were transgendered streetwalkers, of which eleven held "im/migrant" status. This collective group shares their coping strategies exercised on the streets and in the windows, and demonstrate ways in which they must adapt to changes in Dutch prostitution. Their anecdotal knowledge gives some indication of how prostitutes make sense of their professional realm, and also suggest ways they disrupt existing sexual hierarchies. Informants communicated their understanding of how labor processes link to personal self-management styles and to commercial practices affecting their earnings and labor negotiation abilities and their intimate lives. My study draws on social forces driving sex work, and indirectly how the market place reinforces their daily commercial practices, shaping their knowledge about their work. This latter point links social relations to issues of race, class, sexuality, and gender systems; further implicating standardized prostitution in the reproduction of societal inequalities and social resistance to those conditions.

In the Netherlands, where I gathered data for six months over the course of two and a half years, debates of political agency for sex workers are understood from a standpoint of economic legitimacy, transforming sexual labor into a productive activity. This means that labor laws and regulations interpret prostitution like any other form of work. The significance of studying legalized prostitution in the context of the Netherlands holds particular salience as my data suggest. The Dutch regulatory approach to prostitution is a vanguard in terms of European prostitution policy, however social conditions that this system produces generate problems and concerns related to "legalized" and informal sectors that operate there. In the last twenty years, changes in the cultural production of Dutch prostitution sites have transformed the structural organization of sex work and social relations for those who perform erotic labor. The most obvious result has been full legal status granted to the industry. In regard to the human factor, there are other implications for the industry. Namely, in the last twenty-five years, a large influx of many migrant and transgendered sex workers, who are not exclusively but sometimes both transgendered and migrant, have relocated from Latin America, Africa, and Eastern Europe to the Netherlands.[1] Their presence, in particular, has resulted in a disruption of many social arrangements in commercial sex, producing cultural discontinuities and forcing new adaptations at these sites. [2]

The decision of national and city governments to recognize sex work as a form of labor and to refuse giving out residency visas to migrant sex workers who fill an obvious employment demand is just one of the contradictory situations that sets the tone for Dutch prostitution (The Immigration and Naturalization Service brochure, 2002). Recent Dutch immigration reform focuses on the "migrant" as a disruptive presence in the European Union, however fails to answer the question of economic incentives and opportunities that drive migration to the Netherlands. If the Dutch government decides to make migrants' working conditions less exploitative or provides greater rights to them, are they concerned that more "Third World" people will try to work there as well? As long as migrants are considered an invisible underclass, and as long as immigration enforcement continues to occur sporadically, as it has in recent times, migrants will remain a part of an informal labor market and at the losing end of a two-tier prostitution sector. The way to improve this situation for migrants begins with Immigration and Naturalization laws that prohibit administering work visas to erotic laborers (The Immigration and Naturalization Service brochure, 2002). Most other market sectors can "import" human labor if they cannot fill a position with a Dutch employee. This rule applies to all sectors with the exception of prostitution. The only way to assuage this two-tier system is by recognizing that migrant sex workers fill an employment need in the Netherlands, and then granting greater rights to them.

The issues affecting migrants should not take away from issues affecting the quality of life for Dutch and EU sex workers. Competition with migrants has undercut pricing but sex workers who are voluntarily working in the industry face their own struggle to gain other forms of legitimacy. Legal window prostitutes have to deal with a plethora of social and economic issues that are sometimes beyond their control. Many Dutch sex workers complained of physical and emotional drain from their work, but described public judgment and mistreatment of prostitutes as more taxing on them than their actual work. First, Dutch society continues to stigmatize the sex worker. The fact that banks refuse to give prostitutes housing mortgages is just one example of how erotic labor is looked down upon and still not perceived as a legitimate form of work. Second, I do not know if "transforming" the meaning of sex work in the writing of academic papers really changes the nature of the exchange or how larger society interprets sex work. Getting rid of the pimps and middle managers was an excellent way of creating more autonomy for sex workers, but as my description of the sex-clubs suggests, most sex workers are employed in these places that are diminishing their rights and control over their work.

The mechanics of sex work is about getting paid to fulfill other people's sexual needs and fantasies. There is boredom on the job, and close physical contact with people whom sex providers might find undesirable. Most sex workers would agree that they perform this line of work for the money and take little pleasure in the type of work they do. Some sex workers find meaning in the way that they mitigate the loneliness of clients. In reality, the income levels that they can generate drive sex workers. They are also deeply aware of the clientele they serve. Most clients are heterosexual men who have disposable income. Acknowledging this cycle of consumption for clients and the economic incentives the industry provides for many women and transgendered people leads me to realize that this industry will not disappear in my lifetime. As a result of this realization, I have opted to support a regulatory approach in this context.

TRANSGENDERED SEX WORKERS

Social constructionism gives academic license for greater interrogation of previously assumed naturalized notions of gender and sexuality (Gamson, 2004; Lorber, 1994; Sedgewick, 1994 Butler, 1989). Heterosexuality is no longer assumed to be a product of nature but rather a process of normalization. Under this lens, queer theory has emerged as a driving analytical tool through which locating the social production of sexual identities as byproducts of historical forces is made possible. Furthermore, it allows the examination of "the role of the state in the regulation of sexuality" and the value of deploying deconstructive methodologies for exposing how heteronormativity is a "central principle" in the construction of all other sexualities (Gamson; 1995). Hence, it is not possible to write about "homosexuality" or "transgenderism" "outside of the current conception of [hetero]sexuality" (Namaste, 1996). Latin American sexual typologies further confront a Western ideology of sex and gender with alternative ways to interpret and conceptualize sexuality (Cantú, 2002; Sigal, 2002; Nesvig, 2001; Balderston et all, 1997; Kulíck, 1996; Carrier, 1995; Prieur, 1994; Almaguer, 1993; Mendès-Leite, 1993). Inviting a discussion on identity formation for transgendered people draws on such collectivistic tendencies and deconstructive values in the knowledge production of emerging sexualities. The gender performance of trans people, in general, helps to make visible a disruption between "heterosexuality" and "homosexuality" dualisms implying the multiplicity of genders and sexualities and a dismantling a continuum of those discrete systems. Through "incongruous gender performances," self-presentation, and blurred sexual roles, every gendered act emerges as a tactical political strategy for what it means to "do" transgendering. Those embodiments are acts of resistance and in some cases remain under the radar screen of institutions controlling of subjects through labels, pathologizing, and institutionalization of transgendered people and other sexual outlaws in the name of science and medicine.

Dutch social "tolerance' of transgendered people and their life-styles is both an affirmation of their role in society and a form of social control. While gender migration and sex reassignments are more commonplace as a state sponsored procedure, the medicalization of transgenderism falls under the gaze of the medical establishment that determines who and how someone may proceed with a gender reassignment. Under these more "auspicious" conditions, resistance has occurred with transgendered people who opt to have some medical procedures performed and rejecting other recommendations. The notion of a "complete" gender migration is undermined in this example. Hence, new definitions of transgendering are emerging from state intervention. Not unlike the state, public health agencies play a pivotal role in reaffirming some outdated ideas about transgenderism and sex roles.

The growing presence of transgendered sex workers in Dutch prostitution clearly signals a growing need to fills a niche market, as it simultaneously subverts the sexual hierarchy. Their presence and the services they provide on the streets and in the windows challenges popular notions of what are queer or straight client desires and how those desires are fulfilled. Because so many *travestís* working in the Netherlands are from Latin America, they are transporting their sexual typologies and cultural values regarding sexual and gender identities and the services they provide. Sex roles in the commercial exchanges are quickly being reconfigured depending on customer desires. Sexual practices performed by sex workers are a clear indication of how the dominant heterosexual model for role-playing in the sexual act is being undermined. In effect, transgendered sex workers are skewing the sexual order by both taking up public space with their gendered performance and providing the types of services they perform.

NORMALIZATION OF SEX WORK

If society is made up of fields of power, or markets, that produce "spaces of relations of force," as Bourdieu suggests, then the agents who operate inside of prostitution sites are struggling to accumulate status and to dominate this given field with its own modes of capital (Bourdieu, 1998: 34). By Judith Butler's definition, there is a conjunction between fields (prostitution sites) and habitus (beliefs, gestures of sex workers) (1998: 114), as the latter is adjusted by the field and submits to rules of the field. In effect, sex workers become who they are because of their indoctrination into prostitution, but this can also mean that sexualized spaces are "not stationary space[s] but dynamic field[s] constituted by struggles over changing positions" (Butler, 1998: 202, 117). Windows and streetwalking zones are then "poised between stability and change" (Bourdieu: 1989, 5) as a result of a struggle among members who occupy positions determined by the types and amount of capital they possess. This theoretical scenario describes the fight for position, domination, and agency that is inseparable from its relation to capital and so characteristic of most prostitution sites.

Social life in the zone and in the windows is "naturalized" in a number of ways. First, as I point out with the section on the hierarchy of prostitutes, there is a common understanding within classes of prostitutes and the organization of commercial sites that are described as part of the habitus. Sex workers embody their situated understandings and reactions that were often described as an "appropriate response" to their social situation (Bourdieu, 1998: 25; Shusterman, 1998, 4). Sex workers' understanding of their work sites are mediated through bodily inculcations of social relations, and therefore, meanings were never explicitly articulated but understood as part of what rules, and "determined factors," they represent[3] (Pinto, p. 99). As a result, members of prostitution sites often take internalized rules for granted as "normal."

Bourdieu also reminds us that our internalization of a social order keeps agents from other classes or groups from crossing into more desired fields, resulting in reproduction of structures—or relations of unequal power. On appearance, responses, gestures, tastes all look "spontaneous" but at the same time are constrained by a person's situatedness (Shusterman, p. 42). For example, sex workers are initiated into a culture through learned meanings, behavior, dress codes and gestures, which in turn constitute the prostitution site. This occurs partly through an "appropriate" habitus that translates into a "nuanced social position" (Shusterman, p. 42). This means that "embodied rituals of everydayness," in effect, set into motion actions and practices "by which a given culture produces and sustains belief" through "its own obviousness"' (Butler, 1998: 114). This aspect of Bourdieu's work was quite useful in my identifying cultural practices that occur among streetwalkers in the Netherlands. In effect, I learned that self regulation occurs through a modified expression in anticipated reaction, a "euphemized," or self-censored, expression and response. The most obvious example applies to how a prostitute learns to "act," walk, or talk like a prostitute? In this instance a sex workers' "performance" of what she is suppose to behavior like embedded in a type of self-regulation. If she performs outside of those social parameters, she creates a disjuncture between action and markings that qualify her and her social position.

Bourdieu also conceptualizes a more sophisticated definition of "capital" than Marx, though its underlying meaning is similar. Capital is inseparable from the mechanisms that move and shape positions and accumulation in each field. It embodies different forms of power that individuals and institutions desire and use over each other. And, not surprisingly, is unequally distributed and unequally available (Mahar, 1990: 17). The results were hierarchies within any prostitution settings and agents jockeying for better position, and, of course, those who were excluded from entering the field altogether (Bourdieu, 1990: 120). Symbolic forms of capital, such as benefits each prostitution site provided for sex workers, the types of people who frequented the areas where they worked, and types of services sex workers performed, operate at a level that they can "disguise" their material origins across all parts of cultural and social life. These material origins, and the power and position they yield, make capital exchangeable and equal to other forms. The story of Victoria, I think, draws on this principle. For Bourdieu, the perception that this form was often "disguised" leads to an organization of social life through "games" and "strategies," ever concealing and ever coveting for position, accumulation and recognition inside the different fields and therefore, explaining more fully my motivation to write a chapter on "strategies and practices" and turn to Bourdieu's theory of practice as a way to understand prostitution sites (Mahar, et al, 1990: 17).

IN THE INTEREST OF HAVING A PUBLIC HEALTH MODEL TO REGULATE PROSTITUTION

The Dutch sex industry operates through a regulatory system with elaborate laws, rights, and tax schemes. As intermediaries of the state, the police and a host of social service agencies and prostitution rights organizations are actively on the streets enforcing changing regulations. Advocates for prostitutes help to implement public health measures preventing transmission of

HIV and STDs. To this end, underlying all prostitution sites are rational laws and policies closely controlling and regulating sexuality inside commercial spaces. This impression of a host of invasive players and agencies leaves a sense of commercial sexual relations drained of the erotic.

Of course, comparative conditions under which many prostitutes work in the Netherlands can be described as "exemplary" when contrasted with the United States or informal sites throughout the rest of Europe. Many regulatory agencies, local, international, public health, and labor policy oriented organizations play an integral role in the maintenance of the sex trade. Each agency produces rules, expectations, and sanctions deploying control over spaces designated for regulated prostitution and sites where "unregulated" activities take place.

Such public health agencies monitor windows and streets with their own agents in the form of public health workers, social workers, nurses and cultural mediators. Public health models are promoted to benefit the public good, and agencies operating to regulate sexual practices provide STD transmission prevention information to prostitutes in an assortment of languages and mandatory testing for STDs and HIV on a biweekly basis (Haastrecht et al, p. 251–256).

As I observed at the Living Room on a weekly basis, social workers and nurses from area social service and public health agencies came to talk to their caseloads. The public health workers usually arrived in pairs, armed in professional attire, and ready to single out sex workers to discuss safe sex practices and testing. The public health professionals were marked by their own professional code and culture. On occasion, however, social workers rolled a cigarette for a sex worker or performed a favor to produce an air of informality. Meanwhile, they gathered data on the health of sex workers.

This filling out of reports and gathering of data produced what I consider "objectifying knowledge" around the professional activities of sex workers. This is done with the gaze of the public health model that sanitizes and forces cooperation of sex workers who must, in turn, conform to agency guidelines and self-manage their sexual activities. In the case of drug-addicted women in the Living Room, they were given access to smoke and needle rooms after they had registered with the on-site physician. I suggest that in the name of information dissemination, Dutch prostitution is under the careful control of agencies that survey commercial practices and sex workers. The client, however, is not held responsible for their behavior or participation in the exchange. Ultimately, this means that sex workers must fulfill the role as educator for clients who do not practice safe-sex.

Under the auspices of "care," the agencies determine degrees of high-risk behavior and attitudes held by prostitutes and measure their "knowledge" retention in prevention tactics. Documentation produced by local health officials then transform into content presented to legislators and national health agencies across the European Union helping to decide whether city or state should have jurisdiction over the regulations of brothels, windows, clubs and zones or whether prostitution should be constructed as a form of labor at all. Language constructed around activity and space supports a legitimization of the exchange, but also reproduced and disseminated "normative" perceptions within the context of the Netherlands.

FUTURE RESEARCH

In defense of my research methods and findings, I was a lone researcher with limited funding and time to gather data. As stated earlier, my research represents multiple perspectives of sex workers in the Netherlands, however by no means does my work characterize a comprehensive depiction of prostitution there. There are many voices and perspectives missing from my research. Besides the changes to regulation, and the occurrence of employment turnover, there are segments of the industry that are highly inaccessible to many researchers. Certainly my study would gain more concrete elements with the inclusion of other groups who work in the industry.

While I focused on window prostitution and a streetwalking zone, in reality two-thirds of all prostitutes work in venues called "sex-clubs."[4] These prostitution venues are more difficult to enter because of barriers set up to make them more exclusive.[5] Victoria van der Way and Marta, a former club prostitute, pointed out in separate interviews that many of the women working in the clubs have limited choice of clientele, what kinds of services they provide, and what percentage of their earnings they are obligated to hand over to the bar owners. More qualitative research is needed to understand if this kind of venue diminishes the autonomy and rights of women working in these sites. Questions need to be asked about how club prostitutes negotiate services with clients who have sought them out through a request to a third party (bar manager) or after picking them from a lineup on stage. What kinds of communication are club prostitutes able to have with all the actors who operate and participate in this type of commercial space?

The feminization of migration to Western Europe continues to occur with new ethnic groups entering Western Europe each day. Knowledge about who these women are and under what conditions they arrived is part of an ongoing concern of the ILO and other immigration agencies.[6] Many undocumented prostitutes, who are not streetwalking or using the public health sector, are migrants operating deep within an underground economy unbeknownst to authorities. Long-term studies are needed in chronicling the conditions of migrants, their possible deportation, or reentry into prostitution. Further research is needed on what happens to migrants upon returning to their countries of origin, or how they reenter the Netherlands after deportation.

The growing presence of transgendered sex workers intersects with issues related to transnational immigration, globalization, and sexual identity. Additional scholarly attention is required on this subject. Other questions about existing transgendered communities in the Netherlands reflect the issue of aging and its impact on prostitution culture. For instance, what economic sectors are available to older transgendered sex workers once they no longer generate income from prostitution? These questions need to be asked in future research projects.

REDEFINING PROSTITUTION AS PART OF A GENDER DIVISION OF LABOR

Historically, texts on prostitution mostly focus on the institution as part of a sexual division of labor. Constructing a singular representation of the prostitute as a female falls short given changing corporal realities of "doing gender" on the street. Therefore, many of my informants disrupt a metaphor of the female body as the site of sexual colonization, allowing readers to rethink notions of embodiment and performativity as they intersect with agency.

Increased numbers of transgendered sex workers does not suggest complete effacement of gendered power relations, however their presence is re-qualifying everyday interaction for all sex workers, including female-born, with clients and each other. Female sex workers are now competing with transgendered sex workers for clients who are seeking the "exotic" in the form of blurred role-playing or anal-penetration. Hence, as clients "cross the street" they, too, change relations with female and transgendered sex workers and the relations between sex providers. And while changing client expectations and sexual practices may or may not be favorable for female sex workers who are already strained to meet a huge demand for "alternative" sexual practices, this redefinition of their work requires further adjustment in the already changing social and economic climate of the windows and the street. What emerges from this is how sex workers' stories and impressions bear evidence of divergent accounts of life on the streets, therefore locating contemporary prostitution as an ongoing social and cultural product within an historical moment.

Commercial sex in Dutch society continues to change, forcing scholars and advocates to rethink about how diverse sets of prostitution experiences intersect with the fluid social positions of the actors, erotic labor practices, and spatial relations of the contract. Such a concentration of so many social determinants held by each participant in commercial sex reveals the need for understanding what constitutes their social reality, rather than inventing a unified narrative for the sake of a political project, or any representation of prostitution as a uniform phenomenon.

Notes

NOTES TO CHAPTER ONE

1. The area gained its name from the use of red lamps placed in windows where prostitutes worked. During the 1600s, a wall, called *de Wallen*, was built to enclose commercial activities taking place inside the area. Prostitutes who wandered outside the parameters of the district either to openly find clients or provide services could face incarceration if caught by the authorities. Today, the Red Light District is a commercial and residential area in the city center, where prostitution is concentrated. Florescent red lights have replaced kerosene lamps, however this color illuminated from a window still signifies a prostitution site. The Red Light District is also home to an Asian neighborhood.
2. The Mr. A. de Graaf Stichting is known in English as the Institute for Prostitution Issues.
3. The Abolitionists, who fought against all forms of human slavery, declared prostitution a human rights violation.
4. "Between the Lines," Institute for Prostitution Issues: Research, Policy, Advice, Documentation, and Public Information, June 1997.
5. Victoria van der Way
6. This is a euphemistic term for "pimp."
7. This does not include rental agreements in which prostitutes have pay property owners and leasers for a window for a fixed number of days per week.
8. This 1996 estimate comes from the Mr. A. de Graaf Stichting (the Institute for Prostitution Issues). Some of their documents suggest estimates are at a figure closer to twenty thousand sex workers, however this higher figure may include unregistered prostitutes working in underground venues ("Between the Lines," 1997; p. 2).
9. Information based on my interview with Marta, a former sex club prostitute.
10. Including migrant females and transgendered streetwalkers.

11. Since the gathering of my data, as of April 2003, the authorities have clamped down on streetwalking zones enforcing a registration policy and promising to shut down all zones by December 2005.
12. As of today, immigration reform has become a pressing issue among the Dutch populace. This issue became the political platform on which Pim Fortuyn based his right-wing political candidacy. He was assassinated in May 2002, however mainstream political parties have usurped his "anti-immigration platform."
13. Three informants identified themselves as transsexuals; four identified themselves as cross-dressers; and ten identified themselves as *travestís* or "transgendered."
14. Chrys Ingraham identifies "the heterosexual imaginary" as a representation of social life that is "masked to conceal historical and material conditions."
15. This term refers only to "post-operative" transsexuals.
16. This includes "intersexed" persons with male genitals and breast or hip augmentation. They usually take female hormones as well.
17. Not a single informant used the term "post-operative transsexual" to describe themselves or others.
18. Den Apelhaven is a pseudonym for a Dutch city where I conducted research.

NOTES TO CHAPTER TWO

1. Dutch prostitution advocates initially expressed a sharp suspicion towards my presence in the field and, in effect, galvanized my theoretical indoctrination requiring adaptation to this unique cultural environment and the vocabulary that proliferates discussions around Dutch prostitution.
2. GGGD (the public health department), Mr. A. de Graaf Stichling (The Institute for Prostitution Issues), Red Thread (a prostitution rights organization), Department of Labor, etc.
3. Nevada and British Columbia have already legalized prostitution.
4. Much like their name suggests, the ideological origins of the current abolitionist movement can find its roots in the suffrage movement from the 19th century. As found in both movements, the theme of female sexuality is a focal point for social change, constructing it as an obstacle to education, travel, occupation, and diminishment of opportunities rather than as a libratory expression (Chapkis, 1997: 11). Fundamentally, prostitution is interpreted as a form of oppression and therefore must be eradicated.
5. For Anti-Sex Feminists (Dworkin, MacKinnon, the Southern Women's Writing Collective), "woman is constituted through sex," and therefore "sex cannot be a tool for dismantling male supremacy" (Chapkis, 1997: 17, 18). Their premise signifies all women as powerless and therefore unable to reclaim any positive elements from heterosexual relations. Within this radical feminist milieu, therefore, female desires must be recreated outside of contemporary practices of heterosexual culture (18).

6. The "Pro-Sex-Positive" feminists consider prostitution and pornography as "corrupting practices" undermining a "natural foundation of positive sex." Romantic idealization of love and sex free of "distortions of patriarchy" represent the main point of this movement (Chapkis, 1997,13). Female sexuality, therefore, is placed within the confines of monogamous heterosexual practices leaving all other practices as forms of fetishism or perversity (Chapkis, 1997: 13).

7. Inside the "Sex-Radical" movement there is a disjuncture surfacing around prostitution. Classic Sex-Radicalism does not deny modes of domination found in heterosexual practices, but instead approaches the subject believing there are ways of subverting sexual practices as sexual agents within a sexist social order (Chapkis, 1997: 12). Subversion through resignifying sexual language and redefining the sexual order becomes part of the movement's goal. The Libertarian group resists any notions of fixed sexual meaning as "the individual rather than the communal" determines whether an act is "wrong" or not. Female sexuality and beauty are regarded as a source of power, negating historical or political references.

8. Another dominant voice in the Sex-Radical movement is Pat Califia. She acknowledges that meaning is contextually specific, and that the role of the prostitute cannot be reduced to that of passive agent. Califia, Chapkis, and ex-adult film actress Annie Sprinkle, embrace previously stigmatizing nomenclatures such as "slut" and "dyke" as a challenge to the definition of womanhood (30).

9. In the last two decades a flux of undocumented workers from Latin America, Africa, Asia and Eastern Europe entered the Netherlands to work as prostitutes.

10. Study conducted in Australia.

11. An expression used by Jo Doezema in Chapkis' *Live Sex Acts: Women Performing Erotic Labor.*

12. In fact, given Pettiway's disciplinary background and grant stipulations (the research was funded by the National Institute on Drug Abuse) it is fair to ask what motivates Pettiway to focus on subjects who are transgendered, drug-addicted and on the streets hustling if he is theoretically bound to reproduce existing stereotypes of this segment of the population.

13. Through hormone ingestion, silicone injections and adhering to certain aesthetic practices, *travestís* embody mixed gender coding.

14. Boyfriends of *travestís* are "heterosexual" or play the "dominant" sexual role in the relationship.

15. A sexual typology found throughout Latin America.

NOTES TO CHAPTER THREE

1. The Working Sex: Caribbean Development, Tourism, Sex and Work Conference, Kingston, Jamaica, July 1998.

2. A center near the entrance of any streetwalking zone where streetwalkers can changes their clothes, purchase food and beverages, receive medical treatment, or find respite.
3. This should not be problematic because there are numerous "zones" through the Netherlands.
4. Five years of Spanish language instruction did not facilitate any greater ability to communicate with many Latin American sex workers who had been in the Netherlands for only a short time. Consequently, they are mostly excluded from my sample.
5. Desiree
6. The geo-political significance of Albanians as surplus human capital has placed them in many underground European economies including illegal prostitution, human trafficking, auto theft rings, grave robbing, and seasonal agricultural work.
7. Just because my ancestors lived in that region, how do I justify my conduct of research on Eastern European transgenderism?

NOTES TO CHAPTER FOUR

1. On any Saturday night the practice of gazing at window prostitutes becomes a collective event across the District. This practice is an entitlement for pedestrians, cyclists, and motorists entering the Red Light District. On one occasion, I recall two-dozen people stood at a standstill in the middle of the street staring up at a second floor window. The object of attention was a blonde-Northern European woman staring back at pedestrians from behind a glass window.
2. Ramona explained that some of her clients were couples requesting services performed on the female partner.
3. Translated by my companion, a native Italian speaker, who accompanied me into the District.
4. A city law now prohibits large groups of men coming from the United Kingdom from holding their weekend long stag parties here. Their collective behavior has been disruptive and, in some cases, turned to violence.
5. Not the real location.
6. Condoms are worn for oral, anal, and genital sexual contact.
7. She explained that the penile prostheses were there to give an ambiance to the room more than to function as part of the exchange.
8. During this period, many Latin American prostitutes return home for vacation.
9. The pool cue serves two purposes: as a weapon against unwanted intruders or violent clients and a way to push unsightly used condoms deep into the trashcan.
10. I'm not clear whether the client paid 200 guilders for Magdalena to simulate an orgasm or if she was required to ejaculate.

11. Based on my interview with Marta, a former Dutch prostitute who worked in the sex clubs. Estimates reveal that two-thirds of all prostitutes in the Netherlands work in the clubs.

12. French, Portuguese, and Spanish are her dominant languages. Speaking English was an effort for Magdalena, although she spoke mostly English with customers.

13. To estimate how much Diva earns from her window rentals per week, consider the following calculations: Each window produces three eight-hour shifts per day. If a single shift generates 200 Dutch guilders, and a single window has three daily shifts, multiply 200 Dutch guilders by three. That means Diva earns 600 Dutch guilders per day from the rental of a single window. Since she owns three rooms her daily income from rentals amounts to 1,800 Dutch guilders. Multiply her daily rental earnings times seven days and her weekly earning power amounts to 12,600 Dutch guilders ($5,800 or 5,800 Euro) per week.

14. Magdalena used the word "transvestite" when referring to transgendered sex workers who had breast implants, female hormonal injections, but opted to keep their male genitalia.

15. Two years later, when I attempted to speak to the non-Dutch owner of a cluster of windows in the Red Light District, he curtly dismissed me.

16. The day I met Jojo was a day I questioned my trust for Magdalena. I was transfixed by Jojo's resemblance to Magdalena, and wondered if she were playing a joke on me. If it were not for the gap in Jojo's front teeth, her less than streamlined costume, and her mid-day consumption of alcohol, I would have mistaken her for Magdalena. In the end, I spent around thirty minutes talking to Jojo about her experiences in the windows.

17. Most *travestí*s said that their customers knew exactly what kinds of services trangendered sex workers provided. In Chapter Six, Ramona, an Ecuadorian *travestí*, explained that a few of her customers claimed they thought they were having relations with a woman. Ramona believes, however, most of her clients know who she is but simply don't acknowledge they're engaging in sexual relations with a transgendered person. In the past, when she sensed a customer did not grasp her transgendered identity, she concealed her male genitals throughout the sexual exchange and let the client believe he was engaging genital intercourse rather than anal intercourse.

18. Isolated clusters of prostitution windows can be found in different parts of the city.

NOTES TO CHAPTER FIVE

1. An alias name for a Dutch city where I conducted interviews and observations.

2. Based on Bourdieu's definition, symbolic capital, like other capital, is a form of power. Symbolic capital can take cultural or social forms. This refers to knowledge, prestige, or activities that legitimate subjects through

invisible means. Ultimately, status assigned to objects, practices, and gestures conceal their material roots.

3. Here, a habitus is defined as a reproduction of structures, in which unequal relations occur. Through a physical embodiment, a habitus represents a set of understandings and reactions to social relations and their meanings. This inculcation does not require articulation of explicit rules because they operate as an internalized social order that keeps individuals from crossing.

4. Found in The Hague, Utrecht, Rotterdam, Arnhem, Nijmegen, Groningen, and Amsterdam

5. To maintain anonymity, an alias has been given to the city and its streets where I gathered data.

6. Retold to me by Victoria van der Way while giving me a tour of the former streetwalking sites.

7. In order to use the in-house drug facility, drug addicted women had to register with the center. They were given an ID after having a medical exam with the resident doctor.

8. Consumption and distribution of so-called heavy drugs is illegal in the Netherlands. Having an in-house heavy drug dealer was part of an experimental project, based on a medical model, initiated at the center. As stated later in the chapter, during my follow up in January, the city eventually prohibited such an exchange to take place inside the center.

9. Tensions were high because of the habit of the killer to strike during large social events including the Euro soccer games being held in Belgium and the Netherlands at that precise time.

10. Sources report that she is now married and living in another city, but still working on the streets.

11. Reportedly, the winter season is the most commercially active season in the zone.

12. Staff often identified drug addicted female streetwalkers as "girls."

13. In January 2002, Victoria, a Dutch transsexual, relayed this story to me over an elegant Indonesian dinner she prepared for me.

14. Since the time at which this data was collected, the police have enforced registration of the streetwalkers, deported many of the undocumented workers, and promise to close all streetwalking zones in December 2005.

15. Victoria was in a serious intimate relationship, and therefore not working in prostitution, during the time when large numbers of Ecuadorians arrived in the zone.

16. Latinas from Ecuador represent the largest ethnic group of female and transgendered sex workers in the zone. The network they have successfully established protects their street interests, however many of them remain illegal. Perhaps in time they will go the way of Dominicans and Columbians who arrived in the Netherlands in waves in the 1980s and 1990s, but are virtually absent from the street. Through residency status and other legitimating means, they have "graduated" to the windows and clubs. To date, relations

between Dutch and Latinas have not always been hospitable but are becoming more cooperative with new ethnic groups entering the zone.

17. When I first met Veronica, I did not know if she was a pre-operative or post-operative transsexual or a *travestí*. During my follow-up visit she revealed that she was a transsexual.

18. Residency visa are awarded to long-term, registered partnerships. If a relationship with a Dutch or EU citizen terminates, so does the visa.

19. When Pamela first arrived in the Netherlands she worked at a hotel, earning a meager wage. One night, she decided to try her luck selling sex in the zone. In a single night she accumulated three times what she earned in a month at the hotel. To conceal her new employment from her family, she had photographs taken of her working at a hotel to fabricate the source of her income.

20. The field represents "markets," not exclusive to economics that are dynamic and where individuals struggle to attain position and capital. Fields also exist in conjunction with the habitus (beliefs, gestures), but the latter must adjust to the former, not vice versa.

21. Capital is a form of power individuals and institutions use over each other. Economic capital includes money and modes of production.

22. Often gauged by the type of car the client drove, the confidence he displayed or willingness to pay for additional services.

23. As a standard practice, streetwalkers do not disrobe or have mouth-to-mouth contact with clients. It is possible that a Dutch female streetwalker, Anke, along with her colleagues, started the rumor of the Polish women providing theses extra services as a way to discredit them.

24. This definition includes window prostitution, streetwalking zones, clubs, and escort services.

25. Magdalena, Ramona, and Jojo spoke for themselves and colleagues who worked in the windows.

26. Interview with Ramona, an Ecuadorian *travestí,* and Magdalena, a Brazilian *travestí.*

27. Victoria, Anke, Sonja, Veronica, Desiree, Nadine, Steluta, Kasmira, Estrella, Pamela, Nadine, and Agnese.

NOTES TO CHAPTER SIX

1. When considering how to protect the anonymity of this informant, the pseudonym "Victoria Van der Way" came to my mind as an appropriate strong name. "Victoria" approved and then said that this pseudonym translates to "victory from the road" in Dutch.

2. In-depth interviews with Victoria include a ten-hour interview at her home, ten to fifteen hours of casual conversation at the Living Room, two years of e-mail correspondence, numerous phone conversations, an eight-hour follow-up interview at her home one year after our initial interview, and a six-hour follow-up interview at my home the following spring.

3. The name is a pseudonym for a Dutch city where I gathered data.

4. Pseudonym

5. On January 3, 2001, Victoria and I met during my follow-up observation at the *huiskamer*, six months after a series of field observation visits to the site. During this one winter evening, in the capacity as volunteer, I prepared her meal after a slow night on the street. There she invited me to join her after I identified my research intentions.

6. She earns around $15,000 per year from her position as a nurse.

7. This was not the first time I made a personal disclosure of this nature. During the previous summer after keeping my distance from an aloof female sex worker named Betty, we shared our first conversation about her daily struggle caring for her son and her mother who had Alzheimer's disease. The parent's condition had progressed to the point of now having to wear an identity tag in case she wandered from their home. It was this description and Betty's loving responsibility that struck me as only an adult child could feel for her ailing parent. "My mother cared for me as a child, and now it's my turn to care for her, I wouldn't want it any other way," she disclosed, holding my gaze for the first time. We talked about the role of placing a parent in a nursing home, a solution Betty would never consider for her mother. My exchange with Betty, not unlike my growing affinity for Victoria translated into sharing pieces of myself, pieces that I might otherwise have never excavated.

8. During the following summer she had plastic surgery to her nose and cheekbones.

9. Victoria does not relate to "gay," "transvestite," or "transgendered" cultures because she cannot identify with the production of a "gay persona." Once, prior to her "operation," Victoria met a gay man at a bar. She went home with him, and they had anal intercourse that she found painful. At the "Greek bar," however, Greek sailors would buy her drinks thinking she was female because "they didn't know, because of my long hair."

10. Over twenty years ago working as a sex worker would have been impossible without a pimp, however today it is possible to have such autonomy.

11. Victoria refers to her sex reassignment as "the operation."

12. Victoria is a superb cook and takes pride in her ability to prepare elaborate meals.

13. Victoria, Steluta, Valeria, Annike, and Veronica participated in this discussion.

14. Valeria had the most violent reaction to this story.

15. Her father joins us for a cup of coffee upon return from his dog walk. Now in his seventies, Roloph represents a generation who fought in World War II, and as a result have emotionally closed-off after experiencing the brutality of that war. Just before his arrival Victoria disclosed his story to me. Unlike Victoria's parents who had been married fifty-one years, her father's parents separated but did not divorce because of their Catholic faith. Victoria's paternal-grandfather left his wife for another women, forcing many of his six children to find shelter in an orphanage. This paternal abandonment, however, was not the source of their family's shame. The fact that her paternal-grandfather sided with the Germans, forcing Victoria's father, then a teenager of fifteen to fight

for the Germans in Poland was the family secret revealed. This stigma followed Roloph back to the Netherlands, and because of the social weight, Victoria's mother never took her husband's name, since "van der Way" was a name associated with German sympathizers.

Unlike the early hardships of her father's life, her mother, Marian, was "spoiled" by *Oma*, Victoria's beloved materal grandmother. Marian was always treated like a child even while unabashedly pregnant with Victoria's older brother at the time of her marriage to Roloph. By Victoria's account, Marian was a "lady" who led a protected life understood by her refusal to take public transportation. "She never rides the Metro," Victoria retorted.

16. Victoria's victory was temporary. As of April 1, 2003 all streetwalkers must have an ID to enter the streetwalking zone.
17. This name is a pseudonym for the street where the zone is located.
18. As a middle-aged transsexual who spent her entire adult life on hormonal maintenance, Victoria describes a type of menopause much like that of women experiencing a diminishment of hormonal levels. At forty-five, she continues to take Premorin, a hormonal supplement, to prevent menopausal "hot flashes" from occurring.

NOTES TO CHAPTER SEVEN

1. Den Apelhaven is a fictional name given to the city where I interviewed Anke.
2. Prior to the arrival of migrants on the streets, Dutch sex workers reported that they performed either oral sexual services or genital sexual services for the price of fl 50. Since the influx of migrants, there has been a normalization of an intensification of services, since clients have come to expect both a "suck" and "fuck" for the usual fl50 or 25Euro sexual exchange.
3. It should be noted that the public healthcare delivery system in the Netherlands provides universal coverage for all Dutch citizens and residents.
4. Anke expressed interest in working with children but her back went out after a few months of working at a child care center; working as a cashier in a grocery store appealed to her but she saw herself as "too old for that because they want to hire younger people to pay them less"; and working in a *cantina* seemed doable but she became "sick" before she could hold that position.
5. Excluded from this self-analysis of why Anke stayed in sex work is the small detail of Anke's penchant for gambling. Other streetwalkers, and not the informant herself, disclosed this information to me.
6. She was referring to her vagina, implying that her work as a prostitute had not "stretched" her body from excess use.
7. While a transsexual identity represents a permanent gender migration, the definition varies depending upon the culture of origin, economic station, and social support of the informant.

8. This means having male genitals and augmented breasts and hips. This also includes ingesting female hormones.

9. At the age of thirteen, Desiree had her first sexual encounter at a gay club where she met a stranger four years her senior. She "didn't enjoy the encounter" but "[identified] with the act." She admitted to preferring "blow jobs" and hating anal sex. Turning tricks came easy for Desiree. By sixteen years of age, she was picking up clients in the clubs. She reports most of her clients are Dutch, because she has problems interacting with Turkish and Moroccan men.

10. Other sex workers pulled me aside disclosing that Desiree had been talking about this transition for years but had yet to muster up the courage to follow through with the process.

11. Breast augmentation is usually one of the first surgical steps toward a gender transition.

12. At an earlier stage in Steluta's life, she contemplated whether she was meant to live her life as a woman.

13. Statement made by Kasmira.

14. Statement made by Kasmira.

15. Gay men working as transvestites expressed some sexual pleasure during the average transaction.

16. This request requires throwing the contract back into the negotiation stage and costs the client additional fees upwards to 100 Euro or more.

NOTES TO CHAPTER EIGHT

1. "Artist visas" were commonly administered to Latin American women in the 1980s. Now, many Eastern European women come by train on a tourist visa.

2. Previously, Dutch sex workers reported that they performed either oral sexual services or genital sexual services for the price of fl 50 ($25).

3. This part of his theory might be considered too deterministic.

4. De Graaf Stichling statistic

5. The public health department, known as the GGGD, does make the rounds to check on club prostitutes.

6. TAMPEP

Bibliography

Albuquerque, Fernanda Farias de, & Janelli, Maurizio. (1994). *Princesa*, Rome: Sensıbıli alle Foglie.

Alexander, Prisilla. (1995). "Sex Workers Fight Against AIDS: An International Perspective." (Eds.) Schneider and Stoller.

Almaguer, Tomas. (1991). "Chicano Men: A Cartography of Homosexual Identity and Behavior." *Differences* 3: 75–100.

Altink, Sietske. (1995). *Stolen Lives: Trading Women into Sex and Slavery*. London: Scarlet Press.

Andaya, Barbara Watson. (Winter 1998). "From Temporary Wife to Prostitute: Sexuality and Economic Change in Early Modern Southeast Asia." *Journal of Women's History*. Vol 9 No 4.

Balderston, Daniel and Donna J. Guy, (Eds.). (1997). *Sex and Sexuality in Latin America* New York: New York University Press.

Barry, Kathleen. (1995). *The Prostitution of Sexuality*. New York: New York University.

Bell, Laurie (Eds). (1987). *Good Girls; Bad Girls: Sex Trade Worker & Feminists Face to Face*. Toronto: the Women's Press.

Bell, Shannon. (1994). *Reading, Writing, and Rewriting the Prostitute Body*. Bloomington: Indiana University Press.

Bergman, David. (1999). "Beauty and the Beach: Representing Fire Island." *Public Sex: Gay Space*. (Edited by) William L. Leap, New York: Columbia University Press.

"Between the Lines," Institute for Prostitution Issues: Research, Policy, Advice, Documentation, and Public Information, June 1997.

Bindman, Jo and Jo Doezema. (1997). *Redefining Prostitution as Sex Work on the International Agenda*. London: Anti-Slavery International and the Network of Sex Work Projects.

Bogdan, Robert. (1974). *Being Different: The Autobiography of Jane Fry*. New York: Wiley.

Bogdan, R., and S. K. Biklen. (1992). *Qualitative Research for Education: An Introduction to Theory and Methods*. Needham Heights, MA: Allyn and Bacon.

Bornstein, Kate. (1994). *Gender outlaw: On men, women, and the rest of us.* New York: Routledge.

Bordo, Susan. "Feminism, Foucault and the politics of the body." (1993). *Up Against Foucault: Explorations of some tensions between Foucault and feminism.* (Ed) Caroline Ramazanoglu, London: Routledge.

———. *Unbearable Weight: Feminism, Western Culture, and the Body.* (1993). Berkeley: University of California Press.

Bourdieu, Pierre and Jean-Claude Passeron. (1990). *Reproduction in Education, Society and Culture.* London: Sage.

Bourdieu, Pierre. (1992). "In Conversation: Doxa and Common Life." *New Left Review,* no 191, p. 115.

———. *Practical Reason: On the Theory of Action.* (1998). Stanford, California: Stanford University Press.

Broad, K. L. (October 2002). "GLB+T: Gender/Sexuality Movements and Transgender Collective Identity (De)constructions," *International Journal of Sexuality and Gender Studies,* Vol. 7, No 4.

Brock, Deborah R. (1998). *Making Work, Making Trouble: Prostitution as a Social Problem.* Toronto: University of Toronto.

Browne, Jan and Victor Minichiello, (1996). "Research Directions in Male Sex Work," *Journal of Homosexuality.* Vol 31(4).

———. "The Social Meanings Behind Male Sex Work: Implications for Sexual Interaction." (December 1995). *British Journal of Sociology,* Vol 46, n 4.

Butler, Judith. *Gender Trouble: Feminism and the Subversion of Identity.* (1989). New York: Routledge.

———. (1999). "Performativity's Social Magic," *Bourdieu: A Critical Reader,* (ed.) Richard Shusterman, Oxford: Blackwell.

Califia, Pat. (1994). *Public Sex: The Culture of Radical Sex.* Pittsburgh: Cleis Press.

Cantu, Lionel. (2002). De Ambiente Queer Tourism and the Shifting Boundaries of Mexican Male Sexualities *GLQ: A Journal of Lesbian and Gay Studies*—Volume 8, Number 1–2, pp. 139–166.

Carrier, Joseph. (1995). *De Los Otros: Intimacy and Homosexuality among Mexican Men,* New York: Columbia University Press.

Chapkis, Wendy. (1986). *Beauty Secrets: Women and the Politics of Appearance.* Boston: South End Press.

———. (1997). *Live Sex Acts: Women Performing Erotic Labor.* New York: Routledge.

Clatt, Michael C. (1999). "Ethnographic Observations of Men Who Have Sex with Men in Public." *Public Sex: Gay Space,* (ed.) William L. Leap, New York: Columbia University Press.

Clifford, James. (1986). "Introduction." *Writing Culture: The Poetics and Politics of Ethnography,* (Eds.) James Clifford and George E. Marcus, Berkeley: University of California Press.

———. (1986). "On Ethnographic Allegory." *Writing Culture: The Poetics and Politics of Ethnography,* (Eds.) James Clifford and George E. Marcus, Berkeley: University of California Press.

Clough, Patricia Ticineto. (1994). *Feminist Thought: Desire, Power, and Academic Discourse*. Cambridge, Massachusetts: Blackwell.

Coles, Robert. (1997). *Doing Documentary Work*. NY: Oxford University Press.

Davis, Kingsley. (Oct., 1937). "The Sociology of Prostitution." *American Sociological Review*. Volume 2, Issue 5 744–755.

Davis, Nanette. (1971). "The Prostitute: Developing a Deviant Identity." *Studies in the Sociology of Sex*. (Ed.) James M. Henslin, New York: Appleton-Century-Crofts.

Delacoste, Frederique, and Priscilla Alexander. (Ed.) (1998). *Sex Work: Writings by Women in the Sex Industry*, San Francisco: Cleis.

De Vault, Marjorie. (October 1995). "Ethnicity and Expertise: Racial-Ethnic Knowledge in Sociological Research." *Gender & Society*. Vol. 9 No. 5.

———. (1999). *Liberating Method: feminism and social research*. Philadelphia: Temple University Press.

———. (February 1990) "Talking and Listening from Women's Standpoint: Feminist Strategies for Interviewing and Analysis." *Social Problems* Vol. 37, No1.

———. (1996). "Talking Back to Sociology: Distinctive Contributions of Feminist Methodology." *Annual Review of Sociology*.

Delany, Samuel R. (1995). "Aversion/Perversion/Diversion." *Negotiating Lesbian and Gay Subjects*. (Eds.) Monica Dorenkamp and Richard Henke, New York: Routledge.

Denzin, Norman K. (1989). *Interpretive biography*. Newbury Park: Sage.

———. (1997). *Interpretive ethnography : ethnographic practices for the 21st century*. Thousand Oaks, Calif. : Sage Publications.

———. (1992). *Symbolic interactionism and cultural studies: the politics of interpretation*. Oxford, UK: Blackwell.

Dines Gail, Jensen, Robert, & Russo, Ann. (1998). *Pornography: The Production and Consumption of Inequality*. New York: Routledge.

Doezema, Jo. (1998). "Forced to Choose: Beyond the Voluntary v. Forced Prostitution Dichotomy, edited by K. Kempadoo and J. Doezema, *Global Sex Workers: Rights, Resistance, and Redefinition*. New York: Routledge.

———. "Choice in Prostitution." (May 3–5, 1995). *Conference Book: Changing Faces of Prostitution*, Helsinki,. Helsinki: Unioni, The League of Finnish Feminists.

Dworkin, Andrea. (1987). *Intercourse*. London: Secker and Warburg.

Emerson, Robert M., Fretz, Rachel I., & Shaw, Linda L. (1995). *Writing Ethnographic Fieldnotes*. Chicago: University of Chicago.

Enloe, Cynthia H. (1990). *Bananas, Beaches, & Bases: Making Feminist Sense of International Politics*. Berkeley, California: University of California.

Essed, Philomena. (1991). *Understanding Everyday Racism: An interdisciplinary theory*, Newbury Park: Sage.

EUROPAP. (1997). *STD/AIDS Prevention in Prostitution in Amsterdam*. Amsterdam: Municipal Health Services.

Foucault, Michel. (1965). *Discipline and Punishment: the Birth of the Prison*. New York: Random House.

———. (1990). *History of Sexuality: An Introduction*. New York: Vintage.

Gamson, Joshua. (1995). "Must identity movements self-destruct?: A queer dilemma. Soc. Problems. 42:390–407.

Gamson, Joshua & Dawne Moon, "The Sociology of Sexualities: Queer and Beyond," *Annual Review Sociology,* 30: 47–64, 2004.

Geertz, Clifford. (1973). *The Interpretation of Cultures: Selected Essays.* New York: Basic Books.

Glenn, Evelyn Nakano. (1992). "From Servitude to Service Work: Historical Continuities in the Racial Division of Paid Reproductive Labor," *Sign: Journal of Women in Cultures and Society* 18, no 1.

Harvey, David. (1995). *The Conditions of Postmodernity.* Oxford: Blackwell.

Haveman, Roloph. *Voorwaarden voor Stafbaarstelling van Vrouwenhandel.* (1998). Doctoral Thesis, University of Utrecht, Utrecht: Gouda Quint.

Heyl, Barbara. (1979). *The Madam as Entrepreneur: Career Management in House Prostitution.* New Brunswick, N.J.: Transaction Books.

Ingraham, Chrys. (1996). "The Heterosexual Imaginary: Feminist Sociology and Theories of Gender," (eds) Steven Seidman, *Queer Theory/Sociology,* Cambridge: Blackwell.

Jackson, Norman, O'Toole, Richard, & Geis, Gilbert. (1963). "The Self-Image of the Prostitute." *The Sociological Quarterly* 4 (Spring): 150–160.

Jackson, Stevi. (1996). "Heterosexuality as a Problem for Feminist Theory," *Sexualizing the Social: Power and the Organization of Sexuality.* (Eds.) Lisa Adkins and Vicki Merchant, New York: St. Martin's Press.

Jamieson, Lynn. (1996). "The Social Construction of Consent Revisited." *Sexualizing the Social: Power and the Organization of Sexuality,* (Eds.) Lisa Adkins and Vicki Merchant, New York: St. Martin's Press.

Johnson, Mark. (1997). *Beauty and Power: Transgendering and Cultural Transformation in the Southern Philippines.* Oxford & New York: Berg.

Immigration and Naturalization Services brochure, Ministry of Justice, the Netherlands, 2002.

International Organization for Migration, "Information Campaign Against Trafficking in Women from Ukraine Research Report," July 1998.

Liazos, Alex. (1982). People first, an introduction to social problems. Boston: Allyn and Bacon.

Kempadoo, Kamala, & Doezema, Jo. (Eds.) (1998).*Global Sex Workers: Rights, Resistance, and Redefinition.* New York: Routledge.

Kempadoo, Kamala. (Ed.). (1999). *Sun, Sex and Gold: Tourism and Sex Work in the Caribbean.* Oxford: Rowman & Littlefield.

Knopp, Lawrence. (1995). "Sexuality and Urban Space: A Framework for Analysis." *Mapping Desires: Geographies of Sexuality.* (Eds.) David Bell, and Gill Valentine, London: Routlege.

Kulíck, Don, & Willson, Margaret. (Ed.) (1995). *Taboo: Sex, Identity and Erotic Subjectivity in Anthropological Fieldwork.* London: Routledge.

Kulíck, Don. (1995). *Travesti: Transgendered Prostitutes in Brazil,* Chicago: University of Chicago.

Kerkwijk, Carla van. (1995). "The Dynamics of Condom Use in Thai Sex Work with Farang Clients." edited by Han ten Brummelhuis and Gilbert Herdt.

Culture and Sexual Risk: Anthropological Perspectives on AIDS. Amsterdam: Gordon and Breach.

Lopez-Vicuna, Ignacio. (2004). "Approaches to Sexuality in Latin America: Recent Studies on Gay and Lesbian Studies," *Latin American Research Review*. 39. p 238–253.

Lorber, Judith. (1994). *Paradoxes of Gender*, New Haven; Yale University Press.

MacKinnon, Catherine. (1991). *Feminism Unmodified: Discourse of Life and Law*. Boston: Harvard University.

Manderson, Lenore & Jolly, Margaret. (Ed.). (1997). *Sites of Desire, Economies of Pleasure: Sexualities in Asia and the Pacific*. Chicago: University of Chicago.

Margolis, Joseph. (1999). "Pierre Bourdieu: Habitus and the Logic of Practice," *Bourdieu: A Critical Reader*. (Ed.) Richard Shusterman, Oxford: Blackwell.

Maurer, David W. (January, 1939). "Prostitutes and Criminal Argots." *American Journal of Sociology*, Volume 44 546–550.

McDowell, Linda. (1995). "Heterosexual Gender Performances in City Workplaces." *Mapping Desires: Geographies of Sexuality*, edited by David Bell, and Gill Valentine, London: Routledge.

McEwan, Cheryl. (1984). "Encounters with West African Women: Textual Representations of Difference by White Women Abroad," *In Writing Women and Space: Colonial and Postcolonial Geographies*, (Eds.) A. Blunt and G. Rose, New York: The Guilford Press.

McIntosh, Mary. (1996). "Feminist Debates on Prostitution." *Sexualizing the Social: Power and the Organization of Sexuality*, (Eds.) Lisa Adkins and Vicki Merchant, New York: St. Martin's Press.

Mendès-Leite, Rommel. (1993). "The Game of Appearance: The 'Ambigusexuality' in Brazilian Culture of Sexuality," *Journal of Homosexuality* 25.

Mensendiek, Martha. (1997). "Women, migration and prostitution in Thailand." *International Social Work*, Volume 40, Number 2. p 163.

Morse, Edward V., Simon, Patricia M., Balson, Paul M., and Howard J. Osofsky. (August 1992). "Sexual Behavior Patterns of Customers of Male Prostitutes." *Archives of Sexual Behavior*, V21, n4.

———. (March 1, 1991). "The Male Street Prostitute: A Vector for Transmission of HIV Infection into the Heterosexual World." *Social Science & Medicine*, V32, n5.

Mr. A. de Graaf Stitching (Institute for Prostitution Issues), "Between the Lines," 1997.

Mr. A. de Graaf Stitching (Institute for Prostitution Issues), "History of Dutch Prostitution," 1997.

Myslik, Wayne. (1995). Renegotiating the Social/Sexual Identities of Places: Gay Communites as Safe Havens or Sites of Resistance?" Mapping *Desires: Geographies of Sexuality*, edited by David Bell, and Gill Valentine, London: Routledge.

Nagle, Jill. (Ed.). (1997). *Whores and Other Feminists*. London: Routledge.

Namaste, Ki. (1996). "The Politics of Inside/Out: Queer Theory, Poststructuralism, and a Sociological Approach to Sexuality," (Ed.) Steven Seidman, *Queer Theory/Sociology*, Cambridge: Blackwell.

Nesvig, Martin. (2001). "The Complicated Terrain of Latin American Homosexuality, *Hispanic American Historical Review,* 81.3–4 689–729.

Oakley, Ann. (1981) "Interviewing women: a Contradiction in Terms." *Doing Feminist Research,* Edited by Helen Roberts, London:Routledge &Kegan Paul, (1981).

Olesen, Virginia L. (2000). "Feminisms and Qualitative Research At and Into the Millennium." *Handbook of Qualitative Research, Second Edition,* (Eds.) Norman K. Denzin and Yvonna S. Lincoln. Thousand Oaks: Sage.

Pettiway, Leon E. (1996). *Honey, Honey, Miss Thang: Being Black, Gay, and on the Streets.* Philadelphia: Temple University.

Pheterson, Gail. (1996).*The Prostitution Prism.* Amsterdam: Amsterdam Univ. Press.

Pillow, Wanda S. (1997). "Exposed methodology: the body as a deconstructive practice." *Qualitative Studies in Education,* Vol 10, No. 3.

Pinto, Louis. (1999). "Theory of Practice." *Bourdieu: A Critical Reader,* (Ed.) Richard Shusterman. Oxford: Blackwell.

Prieur, Annick. (1998). *Mema's House: Mexico City on Transvestites, Queens, and Machos.* Chicago: University Press.

Pruitt, Deborah and LaFont, Suzanne. (1995). "For Love and Money: Romance Tourism in Jamaica." *Annals of Tourist Research.* Vol. 22. pp. 422–440.

Punch, Maurice. (1986). "Politics and Ethics in Qualitative Research." *The Politics and Ethics of Fieldwork,* London: Sage.

Rabinow, Paul. (1977). *Reflections on Fieldwork in Morocco.* Berkeley: University of California Press.

Ramazanoglu, Caroline. (1993). "Introduction." *Up Against Foucault: Explorations of some tensions between Foucault and Feminism,* (Ed.) Caroline Ramazanoglu, London: Routledge.

Reinharz, Shulamit. (1992). *Feminist Methods in Social Research.* New York: Oxford University Press.

Rubin, Gayle. (1975). *The Traffic in Women: Notes on the Political Economy of Sex: in Rayna Rapp Riter,* 157–210.

Sasson, Saskia. (1996). "Immigration in Global Cities," http://www.interplan.org/immig/im01001.html.

Satz, Debra. (Oct. 1995). "Markets in Women's Sexual Labor." *Ethics* v. 106 p. 63–85.

Sedgwick, Eve. (1994). *Epistemology of the Closet,* Berkeley: University of California Press.

Seidman, Steven. (1994). *Contested Knowledge: Social Theory in the Postmodern Era.* Oxford: Blackwell.

———. (1996). *Queer Theory/Sociology.* Oxford: Blackwell.

Shrage, Laurie. (1994). *Moral Dilemmas of Feminism: Prostitution, Adultery, and Abortion.* New York: Routledge.

Shusterman, Richard. (1999). *Bourdieu: A Critical Reader.* Oxford: Blackwell.

Sigal, Pete. (2002). "Teaching Radical History To Cross the Sexual Borderlands: The History of Sexuality in the Americas," *Radical History Review,* 82 171–185.

Simon, Patricia M., Morse, Edward, Osofsky, Howard, Balson, Paul M, & Gaumer, H. Richard. (1992). "Psychological Characteristics of a Sample of Male Street Prostitutes." *Archives of Sexual Behavior,* Vol 21, No1.

Skrobanek, Siriporn, and Nattaya Boonpakdi and Chutima Janthakeero. (1997). *The Traffic in Women: Human Realities of the International Sex Trade.* London: Zed Books.

Smart, Barry. (1985). *Michel Foucault.* London: Routledge.

Smith, Dorothy. (1987). *The Everyday World as Problematic: A Feminist Sociology.* Boston: Northeastern University Press.

Smith, George W. (November 1990). "Political Activist as Ethnographer." *Social Problems* Vol. 37, No 4, p.629–648.

Somerville, Siobhan B. (2000). "Scientific Racism and the Invention of the Homosexual Body." *Queering the Color Line.* Durham & London: Duke.

Specter, Michael. (January 11, 1998). "Traffickers' New Cargo: Naive Slavic Women." *The New York Times,* page 1, 6.

Stacey, Judith. (1988). "Can there be a Feminist Ethnography?" *Women's Studies International Forum* vol. 11(1), 21–27.

Tampep: Transnational AIDS/STD Prevention Among Migrant Prostitutes in Europe/ Project, October 1996-September 1997.

Thomas, W. I. (1937).*The Unadjusted Girl.* Boston: Little, Brown & Col.

Townsand, Alan R. (1997). *Making a Living in Europe: Human Geographies of Economic Change.* London: Routledge.

Treichler, Paula A. (1996). "How to Use a Condom: Bedtime Stories for the Transcendental Signifier." Edited by Nelson, C. & Gaonkar D. P. *Disciplinarity and Dissent in Cultural Studies,* New York: Routledge.

Truong, Thanh-Dam. (1990). *Sex, Money, and Morality: Prostitution and Tourism in Southeast Asia.* London ; Atlantic Highlands, N.J.: Zed Books.

Valentine, Gil. "(Hetero)sexing space: lesbian perceptions and experiences of everyday spaces." *Environment and Planning: Society and Space,* 1993, volume 11, p. 395–414.

Van der Meer, Theo. (1990). "Private Acts, Public Space: Defining the Boundaries in Nineteenth-Century Holland." *Public Sex: Gay Space,* (Ed.) William L. Leap, New York: Columbia University Press.

Van Haastrecht, H. J. A, Fennema, J. S. A., Coutinho, R. A., van der Helm, T.C. M., Kint, J.P.P.C.M. & van den Hoek, J. A. R. (1993). "HIV prevalence and risk behavior among prostitutes and clients in Amsterdam: migrants at increased risk for HIV infection." *Genitourin Med,* p. 251–256.

Van Maanan, John. "The Moral Fix: On the Ethics of Fieldwork," Ethical and Political Issues in Field Research.

———. (1998). *Tales of the Field: On Writing Ethnography.* Chicago: The University of Chicago.

Vidich, Arthur J. and Lyman, Stanford M., (2000). "Their History in Sociology and Anthropology." *Handbook of Qualitative Research,* Second Edition, (Eds.) N. Denzin and Y. Lincoln, New York: Sage.

Visser, Jan. Press Release, http://www.minjust.nl:8080/c_actual/persber/pb121.htm, August 27, 1998.

Walkowitz, Judith R. (1982). *Prostitution and Victorian Society: Women, Class, and the State.* Cambridge: Cambridge University.

Wax, Rosalie. (June 1979). "Gender and Age in Fieldwork and Fieldwork Education: No Good This is Done by Any Man Alone." *Social Problems,* Volume 26, No5.

Weedon, Chris. (1987). "Discourse, Power and Resistance." *Feminist Practice and Poststructuralist Theory,* Oxford: Blackwell.

Whyte, William Foote. (July, 1943). "A Slum Sex Code." *American Journal of Sociology,* Volume 49, Issue 1), 24–31.

Wijers, Marjan, & Doorninck, Marieke van. (September 2002). "Only Rights Can Stop Wrongs: A critical assessment of anti-trafficking strategies," Paper presented at EU/IOM STOP European Conference on Preventing and Combating Trafficking in Human Beings- A Global Challenge for the 21st Century, 18–20, European Parliament, Brussels, Belgium.

Wijers, Marjan, & Lap-Chew, Lin. (1997). *Trafficking in Women Forced Labour and Slavery-like Practices in Marriage Domestic Labour and Prostitution.* Utrecht: STV.

Wilchins, Ricki Anne. (1997). *Read My Lips: Sexual Subversion and the End of Gender.* Ithaca: Firebrand.

Young, Antonia. (2000). *Women Who Become Men: Albanian Sworn Virgins.* Oxford: Berg, 2000.

Zatz, Noah D. (1997). "Sex Work/Sex Act: Law, Labor, and Desire in Constructions of Prostitution." *Signs,* Volume 22, Number 2. pp. 277.

Index

DATE DUE

DEC 1 7 2009

DEMCO, INC. 38-2931